D1118190

# The
# BEST
## *and*
# WORST
# OF GOLF
# A DEFINITIVE GUIDE
## LES KRANTZ & TIM KNIGHT

# The
# BEST
## *and*
# WORST
## OF GOLF

## A DEFINITIVE GUIDE

## LES KRANTZ & TIM KNIGHT

## TRIUMPH
### BOOKS
#### CHICAGO

The authors are grateful to the following individuals who contributed to this volume:

Sue Sveum: *Manuscript Editor and Contributing Writer*
Dick Krantz: *Contributing Writer*
Kristine Todd: *Photography Editor*
Point West, Inc.: *Interior Design*

ACKNOWLEDGEMENTS: Mitch Rogatz, Publisher of Triumph Books, whose help and good judgement were immeasurable; Tom Bast, Editorial Director, who brought the title into the press; Managing Editor Blythe Hurley at Triumph and other Triumph staffers including: Kristine Anstrats, Production Coordinator; Bilal Dardai, Editorial Assistant; Scott Rowan, Sports Publicist; Fred Walski, General Manager, and Phil Springstead, Director of Sales and Marketing. Also, Jeffrey Lane, Bill Melfi, and Kevin Knight for their advice and consultation.

Copyright © 2002 by Facts That Matter, Inc.
No part of this publication may be reproduced, stored in a retrieval system, or transmitted in any form by any means, electronic, mechanical, photocopying, or otherwise, without the prior written permission of the publisher, Triumph Books, 601 S. LaSalle St., Suite 500, Chicago, Illinois 60605.

Library of Congress control number available on request

This book is available in quantity at special discounts for your group or organization. For further information contact:
Triumph Books
601 South LaSalle Street, Suite 500
Chicago, Illinois 60605
(312) 939-3330
Fax (312) 663-3557

Printed in the United States of America

ISBN: 1-57243-471-6

# PHOTO CREDITS

*Cover: golfballs.com* (tee and ball)

*Left to Right and Top to Bottom:*
Page 2: Everett Collection; Everett Collection; Everett Collection; Everett Collection. Page 4: Everett Collection. Page 5: Everett Collection. Page 7: Courtesy of Gaylord Sports Management. Page 11: Everett Collection. Page 17: Everett Collection. Page 18: Everett Collection. Page 19: Everett Collection. Page 22: Comstock/Fotosearch. Page 23: Corbis/Fotosearch. Page 27: Everett Collection. Page 28: Everett Collection. Page 31: Everett Collection. Page 33: Corbis/Fotosearch. Page 36: Everett Collection. Page 38: Everett Collection. Page 40: Everett Collection. Page 41: Everett Collection. Page 44: PhotoDisc/Fotosearch. Page 45: Everett Collection. Page 47: Everett Collection. Page 49: Corbis/Fotosearch. Page 50: Corbis/Fotosearch. Page 51: Everett Collection. Page 54: Courtesy of Wood Sabold/Pacific Dunes Resort; Courtesy of The Golf Club at Redlands Mesa; PhotoDisc/Fotosearch. Page 56: Courtesy of Wood Sabold/Pacific Dunes Resort. Page 58: GoodShot/Superstock. Page 60: Courtesy of Fox Harbour Resort; Corbis/Fotosearch. Page 62: Corbis/Fotosearch. Page 63: PhotoDisc/Fotosearch. Page 65: Map Resources/Fotosearch. Page 66: Corbis/Fotosearch. Page 69: Corbis/Fotosearch. Page 70: PhotoDisc/Fotosearch. Page 71: PhotoDisc/Fotosearch. Page 73: Courtesy of The Golf Club at Redlands Mesa. Page 74: Corel/Fotosearch. Page 80: Courtesy of Cobra Golf; Courtesy of *Golf Digest*; Everett Collection; Courtesy of PING; Courtesy of Titleist; Everett Collection. Page 85: Courtesy of Titleist. Page 90: Everett Collection. Page 93: Corbis/Fotosearch. Page 94: Courtesy of the National Amputee Golf Association. Page 95: Courtesy of Cobra Golf. Page 97: Corbis/Fotosearch. Page 99: Corbis/Fotosearch. Page 100: Corbis/Fotosearch. Page 103: Courtesy of PING. Page 104: Courtesy of PING. Page 105: Comstock/Fotosearch. Page 106: Courtesy of Callaway Golf. Page 108: Francisco Cruz/Superstock. Page 109: Corbis/Fotosearch. Page 111: PhotoDisc/Fotosearch. Page 112: Corbis/Fotosearch. Page 113: Comstock/Fotosearch; Courtesy of Callaway Golf. Page 114: Courtesy of *Golf Digest*. Page 115: Corbis/Fotosearch. Page 116: Everett Collection. Page 117: Corbis/Fotosearch. Page 119: Courtesy of PING. Page 124: Everett Collection. Page 127: Everett Collection. Page 129: Everett Collection. Page 132: Corbis/Fotosearch. Page 134: Courtesy of Cleveland Golf. Page 135: Courtesy of Cleveland Golf. Page 138: Everett Collection; Everett Collection; Everett Collection; Everett Collection; Everett Collection. Page 141: Everett Collection; Everett Collection. Page 143: Everett Collection. Page 149: Everett Collection. Page 150: Everett Collection. Page 152: Everett Collection. Page 158: Everett Collection. Page 159: Everett Collection. Page 160: Everett Collection. Page 161: Everett Collection. Page 164: Everett Collection. Page 168: Everett Collection. Page 170: Everett Collection. Page 172: Courtesy of Kathy Whitworth. Page 173: Corbis/Fotosearch. Page 174: Everett Collection. Page 175: Everett Collection. Page 178: Everett Collection. Page 179: Everett Collection.

# CONTENTS

# INTRODUCTION

Most people who don't play golf think it's the game of ultimate enjoyment. There's the sunny weather, the luxurious feel of the lush grass at your feet, the camaraderie, the sporty clothes, the great shots, the clubby crowd, the 19th hole and . . . well, it has everything, right?

If you think so, you're one of them—one of those people who don't play the game.

Anyone who's been out for a round or two knows about the slices from the tee, the sand that gets in your shoes in the traps, the triple bogies, the missed shots, and the foursome in front of you who can never find their balls.

In sum, golf is a mix; a mix of the wonderful and woeful, positives and negatives, and satisfaction and frustration. But you, as a golfer, know about that already, so why write a book about it?

We didn't. Instead, we wrote our book about much more, but it focuses on just two things: the pinnacles and the pits.

If something was good, it wasn't good enough to make our lists. It had to be stellar, like "the day for aces," when four pros got holes-in-one on the same day . . . on the same course. Or tournaments for almost every stripe of golfer, including bald men, convicts, and hoboes—even a tourney for anyone whose name happens to be Bob Jones.

And the bad? Just *bad* wasn't good enough to get in our book either. It had to really be the *pits*; like golf courses with cobras or alligators, or a Pennsylvania woman who scored a mind-boggling 161 *on one hole* in a 1913 tournament.

So get ready. You're about to read about a side of golf you hardly knew existed. In reading this book, you're likely to be outraged here and there, maybe even offended in spots, but you'll also be entertained, fascinated, and informed; at least that's what we hoped would happen when we wrote the pages that follow.

Enjoy!

# PEOPLE

# In This Section

**Bob Hope (left) tempts injury by partnering with Vice President Spiro Agnew.**

# AGNEW'S GOLF GAME

## The Vice President's Vice

Spiro Agnew's golf game ranks about on par with his political legacy. Nixon's disgraced vice president was a virtual terror on the golf course, a one-man wrecking crew who took out quite a few spectators with errant shots at pro-am tournaments. Cartoonists had a field day mocking his golf game, yet despite the ridicule, Agnew continued to play in pro-am tournaments, even though he was well aware of his reputation. At the 1971 Bob Hope Desert Classic, Agnew twice sent balls flying into spectators, hitting a woman on the arm and another on the ankle. Always contrite, Agnew would apologize profusely and send his victims autographed golf balls bearing the legend: "You have just been hit by Spiro Agnew." But it wasn't just the spectators who risked injury when Agnew teed off. At the 1970 Bob Hope Desert Classic, Agnew's 3-wood shot slammed into pro Doug Sanders' head. Once he came to his senses, Sanders went on with the match.

Source: *Presidential Lies* by Shepherd Campbell and Peter Landau

# ALL-TIME EARNINGS LEADERS

## PGA

Since turning pro in 1996, Tiger Woods has amassed a staggering fortune, both from golf and a slew of lucrative endorsement contracts. As of this writing, he tops the list of all-time earnings winners on the PGA Circuit by a considerable margin—and will probably continue to do so for years to come. It's all the more impressive (or intimidating, whether you're an aspiring or veteran golf pro) when you consider that Woods is still in his twenties.

Of the 475 golfers on the list, veteran Arnold Palmer just makes the top 200, coming in at No. 199 with career PGA earnings of $1,861,857. Jack Nicklaus, the player who succeeded Palmer as golf's golden boy in the sixties, ranks No. 67 with career PGA earnings of $5,713,991. And one of golf's grand old men, Sam Snead, comes in at No. 335 with $620,126—quite impressive, given that Snead's last victory on the PGA Tour was in 1965.

On a sad note, the late Payne Stewart ranks in at No. 15 with career earnings of $11,737,008. Here are the top 10 all-time PGA earnings leaders as of December 2001. This is the official money earned by a player on the PGA Tour during his career.

| Golfer | Earnings |
| --- | --- |
| Tiger Woods | $26,191,227 |
| Davis Love III | $17,994,690 |
| Phil Mickelson | $17,837,998 |
| David Duval | $15,312,553 |
| Scott Hoch | $14,553,202 |
| Vijay Singh | $14,524,452 |
| Nick Price | $14,477,425 |
| Hal Sutton | $13,885,946 |
| Mark Calcavecchia | $13,409,349 |
| Greg Norman | $13,344,142 |

Source: PGAtour.com.

# ASTROLOGICAL TRAITS

## How Your Sign Affects Your Golf Game

Every golfer has good days and bad days on the links. Even Tiger Woods. We blame the clubs, the ball, the weather. Well, here's the ultimate excuse—your astrological sign.

Author and astrology guru Michael Zullo has watched golfers over the years, recording similarities and patterns based on the golfers' birthdates and astrological signs. While not everyone under a given sign approaches golf the same way, Zullo has found some basic characteristics that may affect a golfer's game, and published them in *Golf Astrology 2000*.

It's probably no surprise to learn that as a Capricorn, Tiger Woods is self-disciplined and goal-oriented, or that Payne Stewart was an eccentric and personable Aquarian. Find your own astrological sign below. Do any of these characteristics sound like you? If so, check out the book to learn how to make the most of those positive traits—and tame the ones that may be hurting your game.

### Aquarius
**January 21–February 19**
complex
analytical
inventive
eccentric
personable

### Pisces
**February 20–March 20**
adaptable
good-natured
considerate
intuitive
noncompetitive

### Aries
**March 21–April 20**
energetic
demonstrative
very competitive
fast playing
aggressive

### Taurus
**April 21–May 21**
practical
easy-going
dependable
consistent
stubborn

### Gemini
**May 22–June 21**
unpredictable
talkative
adaptable
inconsistent
fast-playing

### Cancer
**June 23–July 23**
sensitive
cautious
intuitive
methodical
determined

### Leo
**July 24–August 23**
self-confident
risk-taking
forceful
enthusiastic
charismatic

### Virgo
**August 24–September 23**
analytic
deliberate
down-to-earth
practical
disciplined

### Libra
**September 24–October 23**
perceptive
image-conscious
charming
expressive
balanced

### Scorpio
**October 24–November 22**
passionate
focused
mysterious

*Your golf game may be
written in the stars.*

instructive
intuitive
stoic

**Sagittarius**
**November 23–December 21**
extroverted
optimistic
energetic
fun-loving
daring

**Capricorn**
**December 22–January 20**
self-disciplined
goal-oriented
persistent
patient
dependable

Source: *Golf Astrology 2000* by Michael Zullo

# ASTROLOGICAL SIGNS

## *Signs of the Pros*

We all like to identify with people who are leaders in their field. When Michael Zullo researched pro golfers for his book, *Golf Astrology 2000*, he discovered that the "best" golfers are distributed fairly evenly throughout the zodiac. So even if you noticed some less than stellar traits listed for your own astrological sign, you'll be gratified to find a short list of pros with those exact same traits. If the professionals are able to overcome these obstacles, who knows what you can do?

**Aquarius**
**January 21–February 19**
Carol Mann
Jack Nicklaus
Greg Norman
Payne Stewart
Curtis Strange

**Pisces**
**February 20–March 20**
Amy Alcott
Jim Colbert
Tom Lehman
Hollis Stacy
Vijay Singh

**Aries**
**March 21–April 20**
Helen Alfredsson
Seve Ballesteros
Mark Brooks
JoAnne Carner
Meg Mallon

**Taurus**
**April 21–May 21**
John Daly
Johnny Miller
Betsy Rawls
Hal Sutton
Bob Tway

**Gemini**
**May 22–June 21**
Tina Barrett
Sandra Haynie
Hale Irwin
Phil Mickelson
Sam Snead

**Cancer**
**June 22–July 23**
Billy Casper
Nick Faldo
Juli Inkster
Jerry McGee
Scott Verplank

**Leo**
**July 24–August 23**
Betsy King
Billy Mayfair
Dottie Pepper
Doug Sanders
Colleen Walker

**Virgo**
**August 24–September 23**
Jane Blalock
Raymond Floyd
Arnold Palmer
Larry Nelson
Tom Watson

**Libra**
**September 24–October 23**
Fred Couples
Se Ri Pak
Chi Chi Rodriguez
J. C. Snead
Annika Sorenstam

*Phil Mickelson had the best birdie average on the 2001 PGA Tour.*

**Scorpio**
**October 24–November 22**
David Duval
Gary Player
Patty Sheehan
Dave Stockton
Tom Weiskopf

**Sagittarius**
**November 23–December 21**
Lorie Kane
Tom Kite
Lee Trevino
Lanny Wadkins
Karrie Webb

**Capricorn**
**December 22–January 20**
Ben Crenshaw
Nancy Lopez
Mark O'Meara
Jan Stephenson
Tiger Woods

Source: *Golf Astrology 2000* by Michael Zullo

# BIRDIE AVERAGES

## Pro Golfers

All golfers measure their success in relation to par. Most of us count our strokes *over* par, but the top touring pros count their strokes *under* par. Except for an occasional eagle, or rare double eagle, the pros need birdies to drop well below par and increase their chances to win tournaments. So pros covet birdies. And it seems logical that the best birdie shooter on the tour would enjoy the lowest scoring average and win the most money.

But it didn't happen that way on the 2001 PGA Tour. Phil Mickelson was the top birdie shooter, yet he ranked fourth in scoring and second in winnings. He won about $1.3 million less than Tiger Woods, in fact. And although Tiger ranked fifth in birdies, he was first in both scoring average and prize money.

It is startling to compare Woods' success with that of Kenny Perry, who ranked just behind Tiger in birdies. While Woods averaged 4.30 birdies per round, Perry averaged

4.26 birdies—a slight difference, to be sure. But the gap in their prize money was wide. Woods won about $5.7 million; Perry $1.8 million. And while Woods averaged 68.81 strokes per round, Perry ranked 24th in scoring average, at 70.22 strokes per round.

The lesson here is that champions cannot live by birdies alone. They must also master the art of eliminating bogeys, which neutralize birdies as surely as $-2$ and $+6 = 4$.

### 2001 PGA Tour
### Birdie Average

| Player | Birdie Average |
| --- | --- |
| 1. Phil Mickelson | 4.49 |
| 2. Davis Love III | 4.45 |
| 3. David Duval | 4.31 |
| 4. David Toms | 4.31 |
| 5. Tiger Woods | 4.30 |
| 6. Kenny Perry | 4.26 |
| 7. Chris DiMarco | 4.23 |
| 8. Mark Calcavecchia | 4.22 |
| 9. Vijay Singh | 4.21 |
| 10. Scott McCarron | 4.19 |

### 2001 Senior PGA Tour
### Birdie Average

| Player | Birdie Average |
| --- | --- |
| 1. Tom Watson | 4.50 |
| 2. Larry Nelson | 4.43 |
| 3. Hale Irwin | 4.35 |
| 4. Gil Morgan | 4.33 |
| 5. Allen Doyle | 4.28 |
| 6. Tom Kite | 4.20 |

| | |
|---|---|
| 7. Jim Thorpe | 4.13 |
| 8. Bruce Fleisher | 4.11 |
| 9. Gary McCord | 4.05 |
| 10. Sammy Rachels | 4.04 |

Source: PGAtour.com

# BIRDIE LEADERS

## Par 3 Holes

Nothing seems to shine as brightly on the scorecard of a weekend golfer as a birdie 2 on a par 3 hole. But making that happen usually requires either hitting a great iron shot or sinking a long putt. And most recreational golfers don't card a 2 very often.

You would think that touring pros birdie par 3 holes all the time. But statistics show they really don't. Scott Verplank led the pro tour in 2001 in birdies on par 3 holes, yet he birdied less than 20 percent of all he played. And most golfers on the pro tour don't do nearly as well. Only 20 touring pros shot even par or better on par 3 holes in 2001, while 174 were over par, according to PGA statistics on "Par 3 Performance."

As it turns out, shooting birdies on par 3 holes is only marginally related to success on the pro tour. Of the top 10 birdie shooters on par 3 holes in 2001, three also ranked among the 10 top money winners. They were Scott Verplank, David Toms, and Sergio Garcia. However, Tommy Tolles, who tied for the fifth best birdie shooter on par 3s, ranked only 145th in winnings. Tolles undermined his par 3 birdie success by shooting many bogeys or worse. As a result, he was 29 over par on par 3 holes for the season, and ranked only 139th for par 3 performance.

# BIRDIE LEADERS

## Par 5 Holes

The best golfers on the PGA Tour share a critical ability. It isn't what you might think, such as driving the ball a mile, staying in the fairway, mastering the short game, or even hitting greens in regulation. The vital statistic separating the men from the boys on the pro tour is the ability to birdie par 5 holes.

Need convincing? Look at the record of Tiger Woods, undoubtedly the world's best golfer since he won his first Master's Tournament in 1997. Not surprisingly, Tiger also led the PGA Tour in birdies on par 5 holes in 1997, and every year since. Look, too, at the PGA's leading money winners in 2001. Seven of the eight top winners also ranked in the top 10 for birdies on par 5 holes. They are Woods, Phil Mickelson, Vijay Singh, Davis Love III, Sergio Garcia, Scott Hoch, and David Duval. The only exception was David Toms, the third-leading money winner, at $3.8 million, who ranked 34th in birdies on par 5 holes.

Par 5 holes are where touring pros really take advantage of a golf course and lower their scores. PGA statistics for 2001 list 186 players who birdie at least 25 percent of all the par 5 holes they played, and five who birdied more than 50 percent.

Par 4 and par 3 holes, by contrast, are far more difficult to birdie. Only five players birdied more than 20 percent of par 4 holes, and not one player birdied 20 percent of par three holes. So while long par 5 holes may intimidate weekend golfers, the pros, who routinely hit their drives 275 yards or longer, see them as an opportunity to clean up.

### 2001 Par 3 Birdie Leaders

| Player | Percent Birdies |
|---|---|
| 1. Scott Verplank | 19.7 |
| 2. Jim Furyk | 19.4 |
| 3. Bob Tway | 18.1 |
| 4. Brett Quigley | 17.9 |
| 5. Tommy Tolles | 17.2 |
| David Toms | 17.2 |
| 7. Donnie Hammond | 17.1 |
| 8. Sergio Garcia | 17.0 |
| 9. Mark Brooks | 16.9 |
| John Cook | 16.9 |
| Glen Day | 16.9 |
| Scott McCarron | 16.9 |

### 2001 Par 3 Previous Birdie Leader

| Year | Player | Percent Birdies |
|---|---|---|
| 2000 | Jesper Parnevik | 19.9 |
| 1999 | Jim Furyk | 17.0 |

| 1998 | Paul Stankowski | 19.0 |
| 1997 | David Duval | 17.6 |
| 1996 | Brad Faxon | 18.7 |
| 1995 | Larry Mize | 20.2 |
| 1994 | Loren Roberts | 17.9 |
| 1993 | Tom Kite & Steve Pate | 19.9 |
| 1992 | Doug Tew II | 20.6 |

Source: PGAtour.com

### 2001 Par 5 Birdie Leaders

| Player | Percent Birdies |
| --- | --- |
| 1. Tiger Woods | 55.9 |
| 2. David Duval | 54.5 |
| 3. Vijay Singh | 52.9 |
| 4. Davis Love III | 50.8 |
| 5. Charles Howell III | 50.2 |
| 6. Phil Mickelson | 49.8 |
| 7. Sergio Garcia | 49.2 |
| 8. Stuart Appleby | 48.3 |
| 9. Scott McCarron | 47.9 |
| 10. Mark Calcavecchia | 47.7 |
| Scott Hoch | 47.7 |

### Previous Par 5 Birdie Leaders

| Year | Player | Percent Birdies |
| --- | --- | --- |
| 2000 | Tiger Woods | 55.5 |
| 1999 | Tiger Woods | 54.8 |
| 1998 | Tiger Woods | 48.5 |
| 1997 | Tiger Woods | 51.7 |
| 1996 | Fred Couples | 52.2 |
| 1995 | Greg Norman | 45.1 |
| 1994 | Dennis Paulson | 47.7 |
| 1993 | Greg Norman | 47.8 |

| 1992 | Fred Couples | 47.6 |

Source: PGAtour.com

# CELEBRITY GOLFERS

## Baseball Players

Baseball Hall of Famer Johnny Bench has mastered the art of multi-tasking. In addition to maintaining a full schedule of corporate speaking engagements and sports clinics, the former Cincinnati Reds catcher is an avid competitor on the Celebrity Players Tour, which he helped found in 1996. Two years later, Bench actually received sponsor exemptions to compete in two SPGA tournaments—hard to believe that when Bench made his first appearance at the Bob Hope Chrysler Classic, he couldn't hit the ball off the tee! Needless to say, his game has improved dramatically.

Many of these players have competed alongside Bench on the Celebrity Players Tour, which is now sponsoring 15 pro-am tournaments yearly.

# CELEBRITY GOLFERS

## Hollywood Handicaps

For people whose mantra could be "Never let them see you sweat," a lot of entertainment

### Celebrity Golfers—Baseball Players

| Player | Position | Handicap | Career Best Round |
| --- | --- | --- | --- |
| Johnny Bench | Catcher | 0 | 64 |
| George Brett | Third baseman | 4 | 72 |
| Gary Carter | Catcher | 4 | 70 |
| John Cerutti | Pitcher | 0 | 64 |
| Vince Coleman | Outfielder | 4 | 71 |
| Rollie Fingers | Pitcher | 5 | 69 |
| Carleton Fisk | Catcher | 5 | 68 |
| Doug Flynn | Second baseman | 3 | 69 |
| Bobby Grich | Second baseman | 1 | 65 |
| Charlie Hough | Pitcher | 2 | Not available |
| Bobby Murcer | Outfielder | 5 | 68 |
| Mike Schmidt | Third baseman | 0 | 67 |

Source: *Celebrity Golfer 2001*; cptgolf.com

figures willingly put their golfing skills (or lack thereof) up for public scrutiny in celebrity pro-am tournaments. While many display a genuine aptitude for the game, others learn that their showbiz fortunes don't always transfer to the golf course. Take Jack Lemmon, for instance. The late two-time Academy Award winner was passionate about golf and regularly played in pro-am tournaments, despite the fact that his erratic game had earned him the nickname the "Human Hinge." The following performers are to be commended for revealing their stats with the public, though a few need to work on lowering their handicap—not that we're singling anyone out, Mr. Gumbel.

**Adam Baldwin**
actor
Handicap: 2
Career best round: 68

**Tom Dreesan**
comedian
Handicap: 6
Career best round: 71

**Larry Gatlin**
singer
Handicap: 6
Career best round: 73

**Rudy Gatlin**
singer
Handicap: 3
Career best round: 67

**Steve Gatlin**
singer
Handicap: 6
Career best round: 68

**Bryant Gumbel**
broadcaster
Handicap: 8
Career best round: 72

**Alex Hyde-White**
actor
Handicap: 4
Career best round: 67

**Peter Kessler**
host, The Golf Channel
Handicap: 7
Career best round: 70

**Matt Lauer**
co-anchor, NBC *Today Show*
Handicap: 8
Career best round: 73

**Maury Povich**
host, *The Maury Povich Show*
Handicap: 0
Career best round: 68

**Jack Wagner**
actor
Handicap: 3
Career best round 64

Source: *Celebrity Golfer 2001*

# CELEBRITY GOLFERS

## NBA Players

A fixture on the celebrity pro-am tournament circuit, Michael Jordan is so passionate about golf that he's opened two driving ranges bearing his name in Aurora, Illinois, and Charlotte, North Carolina. Although he's regarded as a fine amateur golfer, Jordan won't be challenging Tiger Woods or David Duval in the world rankings anytime soon. He's one of many NBA stars past and present who like to sink putts when they're not shooting hoops.

# CELEBRITY GOLFERS

## NFL Players

Oakland Raider wide receiver Jerry Rice is widely acknowledged as one of the all-time greats in the NFL. Since turning pro in 1985, Rice has set 14 NFL records and 10 Super Bowl records, and has been named *Sports Illustrated*'s Player of the Year four times. His athletic gifts apparently extend from the gridiron to the fairway as well; Rice made the cut at the 1997 AT&T Pebble Beach Pro-Am Tournament—as if the man needs any further accolades! Rice is one of many NFL players who've taken up golf, which is a lot easier on the knees than football.

# CELEBRITY GOLFERS

## Professional Hockey Players

The term "fish out of water" comes to mind when picturing a hockey player on the golf course. Adam Sandler certainly milked this scenario for all its comic potential in *Happy Gilmore*, which features Sandler duking it out with game show host Bob Barker on the green. The image of hockey players as hulking, toothless jocks prone to fistfights, however, doesn't hold for the NHL stars who regularly leave the ice for the links. Trading in their hockey sticks for golf clubs, these pros are passionate golfers who've never clipped anyone with their 9 irons or spent time in the club penalty box.

# CELEBRITY GOLFERS

## Quarterbacks

From 1957 to 1973, quarterback John Brodie was one of the star players for the San Fran-

cisco 49ers. In addition to being the highest-paid player of the late sixties—he signed a four-year, $827,000 contract with San Francisco in 1967—Brodie was also named the NFL's Player of the Year in 1970. Once he retired, however, Brodie decided to pursue his other great love and became a professional golfer. He joined the SPGA Tour in 1985 and eventually earned over $500,000 from tournament appearances, including a victory at the 1991 Security Pacific Senior Championship.

While none of these other NFL quarterbacks have followed Brodie's lead, they've all taken to the green, which can be a lot more forgiving than AstroTurf.

# CELEBRITY GOLFERS

## Star Golfers from Hollywood's Golden Age

Golf has a rich history in Hollywood—off-screen, that is. During the industry's golden

| Celebrity Golfers—Professional Athletes | | | |
|---|---|---|---|
| **Basketball** | **Position** | **Handicap** | **Career Best Round** |
| Charles Barkley | NBA forward | 14 | 79 |
| Charlie Criss | NBA guard | 3 | 67 |
| Vinny Del Negro | NBA guard | 6 | 72 |
| George Gervin | NBA guard | 6 | 70 |
| Michael Jordan | NBA guard | 3 | not available |
| Bill Laimbeer | NBA All-Star center | 3 | 66 |
| Jerry Lucas | NBA forward | 4 | 66 |
| Dan Majerle | NBA guard | 4 | 71 |
| Jack Marin | NBA forward | 0 | 65 |
| Jason Kidd | NBA guard | 10 | 79 |
| **Football** | | | |
| Bobby Anderson | running back | 3 | 66 |
| Dick Anderson | safety | 1 | 65 |
| Donny Anderson | running back | 2 | 66 |
| Neal Anderson | running back | 5 | 68 |
| Chris Bahr | place kicker | 3 | 68 |
| Jim Brown | running back | 9 | not available |
| Chuck Cecil | safety | 4 | 65 |
| Al Del Greco | place kicker | 0 | 65 |
| Brian Kinchen | tight end | 0 | 67 |
| Jerry Rice | wide receiver | 14 | not available |

Source: *Celebrity Golfer 2001*

| Celebrity Golfers—Professional Athletes (continued) | | | |
|---|---|---|---|
| **Hockey** | **NHL Position** | **Handicap** | **Career Best Round** |
| Don Edwards | goalie | 2 | 68 |
| Grant Fuhr | goalie | 0 | not available |
| Clark Gillies | forward | 3 | 68 |
| Brett Hull | All-Star wing | 4 | 68 |
| Pierre Larouche | All-Star center | 1 | 61 |
| Mario Lemieux | Hall of Fame center | 0 | 65 |
| Stan Mikita | Hall of Fame center | 4 | 67 |
| Bernie Nicholls | center | 2 | 68 |
| Dan Quinn | center | 0 | 65 |
| **NFL Quarterbacks** | | | |
| Dave Archer | | 5 | 71 |
| Steve Bartkowski | | 0 | 66 |
| John Brodie | | 0 | 62 |
| Chris Chandler | | 4 | 67 |
| Trent Dilfer | | 0 | 67 |
| John Elway | | 3 | 68 |
| Dan Marino | | 5 | 71 |
| Jim McMahon | | 0 | 69 |
| Joe Theismann | | 5 | 69 |
| Peter Tom Willis | | 0 | 62 |

Source: *Celebrity Golfer 2001*

age, many of the biggest stars were fixtures on the courses of such elegant country clubs as the Lakeside, the Riviera, and the Hillcrest, among others. Some of the stars' antics have become legendary among caddies and club pros, who watched these big screen luminaries whiff, shank, and slice just like all the other mere mortals.

- **Fred Astaire**: The effortlessly debonair dancer played with about a 10-handicap at the Bel Air Country Club in the forties.

- **Humphrey Bogart**: His nickname of "Bogie" was apparently not a reflection on his golf game. The archetypal film noir antihero used to ride his bike from the Warner Bros. lot to the nearby Lakeside Golf Club.

- **Douglas Fairbanks**: The screen's first swashbuckler, the athletic Fairbanks helped bring the Los Angeles Open to the posh Riviera Country Club in 1929 and contributed $1,000 to the tournament's $10,000 purse.

- **W. C. Fields**: The irascible comedian was a committed golfer who regularly showed up in his pajamas to play at the Lakeside Golf Club on Sunday mornings.

- **Oliver Hardy**: Known as "Babe," the portly comedian once squared off against character actor Adolphe Menjou in a match at Lakeside that ran nearly eight hours long and drew a huge gallery.

- **Katharine Hepburn**: An all-around athlete who learned to play golf when she was five years old, Hepburn regularly played at the Bel Air Country Club. She later put her golf skills to good use in the 1952 romantic comedy *Pat and Mike*, in which she played a character inspired by Babe Didrikson Zaharias.

- **Howard Hughes**: The eccentric aviator once landed his plane on the Bel Air Country Club golf course to play golf with a surprised Katharine Hepburn.

- **Harpo Marx**: Marx once played golf at the Hillcrest Country Club clad only in a shirt

*A passionate golfer, Katharine Hepburn (center) shared the screen with LPGA stars (left to right) Gussie Moran, Beverly Hanson, Helen Dettweiler, and Babe Didrikson Zaharais in the 1952 romantic comedy* **Pat and Mike.**

and underpants. He reportedly had a handicap of 20.

- **Randolph Scott**: The stoic icon of B-westerns got his start in movies after meeting Howard Hughes on a golf course.

- **Johnny Weissmuller**: The screen's best-known Tarzan was a talented golfer who often played with temperamental Mickey Rooney at Lakeside. Weissmuller was also a frequent visitor to Bel Air, where he would often let loose with one of his trademark Tarzan yells—much to the consternation of other golfers.

- Dishonorable Mention: **Jimmy Durante**, who apparently played so badly on the front nine, not even breaking 100, that his frustrated caddie finally asked for the clubs back.

Source: *Hollywood on the Links* by Tom Cunneff; *"And Then Tiger Told The Shark . . ."* by Don Wade

# CELEBRITY PLAYERS TOUR

## *All-Time Earnings Winners*

Founded in 1996 by a group of professional athletes and showbiz personalities, the Celebrity Players Tour has grown from five to fifteen annual tournaments. Each tournament begins with a two-day, pro-am charity event; the players then reconvene to compete in a Low Gross golf tournament with a cash purse. This latter competition is played strictly according to the USGA rules.

Now in its sixth year, the Celebrity Players Tour continues to attract new players from the worlds of sports and entertainment. As of this writing, CPT tournaments have raised over $8 million for various charities.

With the tour since its first season, former baseball star Rick Rhoden is the first CPT player to cross the $1 million mark in all-time earnings. Incidentally, the tour's top 10 career earners all come from the world of sports. Television actor Jack Wagner of *Melrose Place* fame just missed making the top 10, coming in at No. 11 with $195,399 in earnings as of this writing.

# CELEBRITY PLAYERS TOUR

## *All-Time Scoring Leaders*

In the brief history of the Celebrity Players Tour, two players have consistently dominated the field in terms of stroke average. Duplicating their positions on the CPT all-time earnings list, Rick Rhoden and Dan Quinn are currently ranked first and second in all-time CPT scoring. In fact, most of the tour's top 10 earners also appear on this list, the exceptions being Ivan Lendl, Steve

Bartkowski, and Pierre Larouche. Bartkowski, comes in No. 11 with a stroke average of 74.52. Larouche takes the 14th position with 74.76, while Lendl trails a distant No. 36 with a stroke average of 76.03.

# COLLEGE GOLF CHAMPIONS

The NCAA Basketball Tournament is renowned for generating heart-stopping suspense. But in recent years, the NCAA Golf Tournament in June has been generating high drama, too. As in basketball, each team has five players. They compete over 72 holes. And twice in a five-year span teams have finished tied, necessitating a sudden-death playoff.

The first playoff in the tournament's history developed in 1995 when Stanford, with a freshman named Tiger Woods, tied with Oklahoma State. But despite the best efforts of golf's future superstar, Stanford lost to the Cowboys on the first extra hole. The losing Cardinals also had a couple of other future pros on that team—Notah Begay III and Casey Martin, who later successfully sued the PGA for the right to use a golf cart in tournaments because of a disability that prevents him from walking a full 18 holes.

The second playoff, in 2000, again involved Oklahoma State, which tied with Georgia Tech at a record-breaking 36 under par. Both teams featured future pros. The Georgia Tech Yellow Jackets were led by Matt Kuchar, the 1997 U.S. Amateur champion, who astounded the golf world in 1998 by finishing, as an amateur, 20th at the Masters and 14th at the U.S. Open. The Cowboys were led by Charles Howell III, who won the individual NCAA title by shooting a record 23-under-par 265, and would go on, a year later, to win PGA rookie of the year honors.

On the par-4 sudden-death playoff hole, the Yellow Jackets shot four pars and a bogey. The Cowboys also shot four pars, but freshman J. C. DeLeon turned in a birdie to give Oklahoma State the team title. The suspense may not equal basketball's March Madness, but it certainly gave players and spectators the June Jitters.

## NCAA Division 1 Champions

| | |
|------|------------------|
| 2001 | Florida |
| 2000 | Oklahoma State |
| 1999 | Georgia |
| 1998 | UNLV |
| 1997 | Pepperdine |
| 1996 | Arizona State |
| 1995 | Oklahoma State |
| 1994 | Stanford |
| 1993 | Florida |
| 1992 | Arizona |

Source: *ESPN Sports Almanac 2002*; NCAA. com; Stanford University Athletic Department

# DRIVING ACCURACY

## *2001 Pro Tour*

Few would argue that the most accurate pros off the tee lack the charisma of the game's longest hitters. Tournament spectators can't wait to see John Daly or Tiger Woods blast a drive over 300 yards. But who goes out of their way to watch guys like Olin Browne or Billy Mayfair, who rank high in landing drives in the fairway, but typically hit tee shots of 270 yards or less?

Golfers in their more rational moments, however, understand the value of driving accuracy. Better to hit the ball 220 yards down the middle than slice it 280 yards into the deep woods. It might even be logical to conclude that accurate drivers, who stay out of trouble, fare better on the pro tour than the long hitters. But do they?

When you compare the 2001 winnings of the top-10 pros in driving accuracy, with the top-10 in driving-distance, the distance leaders won more prize money. And if you'll pardon the pun, they did it by a long shot. The total winnings for driving-distance leaders was $22.2 million, while the driving accuracy leaders won $12.3 million—that's an 80 percent advantage for the big hitters. It translates to average winnings of about $1,232,000 for the accuracy leaders, compared to $2,224,000 for the longest hitters.

| | | *Driving Accuracy* | |
|---|---|---|---|
| Rank | Player | Percent Fairways Hit | Winnings |
| 1. | Joe Durant | 81.1 | $2,381,684 |
| 2. | Glen Hnatiuk | 77.8 | 434,524 |
| 3. | Fred Funk | 77.2 | 1,237,004 |
| 4. | John Cook | 76.6 | 1,022, 778 |
| 5. | Billy Mayfair | 76.5 | 1,716,002 |
| 6. | Olin Browne | 75.8 | 815,636 |
| 7. | Jim Furyk | 75.7 | 2,540,734 |
| 8. | Tom Byrum | 75.6 | 391,925 |
| | Jose Coceres | 75.6 | 1,502,888 |
| | Brian Gay | 75.6 | 1,299,361 |

Source: PGAtour.com

# DRIVING ACCURACY

## *Percentage of Drives on Target*

Ever worry you can't hit the broad side of a barn with your driver? Don't fret too much. You've got some good company. Tiger Woods, Dave Duval, Davis Love III, and Justin Leonard to name a few, are top professional money winners who have the same problem. In fact, none of the top-10 money winners on the tour are among the top 10 in driving accuracy. And among the top 10 in driving distance, not even one is among the most accurate pros in driving accuracy.

Who then are the real deadeye drivers? During 1999 the following pros were the most accurate. At right is the percentage of drives they place within 10 yards of their target.

| Golfer | Percent of Drives on Target | |
|---|---|---|
| 1. | Fred Funk | 80.2 |
| 2. | Olin Browne | 78.7 |
| 3. | Joe Durant | 78.6 |
| 4. | Corey Pavin | 77.4 |
| | Mike Reid | 77.4 |
| | Loren Roberts | 77.4 |
| 7. | Larry Mitz | 77.2 |
| 8. | Scott Gump | 77.0 |
| | Jeff Maggert | 77.0 |
| 10. | Pete Jordon | 76.0 |

Source: PGAtour.com

# DRIVING DISTANCE LEADERS

## *Heavy Hitters 2001*

What Mark McGwire and Barry Bonds can do to a baseball, John Daly does to a golf ball. That is to say, he hits it out of sight. Daly is certainly the greatest slugger in golf history. In 1999, he became the first player to average more than 300 yards per drive, setting a PGA driving distance record of 305.6 yards. He surpassed that in 2001, averaging 306.7 yards. Daly has led the Tour in driving distance every year but one since 1991, leaving no real contenders for the title of golf's longest hitter.

But Daly's not the only guy who can powder the ball. PGA statistics name 79 touring pros who smashed drives of 350 yards or longer in 2001. What separates Daly from other big hitters, though, is consistency. No one else has yet managed to average more than 300 yards in a season or lead the tour in driving distance for so many years.

Driving distance statistics are interesting for another reason. They show how much more there is to the game than being long off the tee. Although Daly ranked first in driving distance in 2001, he was 61st in prize money, winning $829,000. Tiger Woods was fourth in driving distance, but first in winnings, earning $5.7 million. And Phil Mickelson was seventh in driving distance, but second in prize money, winning about $4.4 million.

### All-Time Celebrity Golfers

| Earnings Winners | Occupation | Earnings |
|---|---|---|
| Rick Rhoden | Major league pitcher | $1,267,174 |
| Dan Quinn | NHL center | $810,878 |
| Shane Rawley | Major league pitcher | $462,657 |
| Al Del Greco | NFL place kicker | $393,680 |
| John Brodie | NFL quarterback | $325,566 |
| Dick Anderson | NFL safety | $314,864 |
| Pierre Larouche | NHL center | $281,886 |
| Steve Bartkowski | NFL quarterback | $240,086 |
| Brian Kinchen | NFL tight end | $219,831 |
| Ivan Lendl | tennis player | $209,555 |
| **Scoring Leaders** | | |
| Rick Rhoden | Major league pitcher | 70.46 |
| Dan Quinn | NHL center | 71.94 |
| Al Del Greco | NFL place kicker | 72.42 |
| Shane Rawley | Major league pitcher | 72.56 |
| Dick Anderson | NFL safety | 73.88 |
| John Brodie | NFL quarterback | 73.89 |
| Brian Kinchen | NFL tight end | 73.93 |
| Jack Wagner | Television actor | 73.98 |
| Trent Dilfer | NFL quarterback | 74.02 |
| Peter Tom Willis | NFL quarterback | 74.27 |

Source: cptgolf.com

The most telling statistics of all, however, belong to Steve Allan, a PGA Tour rookie in 2001 who played three years previously on the European Tour. Despite matching Mickelson in driving distance, averaging 293 yards, Allen won only $157,000 in prize money and finished no better than 19th in 31 tournaments he entered. His record proves conclusively that golfers cannot live by distance alone.

### Average Driving Distance, 2001

| Player | Distance Average |
|---|---|
| John Daly | 306.7 yards |
| Brett Quigley | 298.5 yards |
| Davis Love III | 297.6 yards |
| Tiger Woods | 297.6 yards |
| David Duval | 297.6 yards |
| Charles Howell III | 293.9 yards |
| Phil Mickelson | 293.9 yards |
| Steve Allan | 293.3 yards |
| Chris Smith | 293.2 yards |
| Denny Perry | 292.3 yards |

Source: PGAtour.com

# EAGLE LEADERS

## PGA 2001

As any casual golfer knows, making an eagle can be a thing of rare and deeply satisfying beauty. For at least one brief, shining moment, you get to feel on top of your game.

For the pros on the PGA tour, eagles are business as usual. Here's how the pros ranked in making eagles during the 2001 season:

1. Phil Mickelson: 20 eagles/82 rounds
2. Brad Faxon: 17 eagles/87 rounds
3. Mike Weir: 16 eagles/86 rounds
4. Frank Lickliter II: 15 eagles/102 rounds
5. Jesper Parnevik: 15 eagles/91 rounds.
6. Steve Flesch: 14 eagles/107 rounds
7. Andrew Magee: 14 eagles/94 rounds
8. Tiger Woods: 14 eagles/76 rounds
9. Fred Couples: 13 eagles/68 rounds
10. Shigeki Maruyama: 13 eagles/94 rounds

Source: PGAtour.com

# FAMOUS "CHOKES" BY THE PROS

Golf is a game requiring enormous concentration and nerves of steel. Some days everything will go according to plan and you feel that surge of pride and confidence, only to bottom out the next time you play—to the point that you're so frazzled you miss the easiest of putts.

In the vernacular of the golf world, such a mistake is referred to as a "choke." It is that botched shot that every pro golfer dreads making—particularly in a tournament before onlookers and millions of television viewers. Every golfer, no matter their ability or focus, has "choked" at the most inopportune time, as the list below demonstrates.

1. **Ben Crenshaw:** In the last round of the 1979 British Open, Crenshaw double-bogeyed on the17th hole and lost the tournament, coming in second.

2. **Retief Goosen:** In the final round of the 2001 U.S. Open, the South African–born Goosen putted nearly three feet past the hole on the 18th green. Despite the setback, Goosen miraculously went on to win the title.

3. **Scott Hoch:** At the 1989 Masters, Hoch "choked" on the 10th hole at Augusta and lost the tournament. To this day, he has not won a major title, which lends credence to the belief that "choking" just once can have long-lasting repercussions on a golfer's game.

4. **Greg Norman:** The Shark blew his chance to win the 1996 Masters by shooting a 78 in the final round.

5. **Doug Sanders:** He lost the 1970 British Open after "choking" by missing a three-foot putt at the 18th hole at St. Andrews.

6. **Jean Van de Velde:** His 3-stroke lead going into the final hole at the 1999 British Open ended when he "choked" with a triple-bogey 7.

Source: "The 'C' Word" by John Feinstein in *Golf Magazine*

*In 2001, Fred Couples made 13 eagles in 68 rounds of play.*

# FATHERS AND SONS

## *Pro Golfers*

Back in the 1860s, father and son golfers Old Tom Morris and Young Tom Morris dominated the game, winning four British Opens apiece. Theirs is among the earliest of professional golf dynasties that continue to this day. Here are some other notable father/son golfers who exemplify the adage that "the apple doesn't fall far from the tree."

1. **Willie Park Sr. and Willie Park Jr.**: In the 19th century, Park Sr. won the British Open four times; his son took home the Claret cup once.

2. **Percy and Peter Alliss**: Both have played for Great Britain in the Ryder Cup. Percy was a member of the team three times, while Peter racked up an impressive eight Ryder Cup appearances.

3. **Al and Brent Geiberger**: The SPGA pro and his son competed in the 1998 PGA Championship, the first time a father and son played in the tournament in the same year.

4. **Jack and Gary Nicklaus**: Named for Gary Player, Gary Nicklaus joined the PGA in 1991. He and his father won the 1999 Office Depot Father-Son Challenge.

5. **Bob and David Duval**: Duval's father, Bob, is a member of the SPGA tour. David cad-

*The son also rises: Old Tom and Young Tom Morris.*

died for his father at the 1996 Transamerica, which was the elder Duval's first SPGA tournament.

6. **Davis Love Jr. and Davis Love III**: Davis Love Jr. competed in the 1964 Masters and later became a respected golf teacher. His son turned professional in 1985 and won the 1997 PGA Championship.

7. **Raymond and Robert Floyd**: Now on the SPGA, Ray Floyd won the 1986 U.S. Open; his son Rob has turned pro.

Source: *The Guinness Book of Golf Facts and Feats* by Donald Steel

# FILM AND TV APPEARANCES BY PRO GOLFERS

The track record of professional athletes in film and television is spotty at best. The bravado and natural charisma they display in sports doesn't always come across in their acting attempts—even Muhammad Ali, the very definition of "larger than life," had a difficult time playing himself in the 1977 film version of his autobiography, *The Greatest*.

Unlike Ali or Rosey Grier, who has starred in such classics as *The Thing with Two Heads* (1972), the stars of the golf world have mostly restricted their appearances to cameos or small roles in film and television. Here are some of the golfers who've literally "gone Hollywood" over the years.

1. **Walter Hagen**: The flamboyant golfer played himself in both the 1928 comedy *Green Grass Widows* and the 1930 short *Match Play*, which also features Leo Diegel.

2. **Patty Berg and Babe Zaharias**: The LPGA Hall of Famers made cameo appearances in the 1952 romantic comedy *Pat and Mike*, which was inspired by the Babe herself.

3. **Ben Hogan, Sam Snead, Julius Boros, Jimmy Thomson, and Harry E. Cooper**: A veritable "who's who" of golf greats made cameos in the 1953 Martin & Lewis comedy *The Caddy*.

4. **Jimmy Demaret**: He played himself in a 1954 episode of *I Love Lucy* that found him sharing the course with the disaster-prone redhead.

5. **Arnold Palmer**: He made a cameo in golf aficionado Bob Hope's 1962 film *Call Me Bwana*.

6. **Peter Jacobson**: He appeared in a small role in the HBO adaptation of Dan Jenkins' novel *Dead Solid Perfect* (1988). Ben Crenshaw was the first choice for the part, but turned it down due to the film's racy content and profanity.

7. **Tom Kite**: A cartoon version of the 1997 Ryder Cup captain praised Homer Simpson's golf game in a 1996 episode of *The Simpsons*.

8. **Phil Mickelson**: He gave the Man of Steel some tips in an episode of the ABC series *The Adventures of Lois & Clark: The New Adventures of Superman*, which ran from 1993 to 1997.

9. **The PGA Tour**: Numerous golf pros appeared as themselves in the 1996 Kevin Costner romantic comedy *Tin Cup*, including Fred Couples, Jerry Pate,

*So much for the glamour of Hollywood! Dean Martin (standing, left) looks on while Jimmy Thomson, (kneeling, left), Ben Hogan (standing, right) and Byron Nelson (kneeling, right) give star Jerry Lewis a few pointers in the 1953 comedy,* The Caddy.

Lee Janzen, and Billy Mayfair, to name a few.

Source: imdb.com; *Burried Lies: True Tales and Tall Stories from the PGA Tour* by Peter Jacobsen with Jack Sheehan; *The Guinness Book of Sports Records; Winners and Champions;* all starmovie.com.

# FINAL ROUND SCORING AVERAGES

## *Pro Golfers*

It is easy to see how runners finish a race. Some have strong finishing kicks, while others fade. The way golfers finish tournaments, however, is less visually obvious and seldom discussed. The PGA does keep statistics, though, on final-round scoring averages, and looking at them can be instructive. You discover who finishes strong, who fades, and who remains level with their season scoring averages.

Tiger Woods pretty much stays level. In 2001, he ranked first in season scoring averages, at 68.81 strokes, and second in final round averages, at 68.74 strokes. Davis Love III was also consistent, ranking second in season scoring averages, at 69.06 strokes, and third in final round scoring averages, at 68.88 strokes. That consistency paid off for both

golfers. Woods won $5.7 million in 2001, to rank first in winnings, while Love won $3.2 million and ranked fifth.

The strongest finishing kick in 2001 belonged to Robert Gamez, a touring pro since 1990. His final round scoring average, 68.33, outshone even Tiger's. One problem, though: Gamez ranked 167th in season scoring average for the 22 tournaments he entered. This put him so far back going into the final rounds that he didn't achieve a top-10 finish all year. A final-round 61 that he shot in the Bob Hope Chrysler Classic earned him a tie for 11th place.

Several other strong finishers had the same problem. They entered final rounds far behind and, despite finishing strong, were not in contention to win. This group included Joey Sindelar, who ranked 98th in season scoring averages; Jay Williamson, who ranked 144th: David Peoples, 86th; and Glen Day, who was 81st in season scoring averages.

Some star golfers tend to fade in the final round, the statistics show. Sergio Garcia, who had the third-best season scoring average, at 69.13 strokes, dipped to 26th place in final-round scoring averages, at 70.0 strokes. Phil Mickelson, who was fourth in season scoring averages, at 69.21 strokes, dropped to 55th place in final-round scoring, averaging 70.42 strokes. And David Duval, who ranked seventh in overall scoring, at 69.73 strokes, was 61st in final day scoring averages at 70.47 strokes. Here are the 2001 final-round scoring averages for players on the PGA Tour.

| Rank | Player | Average Score |
|------|--------|---------------|
| 1. | Robert Gamez | 68.33 |
| 2. | Tiger Woods | 68.74 |
| 3. | Davis Love III | 68.88 |
|  | Dudley Hart | 69.00 |
|  | Joey Sindelar | 69.00 |
| 6. | Billy Mayfair | 69.14 |
| 7. | Jay Williamson | 69.17 |
| 8. | David Peoples | 69.24 |
| 9. | Glen Day | 69.33 |
| 10. | Nick Price | 69.35 |

Source: PGATour.com

# GOLF COURSE ARCHITECTS

## American Courses, 1900–1950

A true Renaissance figure in golf history, Charles Blair MacDonald was a founder of the United States Golf Association, the first U.S. Amateur champion, and the preeminent golf course architect in early twentieth-century America. Greatly influenced by the Old Course at St. Andrews, MacDonald began his illustrious career by designing the country's first 18-hole golf course for The Chicago Golf Club in 1894. Prior to MacDonald, there had been no such thing as golf course architecture per se in the United States; in fact, Mac-Donald himself coined the term "golf course architect" in 1902. With his course designs for The Chicago Golf Club and The Old White Course at the Greenbrier, MacDonald paved the way for the following golf course architects, who all rose to prominence in the first half of the century.

1. **Robert Trent Jones**: In his seven-decade career, Jones designed or rebuilt over 400 golf courses in 43 states and 34 countries. English by birth, Jones came to the United States as a child and took up golf as a teenager in Rochester, New York. Reportedly inspired by Donald Ross, Jones began his design career in 1930. His designs include Spyglass Hill in Pebble Beach and Hazeltine National; Jones also reworked such courses as Baltusrol Golf Club, host to seven U.S. Opens, and Oak Hill. Jones was also one of the founders of the American Society of Golf Course Architects. His sons Robert Trent Jr. and Rees have followed in his footsteps.

2. **Alister MacKenzie**: Perhaps best-known today for designing the Augusta National Golf Club course with Bobby Jones, MacKenzie studied medicine before turning to golf course architecture in 1907. After working with Henry Colt, Mac-Kenzie eventually left England for California, where he designed such courses as Cypress Point and Pasatiempo. After befriending Jones at the British Open in the late twenties, MacKenzie collaborated with the golfer on the Augusta National. Unfortunately, MacKenzie died before the course was completed in 1933.

3. **Donald Ross**: With over 400 courses to his credit, the Scottish-born Ross was prolific, to say the least. The former apprentice to Old Tom Morris at St. Andrews, Ross came to the United States in 1899 and immediately began designing courses. Pinehurst No. 2, Oak Hill, the Country Club of Rochester, and Inverness are some of his best-known courses. Ross was also the first president of the American Society of Golf Course Architects.

4. **A. W. Tillinghast**: Nicknamed "Tillie the Terror" for his mercurial temper, Tillinghast was a true character whose flamboyance and drinking binges never got in the way of his course design, which is surprisingly understated. In addition to serving as the PGA's consulting course architect, Tillinghast designed Baltusrol, the Cedar Crest Municipal Golf Course, and the Brackenridge Golf Course, which has the largest clubhouse of any public course in the United States.

Source: golfclubatlas.com; *Historic Golf Courses of America* by Pat Seelig; donaldrosssociety.org

# GOLF COURSE ARCHITECTS

## Golf Pros as Architects

From Old Tom Morris to Tom Weiskopf, professional golfers have long brought their keen eye and hands-on experience to golf course design. Before Charles Blair MacDonald, A. W. Tillinghast, and Donald Ross ushered in the golden age of course design, players like Morris and Willie Park Jr. already had several courses each to their credit, most of them in Great Britain. In the thirties, Bobby Jones collaborated with Dr. Alister McKenzie on the Augusta National. Later, bon vivant Jimmy Demaret designed the Onion Creek Golf Club course. Today, many golf pros team up with certified architects to design courses both here and abroad.

1. **Fred Couples**: Couples and course architect Gene Bates have their own company, Couples Bates Golf Design. As of this writing, they've designed nine courses in the United States and Canada, including the Carolina National Golf Club in North Carolina and the Hamilton Mill Golf Club, which is considered one of the best in metropolitan Atlanta.

2. **Ben Crenshaw**: Crenshaw partnered with architect Bill Coore in 1986 to form Coore & Crenshaw, Inc. Based in Austin, Texas, they have undertaken major renovation projects at such clubs as The Riviera Country Club in Pacific Palisades, California, and the Brook Hollow Country Club in Dallas. The partners also designed the Southern Hills Country Club in Tulsa and Talking Stick in Scottsdale, Arizona.

3. **Jack Nicklaus**: Named by *Golf Digest* in 1999 as one of the most active course designers in the world, Nicklaus collaborated with Pete Dye on the Harbor Town Golf Links in Hilton Head, North Carolina. Many of his courses regularly host professional and national amateur tournaments. Nicklaus has designed, either solo or with a partner, over 200 courses across the world, including such far-flung locales as China and Brunei.

4. **Greg Norman**: Norman has collaborated with Pete Dye and Bob Harrison on courses in Indonesia, the United States, and his native Australia. In 1987, he opened Greg Norman Golf Course Design, which has offices in both Jupiter, Florida, and Sydney, Australia.

5. **Arnold Palmer**: Palmer and noted course architect Ed Seay became partners in 1971. The Palmer Course Design Company has been involved in over 150 projects, most notably the remodeling of the historic Oakmont Country Club. Their courses are spread over 30 states and many countries, including India, Brazil, and Korea.

6. **Tom Weiskopf**: Weiskopf worked with architect Jay Morrish for 12 years before dissolving their partnership in 1994. During their often stormy collaboration, they worked on 25 courses, including Loch Lomond and The Reserve in Palm Desert, California, where Bill Gates has a house above the 18th green.

Source: *Historic Golf Courser of America* by Pat Seelig; golfclubatalas.com

# GOLF COURSE ARCHITECTS

## Notable Architects, 1950–Present

The first half of the 20th century has been christened the "Golden Age" of golf course architecture, when such visionaries as Donald Ross, A. W. Tillinghast, and Robert Trent Jones, among others, designed some of the world's best-loved and most challenging courses: Baltusrol, Pinehurst No. 2, and Oak Hill. These larger-than-life figures set the design bar impossibly high for the next generation of golf course architects, but since 1950, a highly talented and idiosyncratic group of men have risen to the challenge, often in collaboration with professional golfers.

1. **Tom Doak**: The youngest in the group, Doak studied landscape architecture at

Society of Golf Course Architects, Jones has won acclaim for his restoration of the historic Country Club in Brookline, Massachusetts, where Francis Ouimet won the 1913 U.S. Open. He partnered with his father to design the Montauk Downs golf course and later went solo on such projects as Pinehurst No. 7 and the beautiful Sandpines on the Oregon coast.

5. **Robert Trent Jones Jr.**: Like his younger brother Rees, Robert Trent Jones Jr. inherited his father's talent and meticulous eye. After working in his father's firm for 10 years, Jones Jr. struck out on his own in 1972 and has barely stopped to take a breath. As well as designing such eye-catching courses as the Links at Spanish Bay in Pebble Beach and Joondalup in Western Australia, Jones has also devoted his energies to environmental causes as well as writing the best-selling *Golf by Design*.

Source: sportsillustrated.com; golfdigest.com

Cornell University and subsequently won a grant to study 172 golf courses in Great Britain. After working for Pete Dye, Doak gradually established himself as a prodigious talent with his designs for the Heathlands Course at the Legends in Myrtle Beach, South Carolina, and the Stonewall Golf Club near Philadelphia. Doak has also restored the courses of such past masters as Seth Raynor and Charles Blair MacDonald.

2. **Pete Dye**: Named the Golf Course Architect of the Year in 1994 by *Golf World Magazine*, Dye has such courses as Crooked Stick and PGA West on his impressive resume. In addition to being a firm supporter of environmentally safe golf course design, Dye also collaborated with Greg Norman to design The Medalist Golf Club in Florida.

3. **Tom Fazio**: Probably the most celebrated and highest-paid golf course architect today, Fazio learned his craft from his uncle George, a PGA Tour player turned course designer in the fifties. In his nearly 40-year career, Fazio has either designed or restored 125 courses around the world. Restorations include Winged Foot, the Augusta National, and Pine Valley. His design for Shadow Creek, Steve Wynn's opulent Las Vegas golf course, has been hailed as one of the country's all-time greats.

4. **Rees Jones**: The apple didn't fall far from the tree in the case of Rees Jones, the younger of Robert Trent Jones' two sons. The former president of the American

# GOLFERS

## *Demographics*

Just who are our nation's golfers? In an effort to answer that question, the PGA of America conducted their All About Golf II study. After analyzing the results, they separated golfers into eight consumer types by education, age, income, job, level of play, and lifestyle facts. The table on the opposite page shows the groups and their characteristics.

# GOLFERS

## *Who's Typical?*

The expression "typical jock" doesn't have the best connotation, but what about "typical golfer"? Not to worry if you break 90. Only 22 percent of golfers regularly break 90 for 18 holes. Men break 90 only 25 percent of the time. Women break 90 only 7 percent of the time. But what about the rest of us, the "typical golfers"?

*The image of the "typical golfer" has changed considerably from the early days, when most players were proper gentlemen in the country club tradition.*

You may picture the typical golfer to be a white, male country club member with an above-average income, but that stereotype is changing. Golf is growing in popularity among people with incomes below $30,000 and the fastest growing group is junior golfers, ages 12–17. Across the country, 11.9 percent of the population consider themselves golfers. Surprisingly, the north attracts

## Golfers—Demographics

| Category | Percent of Total |
|---|---|
| 1. **Preoccupied Players**<br>Largest group of golfers; play less than other groups, but would like to play more; play 14 rounds a year; typical golfer is male, 38, making $53,000 per year; owns a computer and uses the Internet | 23 |
| 2. **Dilettante Golfer**<br>Avid golfers; play 29 rounds a year; typical golfer is male, 41, making $62,700 per year; often play for business; fashion conscious and computer literate | 16 |
| 3. **Public Pundits**<br>Avid and highly competitive golfers; play mostly public courses; play 39 rounds a year; typical golfer is male, 39; spend vacations golfing; drink sports drinks and soda | 16 |
| 4. **Junior Leaguers**<br>Largest female group; play 22 rounds a year; typical golfer is female, 40, making $58,500 per year; most are not accomplished golfers; most frequent buyers of over-the-counter pain relief | 15.9 |
| 5. **Pull Carts**<br>Retirees who play a lot; play 58 rounds a year, mostly on public courses; typical golfer is 66, making $43,100 per year; most do not own computers; most have no plans to buy a new car | 8.3 |
| 6. **Country Club Traditionals**<br>Most affluent; play 95 percent of rounds on a private course; play 80 rounds a year; typical golfer is male, 59, making $72,400 per year; fastest growing group | 7.6 |
| 7. **Tank Tops and Tennis Shoes**<br>Blue collar males; play 24 rounds per year; typical golfer is 42, making $30,500 per year; most cost-conscious | 7.5 |
| 8. **Swingin' Seniors**<br>Older women; typical golfer is female, 67, making $46,100 per year; rank third in frequency of play; do not buy many golf products or cars | 4.5 |

Source: PGA

more golfers with an average of 20.2 percent living in both Wisconsin and North Dakota.

Power players are golfers who are fanatical about both golf and business. They play 30 rounds or more per year. Here's the lowdown on this group.

Average age: 50
Average years of play: 25
Average score: 91

Another group, known as golf gamblers, take their golf seriously. Their desire to win is intense, with three in four saying that gambling makes the game more enjoyable. Almost half spend more than $500 a year on golf equipment. As many as 64 percent of gamblers admit to cheating on the links, compared with 55 percent of other golfers. Take a look.

Average age: 48
Average Years of Play: 20
Average score: 90

### *What's Average In Golfdom?*

**Average 18-Hole Score**

All golfers: 100
Men: 97
Women: 114

**Average Age**

All golfers: 39
Women: 42
Men: 50

**Average Public Course Green Fees**

Weekday: $36
Weekend: $30

| Average Income | Rounds Played Per Year |
|---|---|
| $65,775 | 20 |
| $68,285 | 15 |

**Miscellaneous**

Average golf holes per 100,000-population: 78
Average number of courses constructed each year: 400

Source: *The Rating Game* by Les Krantz and Sue Sveum

# GOLFING BROTHERS

## *All in the Family*

Taking sibling rivalry to a new level, many brothers have appeared on the links over the years on both the professional and amateur circuits. Fortunately, the family drama has been kept to a minimum—at least before the spectators—even at those tournaments when brothers have played for the title. Such a moment occurred at the 1910 U.S. Open, when Alex Smith defeated his brother Macdonald in a play-off for the title. It was Smith's second U.S. Open title. Four years earlier, he had beaten *another* brother, Willie, who had won the title in 1899. Here are a few other sets of brothers who shared a love for the game.

- **The Turnesa brothers**: Probably the most celebrated golfing brothers are the seven Turnesa brothers, whose father had been a greenskeeper. Six of the Turnesas turned professional, while the youngest, Willie, also known as "Willie the Wedge," won the U.S. Amateur Championship in 1938 and 1948. The sixth-born, Jim, won the 1952 PGA Championship and made the 1953 Ryder Cup team.

- **The Espinosa brothers**: In the twenties and early thirties, Mexican-American brothers Abe and Al Espinosa were familiar figures on the PGA circuit. Winner of the 1928 Western Open, Abe Espinosa later worked as the head pro at a Shreveport, Louisiana, golf course, where he befriended young Tommy Bolt. His brother Al was a runner-up at both the 1927 PGA Championship and the 1929 U.S. Open, and a member of the U.S. Ryder Cup team in 1927, 1929, and 1931.

- **The Hebert brothers**: Jay and Lionel Hebert hit their stride in the late fifties and early sixties. In 1957, Lionel won the PGA Championship and qualified for the Ryder Cup. Jay followed suit, with his 1960 PGA Championship and Ryder Cup appearances in 1959 and 1961.

- **The Ballesteros brothers**: Seve Ballesteros and his brother Manuel hail from the

*He may have given up the throne, but the Duke of Windsor wouldn't give up golf.*

*Mary, Queen of Scots introduced golf to France.*

small town of Pedrena, Spain. One of the game's top players, Seve Ballesteros has three British Opens and two Masters among his many victories. His brother Manuel never emerged from his brother's considerable shadow, but he did well on the European tour and is now president of Spain's PGA.

• **The Wadkins brothers**: From 1971 to 2000, Lanny Wadkins won 21 PGA tournaments, including the 1977 PGA Championship. Growing up in Richmond, he and his brother Bobby won the city's junior championship six times between them. Following in his older brother's footsteps, Bobby Wadkins joined the PGA Tour in 1973, albeit with considerably less fanfare. Now on the SPGA, Bobby Wadkins most recently won the 2001 Lightpath Long Island Classic.

Source: *The Guinness Book of Sports Records: Winners and Champions*; *Links Lore* by Peter F. Stevens

# Golfing Royalty

It may not be known as "the sport of kings" (tennis bears that sobriquet), but golf has a long, royal history, dating back to the fifteenth century. Legend has it that King James II banned "golfe" in Scotland in 1456 because it was distracting his soldiers from archery

practice. Apparently, even defending their kingdom against invaders was a lesser priority than practicing their golf swing.

While King James II may not have looked fondly on golf, many royals since have indulged their passion for the game.

1. **King James IV**: The King of Scotland from 1488 to 1513, King James IV is said to have played the first officially documented match against the Earl of Bothwell in 1504.

2. **Mary, Queen of Scots**: While she is better known for losing her head to Elizabeth I, the ill-fated queen apparently introduced the game to France. The term "caddie" sprang from Mary's use of actual cadets as her assistants.

3. **King Charles I**: The English king reportedly learned of the Irish rebellion while playing golf at Leith in 1641.

4. **The King of Siam**: The King of Siam and other members of the aristocracy regularly played golf at the Royal Hua Hin golf course in the twenties.

5. **The Emperor Franz Josef I**: As well as introducing the sport to Austria, Emperor Franz Josef I actually donated the land to build a course that eventually became the Golf Club Wien in 1901.

6. **The Duke of Windsor**: An avid golfer, he once organized a charity match for the Red Cross at the Bahamas Country Club that

attracted the likes of Walter Hagen, Gene Sarazen and Bobby Jones.

7. **King George VI**: He was elected captain of the Royal and Ancient Golf Club of St. Andrews in 1930, one of five members of the royal family to hold this coveted title.

8. **King Hassan II of Morocco**: The guiding spirit behind the Royal Moroccan Golf Federation, King Hassan II created the Hassan II Trophy in 1971. The tournament is held every November in Dar Es-Salam.

Source: *The Guinness Book of Sports Records: Winners & Champions*; triviagolf.com; *Why Do They Call it a Birdie? 101 Fascinating Facts About Golf* by Frank Coffey; *The Ultimate Golf Trivia Book* by Mike Towle

# GREENS IN REGULATION

## *Pro Golfers*

Any golfer who is hitting green after green in regulation is likely enjoying a low-scoring, high-satisfaction, great-to-be-alive-on-this-beautiful-day round of golf. You are playing as golf was designed to be played—driving the ball well, hitting accurate irons, putting for many birdies, and giving yourself a great chance to break par for the round!

"In regulation" means getting your ball on the green in the number of strokes that, with two putts, will give you a par on the hole. Therefore, to hit greens in regulation, you must reach the green of a par-3 hole in just one stroke; a par-4 hole in two strokes; and a par-5 hole in three strokes.

For touring pros, the percentage of greens in regulation is an important, though not perfect, indicator of how well they're playing. Two of the PGA Tour's top three money winners in 2001, Tiger Woods ($5.7 million) and David Toms ($3.8 million), also ranked in the top 10 for greens in regulation. Phil Mickelson was an exception. He ranked 2nd in prize money ($4.4 million), despite ranking 26th in greens in regulation. And Tom Lehman, who led the tour in greens in regulation, ranked 20th in prize money, winning $1.9 million.

### *Greens in Regulation, 2001*

| Player | Percent in Regulation |
|---|---|
| 1. Tom Lehman | 74.5 |
| 2. Charles Howell III | 73.5 |
| 3. John Cook | 72.9 |
| 4. Joe Durant | 72.1 |
| 5. David Toms | 71.9 |
| Bob Tway | 71.9 |
| Tiger Woods | 71.9 |
| 8. Kenny Perry | 71.4 |
| 9. Hal Sutton | 71.1 |
| 10. Three tied at 71.0 | |

### *Previous Leaders in Greens in Regulation*

| Year | Player | Percent in Regulation |
|---|---|---|
| 2000 | Tiger Woods | 75.2 |
| 1999 | Tiger Woods | 71.4 |
| 1998 | Hal Sutton | 71.3 |
| 1997 | Tom Lehman | 72.7 |
| 1996 | Fuzzy Zoeller | 72.1 |
| 1995 | Lennie Clements | 72.3 |
| 1994 | Bill Glasson | 73.0 |
| 1993 | Fuzzy Zoeller | 73.6 |
| 1992 | Tim Simpson | 74.0 |

Source: PGATour.com

# LONGEST DRIVES

Many golfers enjoy "skins" games and other friendly bets. How many might have wagered, then, that the longest drive measured on the 2001 PGA Tour was hit by John Daly? Probably sounds like a sure winner to golf fans who know Daly's reputation as a slugger. But, in fact, Daly's longest drive of 387 yards ranks only fourth on the PGA's list of atomic blasts.

Even more surprising is that Casey Martin hit the longest drive all year and was the only golfer to break the mind-boggling 400-yard barrier. Martin, of course, gained national fame for successfully suing the Professional Golf Association to win the right to use a golf cart in tournament play. That's because he has a leg disability that prevents him from walking a full 18 holes. While the PGA argued that walking the course is a necessary part of tournament play, Martin's prowess off the tee makes one wonder if the

*Greg Norman averaged 68.81 strokes per round of tournament play in 1994.*

PGA had another reason for wanting him on the sidelines. Coincidently or not, Martin's 409-yard blast makes his old Stanford teammate, Tiger Woods, look like a short-ball hitter. Tiger's longest drive in 2001 was a mere 363 yards, tying him for 28th place.

The PGA's list proves that almost any tour golfer can hit a 300-yard drive. In fact, 212 pros hit drives of 337 yards or longer, and 79 of them smashed drives of 350 yards or more.

| Player | Yards |
|---|---|
| Casey Martin | 409 |
| Shaun Micheel | 398 |
| Jay Don Blake | 393 |
| John Daly | 387 |
| Duffy Waldorf | 378 |
| Carlos Franco | 377 |
| Justin Leonard | 376 |
| Brett Quigley | 376 |
| Steve Allan | 375 |
| Brian Kontak | 374 |

Source: PGAtour.com

# LOWEST SCORING AVERAGES IN A YEAR

## Pro Golfers

In the history of golf, Tiger Woods is the only player ever to average less than 68 strokes per round in a full year of tournament play. He accomplished the feat in 2000, when he entered 20 official tournaments. What did this scoring average achieve for Woods? For starters, he won $9,188,321 in prize money. He was victorious in nine tournaments, including three majors—the U.S. Open, the British Open, and the PGA Championship. He finished second in four tournaments, and was among the top 10 finishers in 17 tournaments. He never missed a cut.

In this record year, Woods played 80 rounds, totaling 1,440 holes. Each hole was on a championship course, configured for tournament play. His average score per hole was 3.77 strokes. His highest score for any round was 75; his lowest 61. He shot 65 or under nine

times. His lowest tournament total was 259 strokes, 21 below par, at the WGC-NEC Invitational, where his scores were 64, 61, 67, and 67, an average of 64.75 per round.

Here's a look at which professional golfers had some of the lowest scoring averages.

| Golfer | Year | Scoring Average |
|---|---|---|
| Tiger Woods | 2000 | 67.79 |
| Byron Nelson | 1945 | 68.33 |
| Tiger Woods | 1999 | 68.43 |
| Tiger Woods | 2001 | 68.81 |
| Greg Norman | 1994 | 68.81 |
| Nick Price | 1997 | 68.98 |
| Greg Norman | 1990 | 69.10 |
| Nick Price | 1993 | 69.11 |
| Sam Snead | 1950 | 69.23 |
| Ben Hogan | 1948 | 69.30 |

Source: triviagolf.com

# LOWEST SCORING ROUNDS

## Pro Golfers

Only four golfers—three men and a woman—have ever shot 59 in a U.S. professional golf tournament. Al Geiberger was the first to break 60, on June 10, 1977, in the second round of the Danny Thomas-Memphis Classic. Because of soggy conditions, however, players were allowed to lift, clean, and place their balls.

More than a decade passed before Chip Beck duplicated the feat, carding 13 birdies

*Since turning pro in 1977, Hall of Famer Betsy King has earned over $7 million.*

and no bogeys in the third round of the Las Vegas Invitational. Despite his record-tying performance in October 1991, Beck did not win the tournament.

Annika Sorenstam is the only woman golfer to break 60. She did it at the Moon Valley Country Club in Phoenix, Arizona, in March 2001.

But the most dramatic 59 of all was David Duval's in the final round of the 1999 Bob Hope Chrysler Classic. His gallery grew steadily that day as he hit one precise shot after another, leaving little need to sink long putts or make spectacular saves.

The man in sunglasses teed up on the par-5 18th, needing an eagle to shoot 59 and win the tournament. He cracked a long, straight drive that settled in the fairway. But to reach the green in two, he needed to carry a distant water hazard. Duval hit a 5-iron shot that sailed over the water, landed in the middle of the green, bit, and rolled backward. The ball stopped at the left and rear of the pin, about 12 feet from the hole.

Spectator Don Spickelmeir described, on pgatour.com, how it felt to be there: "David looked tense as he surveyed the putt. I couldn't imagine how he was keeping it together, because the tension and drama of the moment had me more than a little shaky. I swear, the thousands that lined that fairway and green

were holding their breath as one, as Duval took that putter back.

"I can still see the ball rolling, breaking slightly right, and bending toward the hole...and then it disappeared. I heard the roar and I saw the terminally taciturn Duval pumping both his arms in the air and I remember being stunned by what I had just witnessed. People were screaming and high-fiving each other, couples were hugging each other, and an older gentleman standing quietly next to me had a tear on his cheek."

### Lowest PGA Rounds

| Golfer | Year | Score |
|---|---|---|
| Al Geiberger | 1977 | 59 |
| Chip Beck | 1991 | 59 |
| David Duval | 1999 | 59 |
| Al Brosch | 1951 | 60 |
| Bill Nary | 1952 | 60 |
| Tommy Bolt | 1954 | 60 |
| Ted Kroll | 1954 | 60 |
| Mike Souchak | 1955 | 60 |
| Sam Snead | 1957 | 60 |
| David Frost | 1990 | 60 |
| Davis Love III | 1994 | 60 |
| Steve Lowery | 1997 | 60 |
| Tiger Woods | 2000 | 60 |
| Mark Calcavecchia | 2001 | 60 |

# LPGA

## All-Time Earnings Winners

In terms of both media attention and overall earnings, golf very much remains a man's game—for the moment, anyway. Although

### Lowest Scoring Rounds
**Annika Sorenstam's Record-Breaking Round**

| HOLE | 1 | 2 | 3 | 4 | 5 | 6 | 7 | 8 | 9 | OUT | 10 | 11 | 12 | 13 | 14 | 15 | 16 | 17 | 18 | IN | TOTAL |
|---|---|---|---|---|---|---|---|---|---|---|---|---|---|---|---|---|---|---|---|---|---|
| PAR | 4 | 3 | 4 | 5 | 3 | 4 | 4 | 5 | 4 | 36 | 5 | 3 | 4 | 5 | 4 | 3 | 4 | 4 | 4 | 36 | 72 |
| SCORE | 3 | 2 | 3 | 4 | 3 | 4 | 4 | 4 | 4 | 31 | 4 | 2 | 3 | 4 | 3 | 2 | 3 | 3 | 4 | 28 | 59 |

Source: triviagolf.com; pgatour.com; lpga.com; golfonline.com

they are overshadowed and outearned by Tiger and "El Nino," among others, such LPGA stars as Annika Sorenstam and Karrie Webb are poised to crack the eight-figure mark in prize winnings in the near future.

Hall of Famer Nancy Lopez just missed cracking the LPGA's top 10 earners with $5,310,391 in prize money, while veteran Kathy Whitworth comes in at No. 56 with career earnings of $1,731,770. The legendary Babe Zaharias ranks No. 376 with $66,237 in earnings. Here are the top 10 earners as of November 19, 2001

| Golfer | Earnings |
| --- | --- |
| 1. Annika Sorenstam | $8,306,464 |
| 2. Karrie Webb | $7,698,299 |
| 3. Betsy King | $7,187,444 |
| 4. Dottie Pepper | $6,658,613 |
| 5. Juli Inkster | $6,512,487 |
| 6. Beth Daniel | $6,433,001 |
| 7. Meg Mallon | $5,954,573 |
| 8. Pat Bradley | $5,743,605 |
| 9. Laura Davies | $5,695,525 |
| 10. Rosie Jones | $5,683,934 |

Source: lpga.com

# LPGA

## All-Time Major Championship Leaders

Fans of women's golf will not be surprised that Patty Berg won more major championships than anyone else in LPGA history. She captured all her majors in a 21-year span, from 1937 through 1958, but continued competing for more than four decades. By the time she retired in 1980, she had won 57 LPGA tournaments.

Berg's achievement is all the more impressive when you consider that she competed with the likes of Babe Didrikson Zaharias, Louise Suggs, and Betsy Rawls. During the early years of the LPGA, the 5'2" Berg was known as one of the "Big Four" of women's golf, along with Suggs, Zaharias, and Betty Jameson. Despite her small stature, the red-headed, freckle-faced Berg hit the ball powerfully and was considered a superb shot-maker.

Her major championships included the Women's Amateur in 1938; the U.S. Women's Open in 1946; seven victories in the Western Open; and seven more victories in the Title-holders Championship, which was founded in 1937 as a women's version of The Masters, and was played on the same Augusta National Course in Georgia until 1966.

Here are the LPGA all-time major championship leaders.

| Golfer | Number of Victories |
| --- | --- |
| Patty Berg | 16 |
| Mickey Wright | 13 |
| Louise Suggs | 13 |
| Babe Zacharias | 12 |
| Julie Inkster | 9 |
| Betsy Rawls | 8 |
| JoAnne Carner | 7 |
| Kathy Whitworth | 6 |
| Pat Bradley | 6 |
| Betsy King | 6 |
| Patty Sheehan | 6 |
| Glenna C. Vare | 6 |

Source: *ESPN Sports Almanac 2002*; HickokSports.com; wgv.com; lpga.com

# LPGA

## Highest Earnings for a Single Season

Talk about inflation. In 1951, the legendary Babe Zaharias was the LPGA's top earner for the season with winnings totaling $15,087. Fifty years later, Sweden's Annika Sorenstam became the first LPGA player to cross the $2 million mark with $2,105,868 in earnings for 2001. While that may seem like the proverbial small potatoes compared to what the top winners on the PGA took home, Sorenstam's record-making earnings show just how far the LPGA has come since it was founded in 1950. Here are the top 10 single-season earnings leaders on the LPGA tour

| LPGA | | |
|---|---|---|
| **Golfer** | **Earnings** | |
| 1.  Annika Sorenstam | $2,105,868 | (2001) |
| 2.  Karrie Webb | $1,876,853 | (2000) |
| 3.  Karrie Webb | $1,591,959 | (1999) |
| 4.  Annika Sorenstam | $1,236,789 | (1997) |
| 5.  Annika Sorenstam | $1,092,748 | (1998) |
| 6.  Karrie Webb | $1,002,000 | (1996) |
| 7.  Beth Daniel | $863,578 | (1990) |
| 8.  Pat Bradley | $763,118 | (1991) |
| 9.  Dottie Pepper | $693,335 | (1992) |
| 10. Laura Davies | $687,201 | (1994) |

bestcourses.com

# LPGA

## *Most Career Starts Since 1956*

One of the founders of the LPGA (at age 16!) along with her sister Alice, diminutive Marlene Hagge has been playing golf almost as long as she's been able to walk. A junior champion who made the cut at the 1947 U.S. Women's Open at 13, Hagge won her first LPGA tournament five years later at 18. With this win at the 1952 Sarasota Open, Hagge became the youngest player ever to win an LPGA tournament, a record still standing 50 years later.

During her lengthy career, Hagge won 24 more tournaments, including the 1956 LPGA Championship. Although she's been sidelined by injury in recent years, Hagge has accumulated more career starts on the LPGA Tour since 1956 than any other player—a mind-boggling 939, nearly 100 more than runner-up Kathy Whitworth.

Of the remaining players on the list, three are still actively competing on the LPGA Tour: Pat Bradley, Shelley Hamlin, and Sally Little.

| **Player** | **Career Starts** |
|---|---|
| 1.  Marlene Hagge | 939 |
| 2.  Kathy Whitworth | 846 |
| 3.  Sandra Palmer | 804 |
| 4.  Sandra Spuzich | 698 |
| 5.  Pat Bradley | 692 |
| 6.  Shelley Hamlin | 689 |
|     Sally Little | 689 |

Source: *Golf Magazine*, November 2001

# LPGA

## *Rookie of the Year*

Like their male counterparts in the PGA, not all winners of the LPGA Rookie of the Year Award enjoy great success after their initial seasons. Most, however, are doing very well, thank you. The top three money winners in 2001, as it happens, were all LPGA rookies of the year in the past decade. Annika Sorenstam, the 1994 award winner, topped the 2001 winnings list with $2.1 million. Se Ri Pak, 1998's top rookie, was second in winnings at $1.6 million, and Karrie Webb, 1996 rookie of the year, was a close third, banking $1.5 million in 2001.

The least successful rookies of the year in the past decade were Lisa Hackney, 1997 and Suzanne Strudwick, 1993. Neither woman has yet captured an LPGA tournament victory. Strudwick ranked No. 108 on the 2001 LPGA prize money list, winning $58,861, while Hackney was No. 168, scratching out $9,818 in winnings.

Recent rookie honors show that Korea has become fertile ground indeed for producing top women golfers. Three of the last four LPGA rookie award winners were born in Korea. They are Se Ri Pak; Mi Hyun Kim; and Hee-Won Han. Here's a list of rookies honored over the last decade.

| Year | Player |
|---|---|
| 2001 | Hee-Won Han |
| 2000 | Dorothy Delasin |
| 1999 | Mi Hyun Kim |

He may be small in stature, but Gary Player (right) is a formidable golfer who's won the majors nine times since turning pro in 1952 (at left, Arnold Palmer).

| | |
|---|---|
| 1998 | Se Ri Pak |
| 1996 | Karrie Webb |
| 1997 | Lisa Hackney |
| 1995 | Pat Hurst |
| 1994 | Annika Sorenstam |
| 1993 | Suzanne Strudwick |
| 1992 | Helen Alfredssen |

Source: *ESPN Sports Almanac 2002*; LPGAtour.com; golfweb.com

# LPGA HALL OF FAME

## *Active Honorees*

Now part of the World Golf Hall of Fame, the LPGA Tour Hall of Fame was officially established in 1967. To date, 17 of the game's most celebrated women, including Patty Berg, Louise Suggs, and the late Babe Didrikson Zaharias, have qualified for this honor, which is bestowed upon retired veterans and current members of the tour. LPGA committees have revised the rules for inclusion several times. Since 1999, active LPGA golfers must satisfy the following requirements to be considered for the Hall of Fame.

1. They must have played on the tour for no less than 10 years.

2. They must have won one of the following: a Majors tournament, the Vare Trophy, or the Rolex Player of the Year award.

3. They must accumulate a total of 27 Hall of Fame points. Each LPGA tournament victory, Vare Trophy, and Player of the Year award equals one point; each LPGA major tournament victory earns two points.

Given these requirements, three active members of the LPGA Tour have been inducted into the Hall of Fame since 1999. They join five active Hall of Famers who qualified prior to 1999:

| | Player | Year Inducted | Year Joined Tour |
|---|---|---|---|
| 1. | JoAnne Carner | 1982 | 1970 |
| 2. | Nancy Lopez | 1987 | 1977 |
| 3. | Pat Bradley | 1991 | 1974 |
| 4. | Patty Sheehan | 1993 | 1980 |
| 5. | Betsy King | 1995 | 1977 |
| 6. | Amy Alcott | 1999 | 1975 |
| 7. | Beth Daniel | 2000 | 1979 |
| 8. | Juli Inkster | 2000 | 1983 |

Source: lpga.com; hickoksports.com

# MAJOR CHAMPIONSHIPS

## *Most Won, Amateur and Professional*

Jack Nicklaus and Bobby Jones were undoubtedly the dominant golfers of their eras, just as Tiger Woods is today. And it is tempting, when we see 20 major championships beside Nicklaus' name, to crown the Golden Bear as the greatest golfer who ever lived.

But because few of us were around when Bobby Jones burned up the links in the twenties, it is easy to overlook his amazing record. While it took Nicklaus 24 years (from 1962 to 1986) to capture his 20 major titles, Jones won his 13 majors in only 8 years, from 1923 to 1930.

Since Jones played, the definition of majors has changed. Today, the majors are considered to be The Masters, the PGA, and the United States and British Opens. In Jones' day, the majors were the U.S. and British Opens and the U.S. and British Amateurs.

Bobby Jones never played professional golf, but what he accomplished is unequaled in the sport. He won four U.S. Opens and four U.S. Amateurs, plus three British Opens and one British Amateur—a total of 13 majors! And although Tiger Woods astounded the golfing world by winning four consecutive majors in 2000 and 2001, Jones remains the only golfer ever to win all four majors—the Grand Slam—in a single year! He did it in 1930, and then retired from competitive golf. No wonder he remains the yardstick by which all other golfers are judged.

| Player | Majors Won |
|--------|-----------:|
| Jack Nicklaus | 20 |
| Bobby Jones | 13 |
| Walter Hagen | 11 |
| John Ball | 9 |
| Ben Hogan | 9 |
| Gary Player | 9 |
| Tiger Woods | 9 |
| Arnold Palmer | 8 |
| Tom Watson | 8 |

Source: PGAtour.com; golfeurope.com; *The Majors*, by John Feinstein

# MEN'S GOLFING FIRSTS

Records are broken, victories tallied, and trends set all the time in golf. We've gathered a handful from the firsts of the 20th century, when the game exploded in popularity across America and the rest of the world.

1. **Greg Norman** was the first golfer to exceed $10 million in career earnings.

2. **Gene Sarazen** became the first player in 1922 to win the U.S. Open and the USPGA Championship in the same year, when he was 20 years old.

3. **Bobby Jones** became the first player in 1926 to win the U.S. Open and the British Open in the same year.

4. **Walter Hagen** became the first professional golfer in 1922 to open his own golf equipment company.

5. **Nick Faldo** became the first foreign golfer in 1990 to win the PGA Player of the Year Award.

6. **J. H. Taylor**, one of the preeminent golfers at the turn of the century, became the founder and chairman of the first professional golfer's association in 1901.

7. **Walter Hagen** was the first American golfer to win the British Open when he took the prize in 1922.

8. **Charles E. "Chick" Evans Jr.** was the first player to win both the U.S. Amateur and the U.S. Open in 1916.

9. **Lee Trevino** was the first player to break 70 on all four rounds in the U.S. Open, scoring a 275 in 1968.

10. **Arnold Palmer** was the first PGA golfer to appear on the cover of *Time*.

Source: triviagolf.com; espn.go.com/classic/biography; encarta.msn.com

# MINORITY GOLFERS

Until the emergence of Tiger Woods in 1997, golf was predominantly a white man's game—and not just at the national level. Things are starting to change, but it's a slow process. In 1991 the Minority Golf Association of America was formed for the purpose of introducing inner-city kids to golf. The success of Woods has been another boon to the game. Suddenly kids are not just saying they "wanna be like Mike." Now they want to be like Tiger, too. Here are a few facts about minority golfers in America

• Minority players make up only 3.3 percent of the nation's 26.4 million golfers.

• The number of African-American golfers has doubled since 1996, from 360,000 to 882,000.

• The number of minority golfers has increased by 30 percent over the last 10 years, while the total number has remained the same.

• In 1992 there were only 85 junior golf programs for inner-city youth. Today there are 500.

*The number of African-American golfers in America has doubled since 1996.*

- Nationally there are 400 golf groups for minority men and women.

- There are 200 amateur and pro-am golf tournaments held each year in the U.S. for minority golfers.

- Still lagging is employment in the golf industry. Less than 1 percent of those employed in this field are African American.

Source: *The Charlotte Observer; The Gazette,* in Colorado Springs

# MINORITY GOLFERS

## *African-American Golf Pros*

From the moment he first appeared on the scene, Tiger Woods has been hailed as a role model for African-American golfers. Suddenly, kids from the inner city who had never been outside city limits, much less on a golf course, were clamoring to tee off. Although Woods has endured some racial taunts, he and other African-American golf pros like Jim Thorpe and Calvin Peete owe their current success on the PGA circuit to the efforts of the following African-American golfers, trailblazers all:

1. **John Shippen**: Despite widespread protest by other players, the 18-year-old caddy was permitted to compete in the 1896 U.S. Open, thanks in no small part to the efforts of then USGA President Theodore Havemeyer. Weathering the tension with remarkable poise, Shippen took fifth place and $10. He played in four more U.S. Opens before the PGA enacted Article 3 in 1916, which barred African Americans from tournament play.

2. **Dewey Brown**: The swing coach for John D. Rockefeller, Brown was accepted into the PGA in 1928, but only as a club professional. Unable to compete on the PGA circuit, Brown played on the United Golf Association tour for African-American pros and amateurs.

3. **Bill Spiller**: A star on the UGA circuit, Spiller fought the PGA's "whites-only" clause in court for years. Due to his tireless efforts, the PGA finally revoked Article 3 in 1961.

4. **Charlie Sifford**: The cigar-chomping Sifford became the first African American to win a PGA Tour event with his victory in the 1957 Long Beach Open.

5. **Lee Elder**: Now on the SPGA Circuit, Elder became the first African American to play in The Masters in 1975.

Source: *Links Lore* by Peter F. Stevens

# NICKNAMES

## *Pro Golfers*

Muhammad Ali dubbed himself the "Greatest." Joe Namath went by "Broadway Joe" and Michael Jordan is "Air Jordan." Athletes' nicknames, often coined by sports writers or fans, have become part of sports lore. We all know Aussie Greg Norman as the "Shark," which is a tribute to his intense drive and competitive nature. The following golfers have earned nicknames over the years, although not always to their liking.

1. **Ben "Gentle Ben" Crenshaw**: The easy-going, polite Texan is called this both on and off the links.

2. **Sergio "El Nino" Garcia**: This nickname was given to this talented golfer from Spain, who turned pro at 19.

3. **Ben "Bantam Ben" Hogan**: Famously intolerant, Hogan reportedly hated this nickname, believing that he was hardly small at 5'9" and 160 lbs.

4. **Jack The "Golden Bear" Nicklaus**: Nicklaus earned this moniker after losing weight and letting his hair grow in the seventies. It may not seem like the most flattering nickname, but it sure beats some of his prior nicknames: "Fat Jack," "Blob-O" and "Whaleman."

5. **Gary The "Black Knight" Player**: The driven South African pro always wears black in tournaments, hence the nickname. Player uses the Black Knight as the logo for his company, The Gary Player Group.

6. **Gene The "Squire" Sarazen**: Sarazen was dubbed the "Squire" because of his vast landholdings and his penchant of wearing knickers on the golf course.

7. **Sam "Slammin' Sam" Snead**: Still playing since turning pro in 1936, Snead is known for hitting lengthy drives.

8. **Louise "Miss Sluggs" Suggs**: The Georgia-born founder of the LPGA was given her nickname by none other than comedian Bob Hope.

9. **Eldrick "Tiger" Woods**: Nicknamed for a Vietnamese soldier whom the golfer's father befriended during his tour of duty in southeast Asia.

10. **Mildred "Babe" Didrikson Zaharias**: As in Babe Ruth. An all-around athlete, Zaharias earned her nickname after hitting five home runs in a baseball game.

Sources: PGAtour.com; LPGA.com

# OVERLOOKED GOLF GREATS

So much attention is focused on golf's elite that many deserving players haven't been given their due. Here are seven golfers whose impressive records shouldn't be overlooked.

- **Julius Boros**: Compared to the young players of today, Boros started at the relatively old age of 30. He won 18 PGA titles, however, and finished strong as the oldest player to win a major at age 48. At 55 he lost the Westchester Classic only in a sudden-death playoff. Boros would have been great on the senior tour, but it had not yet been established. Instead, he was instrumental in starting the 50-and-older circuit.

- **Billy Casper**: One of only six golfers to win at least 50 PGA tournaments in their career (he had 51), Casper also won the Vardon Trophy five times. He was the PGA Player of the Year twice and played on the Ryder Cup team eight times. Unfortunately, Casper played during the heyday of the big three—Arnold Palmer, Jack Nicklaus, and Gary Player. Back then, he made news more often for personal traits, such as having 11 children, than for his golf prowess.

- **Jimmy Demeret**: A 31-PGA Tour winner, Demeret was so colorful that his personality overshadowed his own golf game. He is known for his quick wit and stylishly comfortable clothing more than his three wins at The Masters. He went on to fame in five seasons as a commentator on *Shell's Wonderful World of Golf*.

- **Ralph Guidahl**: Guidahl took the golf world by storm, but his whirlwind success soon fizzled out and he quit the circuit after only a short time in the limelight. He won back-to-back U.S. Open titles in 1937 and 1938 and Western Open titles from 1936–1938. By 1940, he was struggling with his swing and he finally left the tour in 1942 when he failed to get back his earlier form.

- **Cary Middlecoff**: A dentist by profession, Middlecoff devoted a decade or so to golf, but never entirely left his practice "in case golf didn't work out." In 1949 he won the U.S. Open as well as six other tournaments. He also won six times in 1951 and 1955, and tallied 40 pro wins in his career.

- **Larry Nelson**: A prominent name on the senior tour today, Larry Nelson never received as many accolades during his PGA career. Along with the well-known names of Nicklaus, Watson, and Ballesteros, Nelson is the only other player to win at least three majors in the eighties. Nelson attributes lack of consistency as the cause of his relatively low profile.

- **Peter Thomson**: An Australian, Thomson saw his share of wins on the pro tour, but few of them on the U.S. Tour. He won five British Open titles as well as numerous second-place finishes. His only U.S win was in the 1956 Texas International Open. The Senior PGA tour, however, has been good to him; he won 9 tournaments in 1985 alone, and 11 overall.

Source: Authors, *The Best and Worst of Golf*

slam" of winning four majors in a row. Woods also won The Players Championship, which some players consider a fifth major. PGA Commissioner Tim Finchem joked that this completed the "Tiger Slam" when he presented Woods with the 2001 Player of the Year Award.

### PGA Players of the Year

| Year | Golfer |
| --- | --- |
| 2001 | Tiger Woods |
| 2000 | Tiger Woods |
| 1999 | Tiger Woods |
| 1998 | Mark O'Meara |
| 1997 | Tiger Woods |
| 1996 | Tom Lehman |
| 1995 | Greg Norman |
| 1994 | Nick Price |
| 1993 | Nick Price |
| 1992 | Fred Couples |
| 1991 | Corey Pavin |

Source: *ESPN Sports Almanac 2002*; tigerwoods.com; sports.yahoo.com

# PLAYERS OF THE YEAR

## PGA

PGA touring pros vote each year on who among them will receive the Jack Nicklaus Award for player of the year. And since Tiger Woods first won the honor in 1997, there has been little doubt each year—save for Mark O'Meara's 1998 award—of the vote's outcome.

In his second year as a pro, Woods received the 1997 award in recognition of four tournament victories, including his electrifying first Masters title. Tiger secured the honor again in 1999 with eight tournament wins, including The Masters and U.S. Open. In 2000 he won the award for no less than nine victories that included the U.S. Open, the British Open, and the PGA Championship.

In 2001 Woods had what might be considered an off-year compared to the standard he set in the two previous years. He won "only" five tournaments. But one of those happened to be The Masters, which completed a "grand

# PGA

## Most Career Starts

In his 30-plus years as a golf pro, Dave Eichelberger has never attracted the media spotlight like many of his contemporaries. Nor has he ever won a majors tournament, though he did take the 1999 U.S. Senior Open. He is one of the many unsung players on the tour, golfers who soldier on through tournament after tournament, often for very little financial reward.

What Eichelberger has accomplished since turning pro in 1966 is nonetheless remarkable, regardless of how his PGA Tour record compares to his peers. The man named the Comeback Player of the Year in 1994 has started on the PGA Tour 783 times—ahead of both Raymond Floyd and Arnold Palmer, who come in second and third, respectively. It may not have the cachet of a majors title or earn him a lucrative endorsement contract—Eichelberger has yet to appear on a cereal box or behind the wheel of a sports car for his PGA starting record—but his persistence needs to be acknowledged.

**No golfer has come close to matching Byron Nelson's record of 11 consecutive victories in 1945.**

The list of most consecutive victories is instructive for what it says about competition on the professional circuit. After Hogan won six in a row in 1948, no pro could manage more than four consecutive wins for the next half century—until Tiger Woods came along and won six tournaments in a row in 1999–2000. Here are the pros with the most consecutive victories.

| Golfer | Year | Number of Wins |
| --- | --- | --- |
| Byron Nelson | 1945 | 11 |
| Ben Hogan | 1948 | 6 |
| Tiger Woods | 1999–2000 | 6 |
| Walter Hagen | 1923 | 4 |
| Joe Kirkwood Sr. | 1924 | 4 |
| Bill Melhorn | 1929 | 4 |
| Horton Smith | 1929 | 4 |
| Jackie Burke Jr. | 1952 | 4 |
| Gary Player | 1978 | 3 |
| Tom Watson | 1980 | 3 |
| Nick Price | 1993 | 3 |

Source: triviagolf.com; golfeurope.com; wgv.com; infoplease.com

| Player | Career Starts |
| --- | --- |
| 1. Dave Eichelberger | 783 |
| 2. Raymond Floyd | 765 |
| 3. Arnold Palmer | 752 |
| 4. George Archer | 733 |
| 5. Bobby Wadkins | 713 |
| 6. Tom Kite | 712 |
| 7. Leonard Thompson | 705 |

Source: November 2001 *Golf Magazine*

# PGA

## Most Consecutive Victories

Two records in sports are considered virtually unbreakable. One is Joe DiMaggio's 56-consecutive-game hitting streak in 1941. The other is Byron Nelson's 11 consecutive victories in 1945. Both records have endured for more than half a century, and many feel that Nelson's feat is the more secure of the two.

Nelson's record of 11 consecutive victories may have been helped by the fact that many top professionals, including Ben Hogan, were fighting in World War II in 1945. Nelson was medically exempt from the draft because his blood was slow to coagulate. Nevertheless, the greatness of "Lord Byron" is unquestioned. In his record-setting year he won 19 tournaments and also set a PGA record for stroke average with 68.33 strokes per round (a record since broken by Tiger Woods). Nelson peaked in 1944–1946, when he won 34 of the 75 tournaments he entered, and finished second 16 times. He finished out of the top 10 only once.

# PGA

## Most Consecutive Years with a Win

Jack Nicklaus' record for the most consecutive years with a PGA tournament win is deceiving because it sounds so minimal. Someone might conclude that Jack, in at least a few of those 17 seasons, must have eked out just one victory that kept the streak going. The idea seems not only plausible, but probable. Care to guess in how many of those years Nicklaus recorded only one win? Go ahead. Then ponder the facts below.

Nicklaus' streak began in 1962, when he won three victories, and ended in 1978, when he also won three times. He averaged nearly four wins per season during the 17 years. His best years were 1972 and 1973, when he won seven victories each season. Among these wins were The Masters and U.S. Open in 1972 and the PGA in 1973. He also had five seasons of five victories; one season of four wins; four seasons of three wins; and five seasons of two wins. There were exactly no years when he had only one win. Nicklaus captured 65 of his 70 career wins during those 17 years.

In comparison, Billy Casper's 16 consecutive years with a win, from 1956 through 1971, included three years when he won only once. He won six times in 1968 and four times in each of six other years. He won 48 of his 51 career victories in 16 consecutive years.

### Most Consecutive Years with a Win

| Golfer | Number of Years |
| --- | --- |
| Jack Nicklaus | 17 |
| Billy Casper | 16 |
| Lee Trevino | 14 |
| Sam Snead | 11 |
| Harry Cooper | 11 |
| Leo Diegel | 11 |
| Arnold Palmer | 10 |
| Lloyd Mangrum | 9 |
| Ben Hogan | 9 |
| Walter Hagen | 9 |

Source: triviagolf.com and PGAtour.com

# PGA

## Most Major Professional Championships

Reasonable people may disagree about the best golfer of all time. Arguments can be made for several of the sport's legends, including Bobby Jones, Byron Nelson, Ben Hogan, Sam Snead, and now Tiger Woods. But if you measure greatness strictly by the number of major *professional* championships won, there is little argument: Jack Nicklaus is the best who ever was. After all, the Golden Bear's 18 major professional victories are 64 percent more than the 11 majors won by Walter Hagen, the flamboyant twenties golf star. And Bobby Jones never played pro golf.

But a close comparison between the records of Nicklaus and Hagen may leave some room for argument, after all. Hagen won

the British Open four times, compared to Nicklaus' three, and they tied with five victories each in the PGA Championship. Nicklaus won the U.S. Open four times, compared to two for Hagen. But the real difference in their records is The Masters tournament. Nicklaus earned six Masters titles, but Hagen was already past his prime when the first Masters was held in 1934. But here's something to ponder. What if there *had* been a Masters in the twenties? Could Hagen have won it six or seven times, between 1920 and 1933, to rival Nicklaus at the top of the professional majors victory list? Like a fantasy fight between Joe Louis and Muhammad Ali, we can guess at the outcome, but we'll never know. The following is a list of players who won the most major professional championships.

| Player | Majors Won |
| --- | --- |
| Jack Nicklaus | 18 |
| Walter Hagen | 11 |
| Ben Hogan | 9 |
| Gary Player | 9 |
| Tom Watson | 8 |
| Harry Vardon | 7 |
| Bobby Jones | 7 |
| Gene Sarazen | 7 |
| Sam Snead | 7 |
| Arnold Palmer | 7 |
| Lee Trevino | 6 |
| Nick Faldo | 6 |
| Tiger Woods | 6 |

Source: PGAtour.com

# PGA

## Most Prize Money in a Season

For crowning the best golfer in any given year, prize money won in a season is an excellent measure. The statistic reflects not merely the number of tournaments won, but also their relative importance, as indicated by the size of the purse. It is little surprise that Tiger Woods, acknowledged as the best golfer in our era, has topped the season's winnings list for four of the last five seasons since 1997.

But in comparing golfers from one era to another, prize money won is a truly useless statistic. For his 70 PGA career wins from 1962 through 1986, Jack Nicklaus earned $5.7 million in prize money. Woods nearly doubled that total in 2000 alone, winning $9.2 million for nine tournament victories. Sam Snead, by comparison, appeared to be a pauper. For his record-setting 81 career victories, from 1936 to 1965, Snead's winnings totaled $620,621.

A landmark was passed in 1988 when Curtis Strange became the first golfer in history to win more than $1 million. But since then the dam has truly burst, and prize money has flooded the golf landscape, so that 55 players won over $1 million each in 2001. On page 46 is a look at the most money won in a season, along with the player who won it.

## Most Tour Victories

If you want to crown someone as the best golfer who ever lived, the very first statistic you would check is career victories. And who stands atop this list? None other than Samuel Jackson Snead, or "Slammin' Sammy," as he was known in his heyday. The man with the Virginia drawl, a trademark straw hat, and the sweetest golf swing of his generation, is arguably the best who ever played the game. His 81 PGA tour victories cover a period from 1936 to 1965, when he competed against all the greatest names in golf, including Sarazen, Nelson, Hogan, Palmer, and Nicklaus. His titles included three Masters championships in 1949, 1952, and 1954; and three PGA championships in 1942, 1949, and 1951. He also won the 1946 British Open. Despite several achingly close

calls, a U.S. Open championship forever eluded him, and the omission stands as perhaps the only flaw in one of the greatest careers the game has ever seen.

Jack Nicklaus occupies second place on the all-time PGA win list, with 11 fewer victories than Snead, but no golfer has won more major tournaments than the Golden Bear. His very first PGA tour victory was the 1962 U.S. Open, while his last was the 1986 Masters—talk about starting and ending with a bang! In his career, Jack managed to win six Masters, five PGA championships, four U.S. Opens, and three British Opens. That's 18 majors—the pinnacle of golfing success that Tiger Woods and all of today's best golfers aspire to equal or beat.

### *Most PGA Tour Wins*

| Player | Number of Wins |
|---|---|
| Sam Snead | 81 |
| Jack Nicklaus | 70 |
| Ben Hogan | 63 |
| Arnold Palmer | 60 |
| Byron Nelson | 52 |
| Billy Casper | 51 |
| Walter Hagen | 40 |
| Cary Middlecoff | 40 |
| Gene Sarazen | 38 |
| Lloyd Mangrum | 36 |
| Tom Watson | 34 |
| Horton Smith | 32 |
| Harry Cooper | 32 |
| Jimmy Demaret | 31 |
| Leo Diegel | 30 |
| Gene Littler | 29 |
| Paul Runyan | 29 |
| Tiger Woods | 29 |
| Lee Trevino | 27 |
| Henry Picard | 26 |

Source: PGAtour.com

## Most Tour Wins in a Season

When we think of the greatest athletes of all time, our thoughts drift naturally to those who shined the brightest in our own era. The greatest golfer: Tiger Woods. The greatest basketball player: Michael Jordan. The greatest home run hitter: Barry Bonds. But sometimes historical statistics tell a different story. It may turn out that the greatest played many years before today's heroes. For example, on basketball's all-time scoring list, Michael Jordan's 30,000 career points (as of early 2002), still lags about 8,000 points behind Kareem Abdul Jabbar's career total of 38,387 points.

And although Tiger Woods is surely the dominant golfer of our day, his 9 PGA tour wins in 2000 are only half of the mind-boggling 18 single-season wins achieved by Byron Nelson in 1945. Ben Hogan and Sam Snead, who preceded Woods by half a century, also won more victories in a year than Tiger. Nelson also holds the records for most wins in two and three consecutive years, while so far, Woods ranks no better than third in either category.

### Most PGA Tour Wins in One Year

| Player | Year | Wins |
|---|---|---|
| Byron Nelson | 1945 | 18 |
| Ben Hogan | 1946 | 13 |
| Sam Snead | 1950 | 11 |
| Ben Hogan | 1948 | 10 |
| Paul Runyan | 1933 | 9 |
| Gene Sarazen | 1930 | 9 |
| Tiger Woods | 2000 | 9 |
| Horton Smith | 1929 | 8 |
| Gene Sarazen | 1930 | 8 |
| Sam Snead | 1938 | 8 |
| Byron Nelson | 1944 | 8 |
| Arnold Palmer | 1960 | 8 |
| Johnny Miller | 1974 | 8 |
| Tiger Woods | 1999 | 8 |

### Most PGA Tour Wins in Two Consecutive Years

| Player | Year | Wins |
|---|---|---|
| Byron Nelson | 1944–1945 | 26 |
| Ben Hogan | 1946–1947 | 20 |
| Ben Hogan | 1947–1948 | 17 |
| Sam Snead | 1949–1950 | 17 |
| Tiger Woods | 1999–2000 | 17 |

### Most PGA Tour Wins in Three Consecutive Years

| Player | Year | Wins |
|---|---|---|
| Byron Nelson | 1944–1946 | 32 |
| Ben Hogan | 1946–1948 | 30 |
| Tiger Woods | 1999–2001 | 22 |

Source: PGAtour.com

# PGA

## Most Wins Before 25th Birthday

Tiger Woods represents the ultimate early bloomer in golf. At age two, he appeared on the *Mike Douglas* television show as a child prodigy, demonstrating his putting while Bob Hope looked on enviously. At age three, he shot 48 for nine holes, and at age five he was featured in a *Golf Digest* article. He won The Masters at age 21, and captured 24 PGA tournaments before reaching his 25th birthday. He is one prodigy who fulfilled his promise, and it's anyone's guess how many tournaments he'll win in his career.

Jack Nicklaus was another early bloomer, winning 12 PGA tournaments before his 25th birthday. But Nicklaus also had great staying power, eventually earning 70 career wins. As it turned out, the Golden Bear earned roughly 17 percent of his wins before his 25th birthday, and 83 percent after. If Woods were to follow the same pattern, he would record an incredible 140 career victories. Only time will tell.

Unlike Nicklaus, young Horton Smith took the golf world by storm, but soon faded from the scene. Smith was a boy wonder from Springfield, Missouri, who took up golf at age 12. He was only 21 when he won his first PGA title in 1929, and he won 16 more before his 25th birthday. But those early wins turned out to be more than half of the 30 total wins Smith would realize in his career. He now stands 12th on the all-time win list.

Jerry Pate also flared brightly at an early age but faded quickly. He won five PGA tournaments by age 25, including the 1976 U.S. Open, when he was 23 years old. But Pate

*Political differences were momentarily put aside when George Bush, Bill Clinton, and Gerald Ford competed in the 1995 Bob Hope Chrysler Classic Pro-Am.*

only won three more tournaments after his 25th birthday, for a total of eight career victories. Here are the players who've tallied the most PGA wins before that magical 25th birthday.

| Player | 25th Year | Wins by 25 |
|---|---|---|
| Tiger Woods | 2000 | 24 |
| Horton Smith | 1933 | 17 |
| Jack Nicklaus | 1965 | 12 |
| Johnny Revolta | 1936 | 9 |
| Paul Runyan | 1933 | 8 |
| Johnny Farrell | 1926 | 7 |
| Gene Sarazen | 1927 | 6 |
| Harry Cooper | 1929 | 5 |
| Vic Ghezzi | 1937 | 5 |
| Jerry Pate | 1978 | 5 |
| Phil Mickelson | 1995 | 5 |

Source: PGAtour.com

# PGA

## *Players with Most Victories*

Since turning pro, such golfers as Phil Mickelson, David Duval, and Vijay Singh have chalked up some impressive victories and taken home the big bucks (and then there's that Woods guy). Still, they've got their work cut out for them if they're going to catch up to

Slammin' Sam, the Golden Bear, and the other players with the most PGA victories to date:

| | | |
|---|---|---|
| 1. | Sam Snead | 81 victories |
| 2. | Jack Nicklaus | 71 victories |
| 3. | Ben Hogan | 63 victories |
| 4. | Arnold Palmer | 60 victories |
| 5. | Byron Nelson | 52 victories |
| 6. | Billy Casper | 51 victories |
| 7. | Walter Hagen | 40 victories |
| | Cary Middlecof | 40 victories |
| 8. | Gene Sarazen | 38 victories |
| 9. | Lloyd Mangrum | 36 victories |

Source: bestcourses.com

# PRESIDENTIAL GOLFERS

When they're not busy running the country, quite a few of our presidents have been known to relax with a few rounds of golf, which can make negotiating peace or reviving the economy seem like a piece of cake. The following presidents all golfed, with wildly varying degrees of ability. Success on the beltway wasn't always repeated on the fairway.

**William H. Taft,** enormously fat, was the first president to take up golf. Although some voters looked upon the president's golf playing as immoral, they were apparently in the

*Never much of a talker, Ben Hogan, whose career was among the longest of pros, 41 years, let his game speak for him.*

minority. During Taft's presidency, the number of players on public courses reportedly doubled.

**Woodrow Wilson,** on the day after he won the presidency in 1912, hit the links with his good friend, Navy Admiral Clay Grayson. Recognized at the 18th hole by other golfers, Wilson cheerfully reported that "The admiral has me three down, but I don't care. I am four states up on yesterday's election."

**Warren G. Harding,** when not boozing it up during Prohibition, or seeing his mistress, played golf weekly at the Chevy Chase Country Club, usually in a cowboy hat and plus-fours.

**Dwight D. Eisenhower** was such a passionate golfer that he had a putting green built outside the Oval Office. A fixture at The Masters, he became extremely close with Bobby Jones and later painted the golfer's portrait.

**John F. Kennedy** was fairly secretive about his golf game and was known to walk off the course if photographers appeared. He typically played late in the evenings when the courses at the Chevy Chase Club were almost empty.

**Richard Nixon** didn't start playing golf until he was 37. An awkward, often clumsy player, he practiced tirelessly to the point that he often scored in the low 90s or high 80s.

**Gerald R. Ford,** despite taking some well-publicized pratfalls, was one of the more athletically inclined presidents. He played golf with a reported 18 handicap and retired to Palm Springs after his presidency to play golf.

**George Bush** inherited his passion for golf from his mother, who adhered strictly to the rules and never took a "mulligan." And like his father, he put a premium on speed over accuracy; Bush and three companions reportedly once played 18 holes in just over 90 minutes.

**Bill Clinton** liked to practice his shots on the South Lawn and once drove a ball 300 yards into a White House fence. In 1995 he joined Gerald Ford and George Bush to play in the Bob Hope Chrysler Classic pro-am event.

Sources: americanpresident.org; *Presidential Lies* by Shepherd Campbell and Peter Landau

# Pro Golfers

## *Playing Over 40 Years*

Most professional athletes are considered well past their prime by the age of 40. The knees are shot, gravity is increasingly cruel, and Ben-Gay is your new best friend. George Blanda may have played professional football into his late forties, but he was the exception.

Unlike such bone-crushing sports as football or basketball, golf is a game that attracts pros for the long haul; can you think of another professional sport where athletes can still *legally* compete for money and collect social security?

Here are just a few professional golfers who played (or are playing) past the age when most athletes' glory days are long behind them.

1. **Ben Hogan** turned pro at 17 in 1929 and played his last competitive round in 1971.

   Career: 41 YEARS.

2. **Jack Nicklaus** turned pro in 1961 and is still playing on the Senior PGA Tour.

   Career: 40+ YEARS

3. **Arnold Palmer** turned pro in 1954 and is still playing on the Senior PGA Tour.

   Career: 47+ YEARS

4. **Gary Player** turned pro at 17 in 1952 and is still playing on the Senior PGA Tour.

   Career: 49+ YEARS

5. **Sam Snead** first played on the PGA tour in 1936 and is now on the SPGA Tour.

Career: 65+ years.

Source PGAtour.com; Authors, *Best and Worst of Golf*

# PUTTING LEADERS

An old golf adage says "drive for show; putt for dough." And we've all seen a victory clinched on the 18th hole when someone drops a dramatic putt. Good putting can also make up for a lot of mediocre shots from the tee and fairway, saving many strokes in a round. But a closer look at PGA putting statistics casts some doubt on the veracity of that old golf saying.

For example, the PGA Tour's 10 leaders in 2001 for average putts per round won combined prize money of $11.5 million—an average of $1,153,000. That seems lucrative until you compare it with the winnings of the Tour's 10 leaders in average driving distance. The long hitters won nearly twice as much, capturing $22,245,000, or an average of $2,225,000.

Only three times since 1992 has the tour's leading putter also been a top-10 money winner in the same season. Payne Stewart did it in 1999, finishing seventh in winnings. Brad Faxon also led the tour in putting 1996 and 1997, and finished eighth and tenth, respectively, in winnings. But putting isn't always for dough. Ask Craig Kanada. He emerged as the leading putter of 2001, but ranked 192nd in prize money, winning only $132,000.

### Putts per Round, 2001

| Player | Putts per Round |
|--------|-----------------|
| 1.  Craig Kanada | 27.90 |
| 2.  David Frost | 27.94 |
| 3.  Steve Stricker | 28.15 |
| 4.  Brad Faxon | 28.17 |
| 5.  Glen Day | 28.19 |
| 6.  Willie Wood | 28.27 |
| 7.  Brian Gay | 28.31 |
| 8.  Bernhard Langer | 28.33 |
| 9.  David Morland IV | 28.37 |
| 10. Bob Estes | 28.38 |
|     Len Mattiace | 28.38 |

### Putting Leaders Previous Years

| Year | Player | Putts per Round |
|------|--------|-----------------|
| 2000 | Brad Faxon | 28.05 |
| 1999 | Payne Stewart | 28.09 |
| 1998 | Rick Fehr | 27.71 |
| 1997 | Brad Faxon | 28.17 |
| 1996 | Brad Faxon | 28.26 |
| 1995 | Jim Furyk | 28.01 |
| 1994 | Ben Crenshaw | 27.88 |
| 1993 | Dick Mast | 28.38 |
| 1992 | Ed Fiori | 28.39 |

Source: PGAtour.com

# ROOKIE OF THE YEAR

## PGA

Being selected as rookie of the year in any sport is certainly a bright beginning to a career. After all, Michael Jordan won the NBA's top rookie award in 1985; Mark McGwire was the American League's honored rookie in 1987; and Tiger Woods won the PGA's rookie of the year award in 1996. Obviously, some top rookies go on to do rather well. But winning the award is not a sure ticket to success, nor does missing out on it doom an athlete to failure.

David Duval is a case in point. He joined the pro tour in 1995, but lost rookie of the year honors to Woody Austin. No matter. The very next year Duval was 10th in prize money, winning nearly $1 million. By 1997 he was second in winnings, banking $1.9 million. And by 1998 he topped the tour by winning $2.6 million in prize money. Duval has ranked in the top 10 in prize money every year since his rookie season.

Phil Mickelson is another example. He turned pro in 1992, but was not selected rookie of the year. That honor went to Mark Carnevale, who won the 1992 Chattanooga Classic. Their fortunes soon reversed. Nearly a decade later Mickelson can count 20 PGA tour victories, while Carnevale managed only one more win in the 1997 Nike Inland Empire Open.

## PGA Tour Rookies of the Year

| Year | Player |
|------|--------|
| 2000 | Michael Clark II |
| 1999 | Carlos Franco |
| 1998 | Steve Flesch |
| 1997 | Stewart Cink |
| 1996 | Tiger Woods |
| 1995 | Woody Austin |
| 1994 | Ernie Els |
| 1993 | Vijay Singh |
| 1992 | Mark Carnevale |
| 1991 | John Daly |

Source: *ESPN Sports Almanac 2002*

# RULE BREAKERS

## Rules Broken by the Pros

The Rules of Golf have gotten much more complicated since the Honourable Company of Edinburgh Golfers in Scotland set down the 13 original rules in 1744. Now overseen by the USGA and The Royal & Ancient Golf Club, the Rules of Golf are often criticized for being vague and confusing; each year, the USGA fields thousands of phone and written queries about particular rulings. And sometimes even the pros get confused about what's acceptable and what's not, much to their chagrin.

**Advice not taken:** Tom Watson was penalized two strokes when he offered a helpful suggestion to another golfer at the 1980 Tournament of Champions, an infringement of the rules. The other golfer unwittingly credited him with the advice in a TV interview. Watson won the tournament, but his margin dropped from five strokes to three after a viewer called to report the violation and Watson was penalized two strokes. This all happened just a few months after Watson had authored a book on the rules of golf.

**Multiple violations:** One rule violation wasn't enough for Lou Graham, who broke four rules in 10 seconds, earning him six penalty strokes at the 1970 Westchester Classic. The official wasn't sure if the penalty should be four or six points and instructed Graham to play it as six while he checked. Upon reaching the clubhouse, he couldn't find the official for the ruling, so Graham took the six and signed his card, missing the cut by just one stroke. As luck would have it, he would have qualified with a stroke to spare—the penalty should only have been four.

**Bodily noises:** Tommy Bolt was hit where it hurt—in the pocketbook. During the 1959 Memphis Open, he played his round by the rules, but was penalized $250 for farting while another player was putting.

**Putter changes:** Don't change your equipment without permission was the lesson learned by Paul Farmer in the 1960 Texas Open. Paint on his putter was flaking, so he exchanged it after nine holes. At the end of the round, officials told him he would need to take a two-stroke penalty for each hole he played with the "new" club—for a total of 18 strokes.

**Wrong ball:** Payne Stewart played the wrong ball in two qualifying tournaments before investing in a magic marker to identify which Titleist was his. The errors cost him two strokes each time.

**Extra clubs:** Bob Dickson took a four-stroke penalty in the 1965 National Amateur tournament after noticing an extra club in his bag. The extra strokes cost him the championship by one point—and it turned out the club wasn't even his.

**Flag holding:** Sam Snead paid for his casual style in the 1959 Buick Open. He tapped in a short putt with one hand while holding the flag with the other. He got a two-stroke penalty and fell to fifth place.

Source: *The Golf Hall of Shame* by Bruce Nash and Allan Zullo; *The Golfer's Sourcebook* by Cliff Schrock

# SCRAMBLING LEADERS

## PGA

Playing golf is part science and part art. Good golfers utilize as much science of the swing as possible. But when shots go awry and greens are not reached in regulation, even the best pros are forced to scramble to save par or grab a miraculous birdie.

And scrambling is pure art. It is the art of blasting out of sand traps, mastering backspin, playing difficult lies, holing chip shots, or

**Gone with the wind: J.C. Snead's straw hat literally blew his chances in a 1977 tournament when his hat blew off and rolled into his ball.**

### Previous Scrambling Leaders

| Year | Player | Percentage |
|------|--------|-----------|
| 2000 | Ernie Els | 67.6 |
| 1999 | Mike Reid | 68.8 |
| 1998 | Payne Stewart | 66.2 |
| 1997 | Bob Estes | 68.8 |
| 1996 | Corey Pavin | 67.1 |
| 1995 | Bob Estes | 66.3 |
| 1994 | Mark McCumber | 68.7 |
| 1993 | Greg Norman | 72.8 |
| 1992 | Nick Price | 68.3 |

Source: PGAtour.com

sinking long and winding putts— any trick a golfer can pull from off the green to get the ball into the cup in a stroke or two.

An ideal golfer should excel in both scrambling and reaching greens in regulation (GIR). Only Tiger Woods ranked in the top 10 in both categories in 2001. He was first in scrambling percentage and tied for fifth in GIR. That combination of skills resulted in Woods winning nearly $5.7 million, tops on the PGA Tour.

Two more golfers ranked high in both scrambling and GIR. One was Davis Love III, who was third in scrambling and 19th in GIR. As a result, he won about $3.2 million and ranked fifth in prize money. The other golfer was Scott Verplank, who tied for sixth in scrambling and 13th in GIR. As a result, he banked nearly $2.8 million in winnings—10th best on the tour.

### Scrambling Leaders, 2001

| Player | Percentage |
|--------|-----------|
| 1.  Tiger Woods | 69.8 |
| 2.  Nick Price | 68.0 |
| 3.  Davis Love III | 67.3 |
| 4.  Scott Hoch | 66.5 |
| 5.  Mark Brooks | 66.1 |
| 6.  Bob Estes | 66.0 |
|     Scott Verplank | 66.0 |
| 8.  Glen Day | 65.5 |
|     Loren Roberts | 65.5 |
| 10. Bernhard Langer | 65.4 |

# SINGLE-SEASON EARNINGS RECORDS

## PGA

No surprises here: Tiger Woods literally breaks the bank yearly on the PGA Tour in earnings. He occupies four of the top five positions in this list of players who've earned the most each year since 1940, when Ben Hogan topped the list with $10,655.

Although Woods has been No. 1 for the last three years in a row, he is still one year shy of Tom Watson's record. From 1977 to 1980 Watson was the top earner on the PGA Tour. While he holds the PGA Tour record of earning at least $100,000 yearly for 26 consecutive years, Watson didn't cross the million-dollar mark in earnings for a single season until 2000, when he took home $1,146,361 from SPGA tournament appearances.

# SNEAD'S HAT

## A Cause for Penalty

In the 1977 Tournament Players Championship, J. C. Snead encountered trouble when his wide-brimmed straw hat blew off his head. He was still 40 yards from his ball when the hat blew off, rolling right into his ball. He was penalized two strokes by officials who said his hat was actually part of his equipment. When a player's ball is unintentionally moved by his own equipment a penalty is assessed. Those two strokes cost Snead $2,750 in prize money when he fell five places to finish the round in 13th.

Source: Authors, *The Best and Worst of Golf*

# SPGA

## *All-Time Earnings Winners*

A three-time winner of the U.S. Open in 1974, 1979, and 1990, Hale Irwin has continued his winning streak since joining the SPGA Tour in 1995. With 33 victories to his credit, including two U.S. Senior Open wins, Irwin has also taken home seven figures annually for six consecutive years, which puts him atop the list of all-time earnings winners on the SPGA Tour.

And what of Career Grand Slammers Gary Player and Jack Nicklaus? Player comes in 25th with total SPGA Tour earnings of $5,642,218, while Nicklaus trails at number 58 with $3,641,125. Just making the top 100 is Arnold Palmer, ranked 92nd with $1,712,430 in earnings. Here are the players who've won the most on the Senior Tour, with earnings through 2001.

| Player | Career Earnings |
|--------|----------------|
| 1. Hale Irwin | $13,921,874 |
| 2. Jim Colbert | $10,553,940 |
| 3. Gil Morgan | $9,749,317 |
| 4. Lee Trevino | $9,426,642 |
| 5. Dave Stockton | $9,140,870 |
| 6. Bob Charles | $8,564,577 |
| 7. Ray Floyd | $8,229,505 |
| 8. Larry Nelson | $8,086,397 |
| 9. George Archer | $8,000,911 |
| 10. Jim Dent | $7,832,042 |

Source: PGAtour.com

# SPGA

## *Career Money Leaders*

Back in the days when Sam Snead and Ben Hogan ruled pro golf, prize money on the PGA tour was a tiny sliver of the gigantic pie it

*Hale Irwin has earned nearly $14 million since joining the SPGA Tour in 1995.*

has become today. In 1955 the combined value of all PGA purses was $782,000, whereas by 1995, purses totaled over $62 million. Even allowing for inflation, the difference is staggering. The result is that a golfing legend like Snead, who amassed a record 81 career wins from 1936 to 1965, won only $620,126. That averages about $7,656 per victory, or less than $21,400 per year. Clearly, getting rich on the golf tour depends less on *how* you played, than *when* you played.

Luckily, though, the booming Senior Tour is giving some older pros a great chance to make up for lost purses. Hale Irwin, who tops the seniors, winning list at nearly $20 million, won less than $6 million on the regular PGA tour. Gil Morgan's success as a senior has nearly tripled his winnings, from $5.25 million on the PGA tour, to over $15 million today. And Bruce Fleisher has struck a gusher as a senior. He had ranked 210th on the PGA career winnings list, with $1.7 million in prize money. But the late-blooming Fleisher has rocketed to 12th place on the seniors' winnings list, with earnings exceeding $9 million. The following list of career earnings includes their winnings on the PGA Tour, Senior Tour, and Buy.com Tour since 1995.

| Golfer | Career Earnings |
|--------|----------------|
| 1. Hale Irwin | $19,905,405 |
| 2. Gil Morgan | $15,042,814 |
| 3. Tom Kite | $13,772,418 |
| 4. Ray Floyd | $13,552,580 |

| PGA—Most Prize Money in a Season | | |
|---|---|---|
| Player | Year | Winnings |
| 1. Tiger Woods | 2000 | $9,188,321 |
| 2. Tiger Woods | 2001 | $5,687,777 |
| 3. Tiger Woods | 1999 | $6,616,505 |
| 4. David Duval | 1998 | $2,591,031 |
| 5. Tiger Woods | 1997 | $2,066,833 |
| 6. Tom Lehman | 1996 | $1,780,159 |
| 7. Greg Norman | 1995 | $1,654,959 |
| 8. Nick Price | 1994 | $1,499,927 |
| 9. Nick Price | 1993 | $1,478,557 |
| 10. Tom Kite | 1989 | $1,395,278 |
| 11. Fred Couples | 1992 | $1,334,188 |
| 12. Greg Norman | 1990 | $1,165,477 |
| 13. Curtis Strange | 1988 | $1,147,648 |
| 14. Corey Pavin | 1991 | $979,450 |
| 15. Curtis Strange | 1987 | $925,941 |

Source: triviagolf.com and PGAtour.com

| | | |
|---|---|---|
| 5. | Lee Trevino | $12,920,970 |
| 6. | Jim Colbert | $12,131,826 |
| 7. | Larry Nelson | $11,979,548 |
| 8. | Tom Watson | $11,969,112 |
| 9. | Dave Stockton | $10,444,151 |
| 10. | George Archer | $9,900,270 |
| 11. | Bob Charles | $9,111,445 |
| 12. | Bruce Fleisher | $9,065,740 |
| 13. | Jack Nicklaus | $8,755,116 |
| 14. | Isao Aoki | $8,518,519 |
| 15. | J. C. Snead | $8,489,691 |

Source: PGAtour.com; triviagolf.com

# SPGA TOUR

## Most Career Starts

Since its launch in 1980, the SPGA Tour has been a financial and professional boon to many players whose PGA records show more guts than glory. Take Miller Barber for instance. After turning pro in 1958 the Louisiana native racked up 11 PGA Tour victories and a reputation as a solid competitor. Since he joined the SPGA in 1981, however, Barber has truly come into his own. With 24 victories between 1981 and 1989, including the 1981 PGA Seniors Championship and three U.S. Senior Opens, Barber is a genuine

late bloomer who also became the first SPGA tour player to earn more than $2 million. He also holds the record for the most career starts on the SPGA Tour, with 565 through September 1, 2002. Add that to his PGA Tour starts, and Barber has over 1,267 career starts, more than any other professional golfer.

Trailing Barber is South African golfer Harold Henning, who joined the SPGA in 1984 after an on-again-off-again PGA career which began in the early fifties.

| Player | Career Starts |
|---|---|
| 1. Miller Barber | 565 |
| 2. Harold Henning | 507 |
| 3. Walt Zembriski | 503 |
| 4. Orville Moody | 490 |
| 5. Dale Douglass | 466 |

Source: *Golf Magazine*, November 2001

# SPGA CHAMPIONSHIP

## Most Victories

Forty-three years before the Senior PGA Tour officially launched in 1980, golf legend Bobby Jones held a tournament for golfers 50 and over at the Augusta National Golf Club in 1937. Thanks to Jones and golf patron Alfred S. Bourne, who contributed $1,500 toward the

*Veteran golfer Miller Barber has started on the SPGA Tour 565 times (and counting).*

tournament's purse of $2,000, veteran golfers could compete against their peers instead of the upstarts on the PGA circuit.

Jock Hutchinson won the first Senior PGA Championship, which was played over 54 holes. Aside from 1939, 1943, and 1944, the tournament has been played yearly, usually at the PGA National Golf Club in Palm Beach Gardens, Florida. In 1979 and 1984 the tournament was played twice. While some of the tournament's early winners are little more than footnotes in golf history today (Otto Hackbarth?), the following luminaries have won the Senior PGA Championship the most times in the tournament's 60-plus year history:

| SPGA Championship, Most Victories | | |
|---|---|---|
| Player | Victories | Years Won |
| 1. Sam Snead | 6 | 1964, 1965, 1967, 1970, 1972, 1973 |
| 2. Hale Irwin | 3 | 1996, 1997, 1998 |
| Gary Player | 3 | 1986, 1988, 1990 |
| Al Watrous | 3 | 1950, 1951, 1957 |
| Eddie Williams | 3 | 1942, 1945, 1946 |
| 6. Julius Boros | 2 | 1971, 1977 |
| Jock Hutchinson | 2 | 1937, 1947 |
| Don January | 2 | 1979, 1982 |
| Arnold Palmer | 2 | 1980, 1984 |
| Paul Runyan | 2 | 1961, 1962 |
| Gene Sarazen | 2 | 1954, 1958 |
| Lee Trevino | 2 | 1992, 1994 |

Source: *The Golfer's Sourcebook* by Cliff Schrock; sportsillustrated.com

# SPGA

## Single-Season Earnings Records

A member of the SPGA Tour since 1998, Allen Doyle is truly a late bloomer. Unlike Hale Irwin or Larry Nelson, PGA veterans with four U.S. Open victories between them, Doyle hadn't made much of an impression during his brief PGA Tour career; his highest finish was a tie for seventh at the 1998 Deposit Guaranty Classic. After winning several amateur tournaments in Georgia, Doyle joined the BUY.COM Tour in the early nineties and won three tournaments. It is only since Doyle qualified for the SPGA Tour, however, that he has been recognized as a talented golfer and worthy competitor. In 34 starts on the tour, Doyle has finished in the top ten 25 times, just shy of Lee Trevino's record. With earnings of $2,553,582 for the 2001 SPGA Tour, Doyle comes in third on the list of the tour's highest single-season earnings since the SPGA's inaugural year of 1980.

### SPGA Single-Season Earnings Records

| Player | Earnings | Year |
|---|---|---|
| 1. Hale Irwin | $2,861,945 | 1998 |
| 2. Larry Nelson | $2,708,005 | 2000 |
| 3. Allen Doyle | $2,553,582 | 2001 |
| 4. Bruce Fleischer | $2,515,705 | 1999 |
| 5. Hale Irwin | $2,343,364 | 1997 |
| 6. Jim Colbert | $1,627,890 | 1996 |
| 7. Jim Colbert | $1,444,386 | 1995 |
| 8. Dave Stockton | $1,402,519 | 1994 |
| 9. Lee Trevino | $1,190,518 | 1990 |
| 10. Dave Stockton | $1,402,519 | 1993 |

Source: bestcourses.com

# TEACHERS

## Great Golf Teachers and Their Star Pupils

When the pros need help with their swing or course strategy, they usually turn to the nation's best golf teachers, who offer specialized instruction at golf schools both here and abroad. The following golf teachers have become veritable cottage industries, opening schools, writing books, designing courses, and helping pros and amateurs alike improve their golf game.

1. **Butch Harmon**: Best known as Tiger Woods' coach, Harmon has also worked with Darren Clarke and Mark Calcavecchia. The son of Claude Harmon, the 1948 Masters champ, Harmon currently operates schools in Henderson, Nevada, and the Bahamas. He has written several books and was recently picked as the nation's best golf teacher in an August 2001 *Golf Digest* poll. Website: www.butchharmon.com

2. **Dave Pelz**: A former NASA research scientist who left the agency in 1975 to devote his energies to golf research and development, Pelz has worked with such pros as Peter Jacobson, Vijay Singh, the late Payne Stewart, and LPGA star Beth Daniel. He has schools in Boca Raton, Florida, Palm Springs, California, and Edwards, Colorado. Books include *Dave Pelz's Putting Bible* and *Dave Pelz's Short Game Bible*. Website: www.pelzgolf.com

3. **Jim McLean**: Named the PGA of America Teacher of the Year in 1994, McLean has worked with Gary Player, Hal Sutton, and Tom Kite, among others. Based in Miami, he has written for several magazines and appeared on the Golf Channel. His book *The Eight Step Swing* is widely considered one of the best golf instruction manuals. Website: www.jimmclean.com

4. **David Leadbetter**: Leadbetter has opened several golf academies in the United States, Europe, and Asia. Both Nick Price and Nick Faldo have turned to Leadbetter for assistance with their games. His books include *The Fundamentals of Hogan* and *The Golf Swing*. Website: www.leadbetter.com

5. **Jim Flick**: Named one of the 10 best golf teachers of the 20th century in 1999 by *Golf World,* Flick is the director of training and education for the Nicklaus/Flick Golf School in Scottsdale, Arizona. He has worked with both Nicklaus and Palmer and coached Tom Lehman, the 1996 British Open winner. Website: www.nicklaus.com/flick2000

Source: "50 Greatest Teachers," *Golf Digest,* August 2001

# WOMEN GOLFERS

## A Lowdown

The number of women golfers is on the rise. Some are taking to the links for pleasure and others are finding a new, more casual way to conduct business. *Golf Digest* has started a new magazine especially for the fairer sex, *Golf for Women*, that already boasts a circulation of 380,120. Advertisers are jumping on the bandwagon, touting clothing and equipment for women only. There are now golf schools just for women and courses that are female-friendly. The LPGA is attracting attention among men and women golfers alike. Here are a few more facts about women and golf.

**Women now comprise 22 percent of all golfers.**

- Rounds played per year by the average woman golfer: 15

- Percent of golfers who are women: 22 percent

- Number of women golfers: 5.7 million

- Currently taking golf lessons: 35 percent

- Have ever taken a golf lesson: 61 percent

- Regularly practice golf: 36 percent

- Annual consumer spending on golf by women: $3 billion

- Average age of women golfers: 42

- Average household income of women golfers: $68,285

Source: ngf.com

# WOMEN GOLFERS

## Golfing Firsts

Trailblazers whose achievements cut across gender lines, these women have all brought worldwide attention to the game from the twenties forward.

1. **Kathy Whitworth** was the first LPGA player to earn $1 million in career earnings in 1981.

2. **Karrie Webb** became the first LPGA player to earn $1 million in one year in 1996.

3. **Nancy Lopez** was the first LPGA player to be named Rookie of the Year and Player of the Year simultaneously in 1978.

4. **Patty Berg** was the first woman pro to give an exhibition in Japan in 1962.

5. **Laura Rankin** was the first LPGA player to hit the six-figure mark in single-season earnings, taking home $150,734 in 1976.

6. **Babe Didrikson Zaharias** was the first American to win the Ladies' British Open Amateur in 1947.

7. **Beverly Hanson** won the first LPGA Championship in 1955.

8. **Bonnie Bryant** was the first left-hander to win a LPGA event, the 1974 Bill Branch Classic.

9. **Smriti Mehra** was the first native of India to join the LPGA tour, in 1997.

10. **Edith Cummings,** a beautiful amateur, was christened the "Golden Girl of Sports" in the early twenties, and was the first golfer to appear on the cover of *Time* magazine, in 1924.

Source: World Golf Hall of Fame website; *Links Lore* by Peter F. Stevens; *Ultimate Golf Trivia* book; bestcourses.com

## WOMEN GOLFERS

### *Taking Care of Business*

According to Audrey Gusky, marketing professor at Duquesne University in Pittsburgh, as much as 40 percent of all business deals are discussed on the golf course. It's no wonder, then, that women golfers are on the rise. Women now account for 21 percent of the nation's golfers, up from 19 percent in 1993. They are also more apt to take lessons than their male counterparts. And advertisers will be interested to note that women are much more concerned about fashion on the links.

Here are some other observations about women who conduct business on the links

- 38 percent of women golfers hold management level jobs

- 8 percent currently play golf for business reasons

- 14 percent say that have played golf for business

- 19 percent expect to play golf for business in the future

- 35 percent of all new golfers are women, but less than half of them stick with the sport

- Women spend $3 billion on golf-related merchandise annually.

- Women golfers spend $200 million on golfwear alone.

Source: Audrey Gusky

## WORLD GOLF HALL OF FAME

### *Behind the Scenes Inductees*

At first glance the World Golf Hall of Fame roster of inductees evokes Claude Rains' famous line in *Casablanca*: "Round up the usual suspects." As expected, all the greats are represented—Vardon, Hogan, and Palmer, to name a few—but there are also inductees whom most sports fans would be hard pressed to identify. Working behind the scenes rather than on the green, these Hall of Famers did everything from popularize the game to establish the rules. Because of their efforts, golf has truly become an international sport that continues to attract new players and fans yearly. Without their contributions, golf would never have flourished in 20th century America and abroad.

1. **Joseph C. Dey**: A 1974 inductee, Dey was the executive director of the USGA from 1935 to 1969. He immediately segued from the USGA to the PGA Tour, where he served as commissioner from 1969 to 1974. In 1975, he was named captain of the Royal and Ancient Golf Club of St. Andrews. During his tenure at the USGA, he played a key role in unifying the rules of the USGA and the R&A.

2. **Fred Corcoran**: Also inducted in 1974, Corcoran wore many hats during his career. One of golf's first agents (Sam Snead and Tony Lema were clients), Corcoran served as a PGA Tournament manager from 1937 to 1948 and founded both the Golf Writers Association of America and the LPGA. In addition to being the LPGA Director from 1949 to 1961, Corcoran also worked as the PGA promotional director from 1952 to 1955.

3. **Herb Graffis**: A 1977 inductee, Graffis was a sportswriter for the *Chicago Sun-Times* who founded the National Golf Foundation and the Golf Course Superintendents Association with his brother Joe. Graffis also founded two magazines,

*The incomparable Babe Didrikson Zaharias was posthumously inducted into the World Golf Hall of Fame.*

*Golfdom* and *Golfing Magazine*, in 1919 and 1933, respectively.

4. **Clifford Roberts**: A 1977 inductee, Roberts is best remembered as the stern taskmaster who cofounded The Masters Tournament with Bobby Jones. A Wall Street financier by trade, he later oversaw The Masters when Jones was felled by illness. Run with military-style precision, the Masters is Roberts' legacy.

5. **Robert Harlow**: A Hall of Famer since 1988, Harlow began his golf career as Walter Hagen's business manager from 1921 to 1929. A tireless, charismatic promoter, he became the PGA Tournament Manager in 1930. For the next five years, Harlow devoted his considerable energies to keeping the PGA alive in Depression-era America. He later founded *Golf World* magazine in 1947.

Source: wgv.com

# WORLD GOLF HALL OF FAME

## *Original Inductees*

Want to test someone's knowledge of golf history? Ask them to name the 13 players who were the original inductees into the World Golf Hall of Fame. Since it opened in 1974 the World Golf Hall of Fame has honored both professional and amateur golfers, sportswriters, golf architects, and three Hollywood handicappers (Bob Hope, Bing Crosby, and Dinah Shore). The men and women who first received this honor, however are undeniably golf's "Who's Who": the players whose skills, charisma, and resilience made them true champions. Of these original honorees, four are still active on the SPGA Tour.

### 1974 World Golf Hall of Fame Inductees (in alphabetical order)

Patty Berg
Walter Hagen
Ben Hogan
Bobby Jones
Byron Nelson
Jack Nicklaus
Francis Ouimet
Arnold Palmer
Gary Player
Gene Sarazen
Sam Snead
Harry Vardon
Babe Didrikson Zaharias

Source: wgv.org

# WORLD GOLF RANKINGS

There's no rest for the weary golf statisticians in charge of compiling the Official World Golf Rankings. Each Monday the rankings must be updated according to the latest results from nine distinct tours: the six comprising the International Federation of PGA Tours, the Canadian Tour, the Buy.com Tour, and the European Challenge Tours. Players' standings and tournament fields are scrutinized closely on several levels, with particular weight given to the majors, to award a set number of points to a player. To be considered for the ranking, each player must play a minimum of 40 tournaments over the two-year ranking period, which has been sanctioned by none other than the Royal & Ancient Golf Club.

To no one's surprise, Tiger Woods tops the list with points accumulated from appearances in 44 tournaments. In fact, Americans make up half of the top 20 golfers, per the latest rankings to date.

| Player | Country |
|---|---|
| 1. Tiger Woods | USA |
| 2. Phil Mickelson | USA |
| 3. David Duval | USA |
| 4. Sergio Garcia | Spain |
| 5. Ernie Els | South Africa |
| 6. David Toms | USA |
| 7. Retief Goosen | South Africa |
| 8. Davis Love III | USA |
| 9. Vijay Singh | Fiji |
| 10. Mike Weir | Canada |
| 11. Chris DiMarco | USA |
| 12. Darren Clarke | N. Ireland |
| 13. Padraig Harrington | Ireland |
| 14. Jim Furyk | USA |
| 15. Bernhard Langer | Germany |
| 16. Kenny Perry | USA |
| 17. Scott Verplank | USA |
| 18. Colin Montgomerie | Scotland |
| 19. Toshi Izawa | Japan |
| 20. Bob Estes | USA |

Source: usatoday.com

# WRITERS

In 1857 H. B. Farnie wrote what is generally considered the first golf book, *The Golfer's Manual*. Since its publication, scores of writers, ranging from novelists to newspaper sportswriters, have brought the sport vividly to life for generations of readers. The truly great writers, a few of whom are listed below, go beyond mere reporting on tournaments and player statistics. They instead depict the personalities, philosophies, and politics that have shaped the golf world over the years.

1. **Bernard Darwin**: The grandson of Charles Darwin, he abandoned his legal career to become one of the most articu-

late and witty essayists on the sport. A fine golfer who learned the game at Cambridge University, Darwin won many amateur tournaments and reported on golf for the *London Times* for 46 years. *The Happy Golfer* is a collection of some of his most memorable essays.

2. **Grantland Rice**: One of the first American sportswriters, Rice is credited with discovering Babe Didrikson. He chronicled golf's increasing popularity in *The Duffer's Handbook of Golf*, which features cartoons by Claire Briggs.

3. **Herbert Warren Wind**: Both a *New Yorker* staff writer and *Sports Illustrated* golf editor, Wind also collaborated with Gene Sarazen and Jack Nicklaus on books. His book *The Story of American Golf, 1888–1941*, is a monumental history of the game.

4. **Henry Longhurst**: A witty television commentator who enlivened many a golf tournament broadcast, Longhurst also wrote a column on golf for the *Sunday Times*.

5. **Dan Jenkins**: A novelist and sportswriter with a raucous sense of humor, Jenkins also sponsors his own charity golf tournament. *Fairways and Greens* is a fine collection of his golf articles from both *Golf Digest* and *Sports Illustrated*.

Source: Authors, *The Best and Worst of Golf*

# YOUNGEST PGA QUALIFIER

The youngest player ever to qualify for the PGA Tour is Ty Tryon. In 2001, the 17-year-old from Orlando, Florida, shot a six-under-par 66 on the last day of Qualifying School. After the six-day shootout, he emerged 23rd out of 1,200 entrants. His solid play in two PGA events in 2001 earned the high schooler an endorsement with Callaway Clubs and Target, for $1 million a year.

Source: *People* magazine

# PLACES

# In This Section

# AMERICA'S BEST COURSES

The perennial butt of jokes, New Jersey is thought of more as one big turnpike than a haven for golfers. However, the editors of *Golf Magazine* would heartily disagree with this dire assessment of the Garden State. In their survey of the nation's best golf courses, they ranked the Pine Valley Golf Club in Pine Valley, New Jersey, Number 1. The birthplace of target golf, now the dominant motif of golf course architecture, the Pine Valley Golf Club has changed little since it was built in 1922. Nine years in the making, the Pine Valley Golf Club truly challenges golfers with its huge bunkers, dense patches of rough, and elevated greens (Pine Valley is 200 feet above sea level.)

In 1960 the producer of television's *Shell's Wonderful World of Golf* chose Pine Valley to host a match between Byron Nelson and Gene Littler. It was an awkward experience, both for the pros and the television crews, but despite some technical glitches, the match was ultimately a success.

Today the Pine Valley Golf Club also boasts a 10-hole short course designed by Tom Fazio, where less confident golfers might practice before moving onto the 18-hole course designed by club founder George Crump and English architect H. S. Colt.

| Course | Year Opened |
|---|---|
| 1. Pine Valley Golf Club | 1922 |
| 2. Cypress Point Club | 1928 |
| 3. Pebble Beach Golf Links | 1919 |
| 4. Augusta National Golf Club | 1933 |
| 5. Shinnecock Hills Golf Club | 1931 |
| 6. Pinehurst Country Club #2 | 1935 |
| 7. Merion Golf Club East | 1912 |
| 8. Sand Hills Golf Club | 1995 |
| 9. Oakmont Country Club | 1903 |
| 10. Seminole Golf Club | 1929 |

Source: *Golf Magazine*; *Historic Golf Courses of America* by Pat Seelig

# AMERICA'S BEST NEW COURSES

America is known for it's innovative ideas in nearly every arena, from art to technology. Golf courses are no exception. In addition to the traditional links, new courses are springing up all over. With the exception of Ocean Hammock Golf Course in Florida, the new upscale courses listed below are north of the

**The breathtaking views from Pacific Dunes course on the Oregon coast.**

Mason-Dixon line. Although the Yanks may not be able to play golf all year long, they appreciate a good course when they see one. And at a price of at least $50 per round, they're willing to pay for the best.

# Best New Courses in the U.S.

**Pacific Dunes**
   Bandon, Oregon

**Wild Horse Golf Club**
   Gothenburg, Nebraska

**Victoria National Golf Club**
   Newburgh, Indiana

**Shenendoah Golf Course**
   Verona, New York

**Arcadia Bluffs Golf Course**
   Arcadia, Michigan

**Stonebridge Country Club**
   Goffstown, New Hampshire

**Gary Player Course at Geneva National**
   Lake Geneva, Wisconsin

**Great River Golf Course**
   Milford, Connecticut

**Wolf Creek at Paradise Canyon**
   Mesquite, Nevada

**Ocean Hammock**
   Palm Coast, Florida

**Lost Dunes**
   Bridgman, Michigan

Source: Authors, *Best and Worst of Golf*

# ANIMAL ANTICS ON THE COURSE

Golf courses, by their very nature, are home to a variety of wildlife. Chipmunks, squirrels, birds, and even deer are common sights along the fairways. But some animals are peskier than others. And then there are some that are downright dangerous. Here are a few animal tales from golf courses around the world.

- **Yellowknife Golf Club** (Yellowknife, Northwest Territories, Canada): One of the northernmost courses in the world, Yellowknife causes golfers problems in more ways than one. Not only is the entire nine-hole course made of sand, it is plagued by a brave band of eagle-sized ravens, that have been stealing golf balls since 1950. The birds watch from their perch, some 200 yards from the green. When a ball lands, a raven swoops down, picks up the ball, and makes his get-away. A club official notes that several golfers have lost as many as six balls in a single round. Rule Number 6 on the Yellowknife scorecard? "No penalty shall be assessed when ball carried off by raven."

- **Singapore**: Golfer Jimmy Stewart approached his ball on the third hole of the 1972 Singapore Open when a 10-foot-long cobra slithered into his path. Thinking quickly, Stewart used his 3 iron to kill the slippery beast. As he turned his attention back to his shot, he saw a smaller snake crawl from the mouth of the lifeless cobra. Stewart had no choice—he killed that one, too.

- **Elephant Hills Country Club** (Victoria Falls, Zimbabwe, Africa): Designed by Gary Player, this course takes the natural jungle habitat to extreme. Elephant Hills is home to elephants, hippopotami, warthogs, snakes, ants, crocodiles, lions, and leopards. Although elephants leave large footprints on the green, surprisingly, it's those pesky warthogs that give golfers the biggest problem, digging holes on the fairways. Golfer Nick Price once hit a running warthog, toppling the animal to the ground. The good news? No penalty stroke was assessed, as rules dictate that after hitting a moving animal, the ball will remain in play.

- **Borders Club** (England): This course is bordered by a herd of cows with legal grazing rights along the edge of the third fairway. In 1967 the bovine suddenly made themselves known when they started eating the golf balls that came their way. The cows didn't just carry the balls away, they actually swallowed them whole. In fact, they've become such a problem—one golfer lost four balls in just two holes—that the rules have been changed to allow golfers to drop a new ball with no penalty

*Golfer Jimmy Stewart had a memorable run-in with a cobra at the 1972 Singapore Open.*

- **Oso Beach (Texas) Municipal Golf Course**: A six-foot alligator, who used to sun himself on a mud flat near the 15<sup>th</sup> hole, met his end when game wardens and police were unable to capture him in a ditch that ran between the golf course, Cullen Park, and Cullen Middle School. Although the gator was a fixture on the links for years, officials felt the students might be in danger, and shot the reptile. He will be missed by neighbors, students, and golfers, who have all filed complaints about his demise.

Source: Authors, *The Best and Worst of Golf*

"if a player's golf ball is consumed by a cow during the course of play."

- **Staunton Course** (England): Cows were also the cause for alarm during the 1984 St. Andrew's Trophy Match. Four golfers on the 18<sup>th</sup> green were suddenly stampeded by a herd of 40 to 50 cattle. Grabbing a red flag, the tournament official and his committee headed them off at the last moment.

- **The Chembur Golf Course** (Bombay, India): This course has been having a problem with local birds called kites. Thinking the balls are eggs, they swoop down to retrieve them. Course officials, however, have taken action to prevent the problem. They have hired forecaddies to run out after the ball and cover them with red cloths until the players reach them to take their next shot.

- **Atlanta Classic**: During a 1972 tournament, three players approached the ninth hole, each shooting for a birdie. The scene at the edge of the green drew the crowd's attention away from the golfers, however. Two ducks, that were not in the least deterred by the golfers or their fans, were attempting a mating dance on the carpet of grass. A tournament marshal shooed the pair off the green and all three golfers got their birdie.

# AUDUBON SIGNATURE SANCTUARIES

Golf magazines, pros, and fans regularly weigh in on which golf courses are the most difficult, the most scenic, or the most historic. Thanks to the work of Audubon International, we can now add yet another qualifier to the mix: which golf courses are the most eco-friendly.

Over the past few years, Audubon International has been working with golf course architects, managers, and key personnel regarding conservation, energy usage, waste management, and wildlife habitat in and around golf courses. Those courses that satisfy Audubon's rigorous and ongoing environmental requirements are certified as Audubon Signature Sanctuaries. To date, 21 courses both here and abroad have achieved this rating, while others are currently awaiting review. See table on opposite page.

# CANADIAN COURSES

## *Best New Courses*

If America is building new golf courses at an astonishing rate, our Northern neighbor is not far behind. Here's a look at some of the links decorating the Canadian country-side. Reviewing the courses for beauty and

| Audubon Signature Sanctuaries | |
|---|---|
| **Golf Course** | **Location** |
| 1. Bonita Bay Club East | Naples, Florida |
| 2. Cateechee Golf Club | Hartwell, Georgia |
| 3. Colbert Hills | Manhattan, Kansas |
| 4. Collier's Reserve | Naples, Florida |
| 5. Cypress Ridge Golf Course | Arroyo Grande, California |
| 6. Granite Bay Golf Club | Granite Bay, California |
| 7. Haymaker Golf Course | Steambrook Springs, Colorado |
| 8. Indian River Club | Vero Beach, Florida |
| 9. Legacy Club at Alaqua Lakes | Longwood, Florida |
| 10. Longaberger Golf Club— The Hills Course | Nashport, Ohio |
| 11. Lost Key Golf Club | Perdido Key, Florida |
| 12. North Hempstead Harbor Links | North Hempstead, New York |
| 13. Oak Grove Golf Course | Harvard, Illinois |
| 14. PGA Golf Club | Port St. Lucia, Florida |
| 15. Pinehurst No. 8, Centennial | Pinehurst, North Carolina |
| 16. Quinta da Marinha Oitavos Golfe | Cascais, Portugal |
| 17. Red Hawk Golf Club | Sparks, Nevada |
| 18. Sanctuary Golf Club at WestWorld | Scottsdale, Arizona |
| 19. Sand Ridge Golf Club | Chardon, Ohio |
| 20. Stevinson Ranch— Savannah Course | Stevinson, California |
| 21. Summer Grove Golf Club | Newman, Georgia |

Source: audubonintl.org

challenge, among other things, these six get the nod for "must play."

### Best Canadian Golf Courses

**Fox Harbour Resort**
Wallace, Nova Scotia

**Silver Lakes Golf and Country Club**
Newmarket, Ontario

**Le Club de Golf Lac Brome**
Ville de Lac Brome, Québec

**Stewart Creek Golf Course**
Canmore, Alberta

**Bridges Golf Course**
Starbuck, Manitoba

**St. Eugene Mission Golf Course**
Cranbrook, British Columbia

Source: Canadiangolfcourse.com

# CITIES FOR GOLFERS

## Big Cities to Avoid

Few cities captivate the imagination like New York—or cater less to golfers, we're sorry to report. Home to Broadway, the Yankees, and Rudy Giuliani, New York came in last in Golf Digest's rankings of America's big cities in regard to the number and quality of municipal, private, and public golf courses per the estimated golfer population. Golfers in Long Island fare better; Nassau, New York came in seventh on the list of America's best cities for golf.

In reverse order (worst being first), here are metropolitan areas that comprise *Golf Digest*'s bottom 10.

1. New York, New York
2. Bergen, New Jersey
3. Charlotte, North Carolina

*The Fox Harbour Resort golf course overlooks the Northumberland Strait off Northern Nova Scotia.*

4. Philadelphia, Pennsylvania
5. San Francisco, California
6. Orange County, California
7. Oakland, California
8. Raleigh, North Carolina
9. Washington, D.C.
10. San Jose, California

Source: *Golf Digest*

**New York is the least "golf-friendly" of America's big cities.**

## CITIES FOR GOLFERS

### *Top Picks*

Until the 2002 Winter Olympics, Salt Lake City was thought of mainly as the world head-quarters of the Mormon church. Thanks to the editors and researchers at *Golf Digest*, Salt Lake City can now also proclaim itself the best of America's big cities for golfers. Working closely with professors from Oklahoma State University's geography department, the editors and researchers at the magazine analyzed over 300 American metropolitan areas (defined as a "city" in the survey.) If a city had a sufficient number of public, municipal, and private golf courses to accommodate its golfer population, *and* those courses were adequately designed or maintained, then the city received a favorable rating. In the category of metropolitan areas with populations over one million, Salt Lake City came in first. Here are the top 10 big cities for golfers as chosen by *Golf Digest*:

1. Salt Lake City, Utah
2. Greensboro, North Carolina
3. Minneapolis, Minnesota
4. Cleveland, Ohio
5. Oklahoma City, Oklahoma
6. Austin, Texas
7. Nassau, New York
8. San Antonio, Texas
9. Milwaukee, Wisconsin
10. Denver, Colorado

Source: *Golf Digest*

# DANGEROUS GOLF COURSES

Do you have a fully paid up insurance policy? You should if you're playing in Sun City, South Africa. You might also want to consider hiring a caddy with a large-caliber rifle to protect against 15-foot alligators. Or, if you're in Singapore playing a round, you might want to trade your spiked golf shoes for a sturdy pair of Wellingtons to protect your calves from cobra bites. In Southern California, on the other hand, you might want to be accompanied on your rounds by a cordon of helmeted police. At Lost City Golf Course in Sun City, South Africa, a stone pit filled with crocodiles, some 15-feet long, fronts the 13th green. At Elephant Hills Country Club in Victoria Falls, Zimbabwe, craters caused by mortar shells fired across the Zambezi River sometimes mark the fairways. The Compton Par-3 Golf Course in Compton, California, has particularly high-caliber excitement when the Crips versus Bloods trouble flares. Following are other courses you would do well to avoid if you're faint of heart.

Below are the links for real men.

1. **Machrie Hotel Golf Course**
   Islay, Scotland
   On this old-fashioned, lay-of-the-land links, virtually every drive and approach is blind, played over huge sand dunes.

2. **Scholl Canyon Golf Course**
   Glendale, California
   Built on a landfill, it ran into difficulties when golfers snagged clubs on buried tires and methane gas rose up from the divots. They now pump the gas to the local power company.

3. **Pelham Bay and Split Rock Golf Courses**
   Bronx, New York
   Pelham's remote location makes it ideal for dumping unfortunate souls. In a recent 10-year period, 13 bodies were said to have been found.

4. **Singapore Island Country Club**
   **Singapore**
   In the 1982 Singapore Open, pro Jim Stewart encountered a 10-foot cobra. He killed it, only to watch in horror as another emerged from its mouth.

5. **Beachwood Golf Course**
   Natal, South Africa
   Mrs. Molly Whitaker successfully executed a bunker shot here a few years back, but was then attacked by a monkey who leaped from the bush and tried to strangle her. An alert caddie dispatched the mischievous primate.

6. **Plantation Golf and Country Club**
   **Gretna, Louisiana**
   With 18 holes shoved into 61 acres (less than half the norm), players must huddle against protective fencing while waiting their turn.

7. **Lundin Links**
   Fife, Scotland
   Enjoyable links near St. Andrews, unless you're Harold Wallace, who in 1950 was hit by a train while crossing the tracks beyond the fifth green.

Source: *Men's Health*, April 1997.

# DESERT COURSES

## *Top 10 Arid Courses*

America's golfers expect a lot from their courses. They want them to be challenging, but not too hard. They want the green fees to be affordable, yet expensive enough that they feel they are getting something of value. And of course, they want beauty. Picture lush greens surrounded by flowering cactuses and warm weather all year round.

That mild (okay, hot) climate is what attracts golfers from around the country to spend their vacations golfing in the dry southwest. In the November 2001 issue, *T&L Golf* rated the nation's top desert courses. Here's how they stack up.

*Golfers flock to the Sunbelt, which boasts some of America's most spectacular and challenging courses.*

1. **Pinnacle Course**
   Troon North Golf Club
   Scottsdale, AZ
   Yardage: 7,044
   Fees: $75–$240
   480-585-7700

2. **Monument Course**
   Troon North Golf Club
   Scottsdale, AZ
   Yardage: 7,028
   Fees: $75–$240
   480-585-7700

3. **Mountain Course**
   The Lodge at Ventura Canyon
   Tucson, AZ
   Yardage: 6,907
   Fees: $99–$199
   800-828-5701

4. **Talon Course**
   Grayhawk Golf Club
   Scottsdale, AZ
   Yardage: 6,973
   Fees: $50–$225
   480-502-1800

5. **South Course**
   The Boulders Resort
   Carefree, AZ
   Yardage: 7,007
   Fees: $110–$220
   1-480-488-9009

6. **Reflections Bay Golf Club**
   Lake Las Vegas Resort
   Henderson, NV
   Yardage: 7,261
   Fees: $200–$250
   702-740-4653

7. **Mountain Course**
   La Quinta Resort & Club
   La Quinta, CA
   Yardage: 6,756
   Fees: $75–$235
   800-598-3828

8. **Raven Golf Club**
   Sabino Springs
   Tucson, AZ
   Yardage: 6,776
   Fees: $55–$170
   520-749-3636

9. **Paa-ko Ridge Golf Club**
   Sandia Park, NM
   Yardage: 7,562
   Fees: $38–$66
   866-898-5987

10. **Desert Course**
    Primm Valley Golf Club
    Primm, NV
    Yardage: 7,131
    Fees: $80–$195
    800-386-7867

Source: *T & L Golf*

*Whether you're practicing your swing or just blowing off steam, an afternoon at the driving range can be just what the doctor ordered.*

# DRIVING RANGES

## Top Rated Practice Tees

Regular sessions at a driving range are key to improving your golf swing. Some driving ranges are admittedly rather low-rent establishments—little more than a line of hitting stalls facing an open field—while others are plush, indoor facilities offering golfers a wide range of amenities, from electronic swing analysis to personal instruction from certified PGA teachers. If you have the time and resources, check out any of the following driving ranges, which are considered among the nation's best.

1. **Callaway Golf Center**: Conveniently located outside Las Vegas, the Callaway Golf Center offers golfers both a driving range and a nine-hole golf course, where they can try out their new and improved golf swing. Critics praise the tiered driving range and its challenging target greens, including one doozy completely surrounded by water. Be prepared to fork over some cash to use Callaway's facilities, however. Hourly rates run from $13 to $18, depending on whether you hit from a mat or grass.

2. **PGA Golf Learning Center**: More than just a driving range, the PGA Golf Learning Center in Port St. Lucie, Florida, currently has over 100 full swing practice stations where golfers hit from Tifway 419 Bermuda turf grass. You can also practice your putting skills at a 7,000-square-foot practice putting green, enroll in one or more of several classes, or take private lessons from one of the PGA teaching professionals.

3. **Hank Haney Golf Ranch**: One of Haney's seven golf schools in Texas, the Hank Haney Golf Ranch features a top-notch driving range and a nine-hole golf course designed by noted golf course architect Pete Dye. Former LPGA pro Jane Blalock and Denis Pugh, coach to European pro Colin Montgomerie, provide lessons and lead seminars.

4. **Michael Jordan Golf Center**: This Charlotte, North Carolina, facility was named the best golf range in North America by the Golf Range Association of America. Catering to beginners and experienced golfers, the Michael Jordan Golf Center driving range has elevated greens, heated and covered tees, and bunkers galore to make it both challenging and fun.

5. **The Golf Club at Chelsea Piers**: Billed as the most technologically sophisticated driving range in the country, this year-round, multi-tiered, outdoor Manhattan facility has 52 heated and weather-protected hitting stalls on four levels (this is New York, so space is at a premium). Using the computerized automatic ball tee-up system, golfers hit balls onto a 200-yard, net enclosed artificial turf fairway.

Sources: golfrange.org; Las Vegas Review-Journal online (lvrj.com); PGA.com; cbs.sportsline.com/u/jordan/career/feature_golf.html; golfspan.com/instructors/hhaney/ranch.asp; chelseapiers.com/gc01.htm

# GOLF COURSES

## Best Lady Links

Commercials tout a variety of products that are specially made for women: deodorant, razors, and shampoo, to name a few. But golf courses? Well, maybe none are made for women only, but there are certainly courses that are friendlier to women golfers than others. *Golf For Women* magazine looked at America's daily-fee courses to find links that were favorable to women in several areas.

Some courses are more female-friendly when it comes to leagues, instruction, events, and women pros on staff. Facilities such as the pro shop, locker rooms, and practice areas are also important to women. And as for the course itself, consideration was given to yardage, minutes between tee times, and, of course, rest room facilities.

The courses below received top ranking.

## Atlantic Courses

Province Lake Golf Course, Parsons
    Field, ME
Beechtree Golf Club, Aberdeen, MD
Marlton Golf Club, Upper Marlboro, MD
The Timbers at Troy, Elkridge, MD
Ballyowen Golf Club, Hardyston
    Township, NJ
Blue Heron Pines Golf Club, Cologne, NJ
Charleston Springs Golf Course, Millstone, NJ
Seaview Marriott Resort, Absecon, NJ
Centennial Golf Club, Carmel, NY
Hillendale Golf Course, Ithaca, NY

## Hawaii's Courses

The Challenge at Manele, Lana'i
Hapuna Golf Course, Kohala Coast
Luana Hills, Kailua
Princeville Resort, Kauai
Wailea Golf Resort, Maui

## Midwestern Courses

Buffalo Grove Golf Course, Buffalo Grove, IL
Shepherd's Crook Golf Course, Zion, IL
Hoosier Links Golf Club, Milan, IN
Morningstar Golf Club, Indianapolis, IN
Black Lake Golf Club, Onaway, MI
Thousand Oaks Golf Club, Grand Rapids, MI
Dacotah Ridge Golf Club, Morton, MN
Deacon's Lodge Golf Course, Breezy
    Point, MN
Stone Ridge Golf Club, Stillwater, MN
Longaberger Golf Club, Nashport, OH

## Southern Courses

Robert Trent Jones Trail, AL
Emerald Dunes Golf Course, West Palm
    Beach, FL
Halifax Plantation Golf Club, Ormond
    Beach, FL
Ocean Hammock Golf Club, Palm Coast, FL
Sandestin Golf and Beach Resort, Destin, FL
Stone Mountain Golf Club, Stone
    Mountain, GA
Pine Needles Resort & Golf Club, Southern
    Pines, NC
Wil-Mar Golf Club, Raleigh, NC
King's North at Myrtle Beach National, Myrtle
    Beach, SC
Southcreek at Myrtle Beach National, Myrtle
    Beach, SC

## Western Courses

Camelback Golf Club, Scottsdale, AZ
Raven Golf Club at Sabino Spring,
    Tucson, AZ
Cascades Golf Course, Sylmar, CA
The Golf Club at Quail Lodge, Carmel, CA
Pelican Hill Golf Club, Newport Coast, CA
Resort at Squaw Creek, Lake Tahoe, CA
Vail Golf Club, Vail, CO
Pinon Hills Golf Course, Farmington, NM
Sunriver Resort, Sunriver, OR
Coral Canyon Golf Course, Washington, UT

Source: *Golf for Women*

# GOLF COURSES

## *Just the Facts*

Or as Woody Allen might put it, "Everything You Wanted to Know About Golf Courses, but Were Afraid to Ask."

Before they transform a barren desert into a lush green fairway, or incorporate a nearby ocean into their design (the biggest water hazard of them all), golf course architects everywhere start with basically the same list of general course requirements, such as the number of holes, distances, and cup size and depth. They will then manipulate and transform these requirements through hazard placement, landscaping, and location to make every golf course unique.

1. **Number of holes per golf course**: 9 or 18

2. **Average golf course size**:
   9 holes: 65 acres
   18 holes: 150 acres
   18 holes are usually 6,500–7,000 yards
   in length

3. **Par**:
   9 holes: 35 or 36
   18 holes: 68–74

4. **Men's par**:
   Men's par 3: 250 yards or less
   Men's par 4: 251–470 yards
   Men's par 5: 47 yards or more
   Women's par is based on slightly
   shorter yardage

5. **Typical distribution of pars on an 18-hole course**:
   Par 3: 4
   Par 4: 10
   Par 5: 4

6. **Design**: Courses are laid out in loops so the starting and ending holes are next to each other. Holes are planned so there are an equal number of holes into the wind as against the wind

7. **Tee**: usually 15-yards wide

8. **Green**: 6,000 square feet or more of the carpet-like grass

9. **Cup**: 4¼ inches in diameter and 4 inches deep

10. **Hazards**:
    sand traps
    bunkers
    rough (taller grass)
    woods (trees and shrubs)
    water

Source: *Compton's Interactive Encyclopedia*

# GOLF COURSES

## States with the Most

For the serious golfer (translation: addict), the prospect of being stuck out in the boonies, far

*A golfer's paradise: over 1,200 courses and The World Golf Hall of Fame.*

from any course, is the worst-case scenario. Happily, this nightmare need not come true. Heck, even Death Valley has a golf course—the appropriately named Furnace Creek Resort—which is the world's lowest course at 214 feet below sea level.

According to the 2001 edition of the National Golf Foundation's publication *Golf Facilities in the U.S.*, there are just over 17,000 golf courses in the country. Of these, more than 12,000 are open to the general public.

The following five states have the most golf courses, but bear in mind that the numbers are constantly changing; as of 2000, plans were in the works to build more than 1,000 new golf courses in the United States.

## States with the Most Courses

1. **Florida**: 1,261 courses

2. **California**: 1,007 courses

3. **Michigan**: 971 courses

4. **Texas**: 906 courses

5. **New York**: 886 courses

Splitting even more hairs, the National Golf Foundation reports that the average

*Many of the game's greatest players literally grew up on the golf course.*

number of golf holes (public and private) per 100,000 population among the nation's 317 Metropolitan Statistical Areas [MSAs] is 80. The following metropolitan areas rank highest on the NGF list.

## Number of Holes Among Top Metropolitan Statistical Areas

1. **Myrtle Beach, SC**: 721 holes

2. **Naples, FL**: 640 holes

3. **Barnstable, MA**: 289 holes

4. **Wilmington, NC**: 287 holes

5. **Ft. Myers/Cape Coral, FL**: 326 holes

Source: *Golf Facilities in the U.S.—2001 edition*; furnacecreek.com

## GOLF COURSES

### *Where the Pros Learned*

Many golfing legends discovered the game at some of America's most historic and prestigious country clubs. It is at these clubs that many picked up a golf club for the first time and experienced that peculiar mix of elation and exasperation that characterizes golf. Here are six clubs where pros teed off for the first time.

1. **East Lake Country Club**: Bobby Jones began his fabled career at age five on the courses of this Atlanta, Georgia country club was built in 1901.

2. **Country Club of Rochester**: Walter Hagen took his first swing here at age five, thanks to the efforts of this country club's resident pro. Hagen later worked as a caddie at the club, making 10 cents an hour in 1900.

3. **Glen Garden Country Club**: Both Ben Hogan and Byron Nelson started out as caddies at this Fort Worth, Texas, country club.

4. **Latrobe Country Club**: Arnold Palmer's father was the head pro and greenskeeper at this club, 50 miles east of Pittsburgh. Young Palmer started playing golf when he was five years old, using a ladies iron that his father had cut down to size.

5. **Kansas City Country Club**: Tom Watson began playing at age six at this Shawnee Mission, Kansas, country club. Coached by his father, and later the club pro, Watson broke 80 here for the first time when he was 12 years old.

6. **Scioto Country Club**: Jack Nicklaus started playing golf at this Columbus, Ohio, country club when he was 10 years old, and shot a 51 for nine holes.

Source: *Historic Courses of America* by Pat Seelig

## GOLF MUSEUMS

Ever wondered what became of the golf club that astronaut Alan Shephard used on the moon in 1971? Or what kind of clubs the Scots used in the 1700s? Then it's high time to visit any of the golf museums currently open in the United States and Scotland. From feathery golf balls to rare books to player memorabilia, these golf museums preserve the sport's illustrious past for today's golf enthusiasts.

1. **American Golf Hall of Fame**: Housed in the Foxburg Country Club in Foxburg, Pennsylvania, the American Golf Hall of Fame has over 400 years worth of golf artifacts and history. The museum is open April through October, seven days a week.

2. **The British Golf Museum**: Located in St. Andrews, the British Golf Museum traces the history of golf from the 15th century to today's champions. While in St. Andrews, make a pilgrimage to the Old Course, where Old and Young Tom Morris are buried. Website: www.britishgolf museum.co.uk

3. **Jack Nicklaus Museum**: Scheduled to open in the spring of 2002, the Jack Nicklaus Museum will be housed in an 18,000-square-foot facility on the campus of the Golden Bear's alma mater, Ohio State. Website: www.nicklausmuseum.org

4. **U.S. Golf Association**: In addition to housing Alan Shephard's lunar club and numerous art pieces, the USGA museum has a library of over 8,000 volumes for public use. Based at the USGA headquarters in Far Hills, New Jersey, the USGA museum and library is free to the general public. Website: www.usga.org

5. **World Golf Hall of Fame**: Previously housed in Pinehurst, North Carolina, the World Golf Hall of Fame is now based in St. Augustine, Florida. Along with exhibits commemorating the Hall of Fame inductees, the 75,000-square-foot Hall of Fame features a variety of interactive exhibits that test patrons' knowledge of the rules and assess their swing. Website: www.wgv.com

Source: *The Golfer's Sourcebook* by Cliff Schrock

# GOLF SCHOOLS

## *Four-Year Schools Offering PGA-PGM Programs*

Head golf professionals, working at a golf course, generally have a college degree. Most are also PGA members. This means they have passed the PGA's Playing Ability Test (PAT) and other training required by the PGA. Not too long ago, the college coursework and PGA certification were two separate entities. They each had their own fees, their own time requirement, and their own methods of testing.

Times have changed, however, and those looking toward careers in the golf field can fulfill both these requirements at once with the PGA's Professional Golf Management Program (PGM). The PGM began in 1975 with only a couple of participating colleges in the U.S. Since then, 1,900 students have graduated from the program. Another 1,300 are currently enrolled in the program at one of 11 accredited four-year colleges.

To qualify, candidates must have a handicap of 8 or less. Students prepare for a career in the golf industry through classroom studies, internships, and player development. They can choose a major in one of several areas including business administration, marketing, hospitality administration, recreation, or park management. The following universities offer PGM programs.

**Arizona State University East PGM Program** (1999)
Richard Grinage, Director
7001 East Williams Field Road
Building 20
Mesa, AZ 85212
(480) 727-1017
(480) 727-1961—fax
grinage@asu.edu

**Campbell University PGM Program** (1999)
Ken Jones, Director
P.O. Box 218
Buies Creek, NC 27506
(910) 893-1395
(800) 334-4111 ext. 1395
(910) 893-1392—fax
jonesk@mailcenter.campbell.edu

**Clemson University** (2001)
Dan Drane, Director
263 Lehotsky Hall
Box 340701
Clemson, SC 29634-0701
(864) 656-2230

(864) 656-2226—fax
ddrane@clemson.edu

**Coastal Carolina University PGM
   Program** (1999)
Andy Hendrick, Director
E. Craig Wall, Sr. School of Business
P.O. Box 261954
Conway, SC 29528-6054
(843) 349-2647
(843) 349-2455—fax
Hendrick@coastal.edu
David Hackney, Intern Coordinator (843)
   349-2972
Hackney@coastal.edu

**Ferris State University PGM
   Program** (1975)
Matt Pinter, Director
1506 Knollview Drive
Big Rapids, MI 49307-2290
(231) 591-2380
(231) 591-2839—fax
PinterM@Ferris.edu
Jean Shaw, Administrative Assistant
ShawJ@Ferris.edu

**Florida State University PGM
   Program** (1999)
Jim Riscigno, Director
Hospitality Department
University Center, Building B
One Champions Way, Suite 4100
Tallahassee, FL 32306-2541
(850) 644-9494
(850) 644-5565—fax
Jriscign@cob.fsu.edu

**Methodist College PGM Program** (1999)
Jerry Hogge, Director
5400 Ramsey Street
Fayetteville, NC 28311-1420
(910) 630-7144
(910) 630-7254—fax
Jhogge@methodist.edu

**Mississippi State University PGM
   Program** (1985)
Scott Maynard, Director
P.O. Box 6217
Mississippi State, MS 39762-5513
(662) 325-3161

(662) 325-1779—fax
Scott@coop.msstate.edu

**New Mexico State University PGM
   Program** (1987)
Pat Gavin, Director
P.O. Box 30001/Dept. PGM
Las Cruces, NM 88003-8001
(505) 646-7686
(505) 646-1467—fax
Pgavin@nmsu.edu

**North Carolina State University PGM
   Program** (2002)
Dr. Michael A. Kanters, Director
Department of Parks, Recreation & Tourism
   Management
Campus Box 8004
NC State University
Raleigh, NC 27695-8004
(919) 515-8792
(919) 515-3687—fax
michael_kanters@ncsu.edu

**Penn State University PGM
   Program** (1990)
Dr. Frank B. Guadagnolo, Professor
   in Charge
201 Mateer Building
University Park, PA 16802
(814) 863-8987
(814) 863-2624
(814) 863-4257—fax
Fbg@psu.edu

Source: PGA

# GOLF SCHOOLS

## *For the Amateur Golfer*

OK, so you've tried everything to improve your game—regular visits to the local driving range, instructional books and videos, visualization exercises, chanting "Be the ball" over and over again—but you're still spending an inordinate amount of time in the bunker and setting a new course record for slicing. Short of lighting votive candles before a picture of Bobby Jones, what's a golfer to do (besides drowning a few sorrows at the clubhouse bar?)

Well, if you have the time and the money, why not enroll for a refresher course at any of the following golf schools? Lasting anywhere from a half day to a week, these intensive programs give golfers the opportunity to hone and refine their skills under the critical gaze of PGA-certified instructors.

1. **Lyford Scottsdale Golf School**: Located in Scottsdale, Arizona, this school offers a two-day weekend course that runs from $500 to $600 (hotel not included.) For information, call 800-238-2424 or log onto www.swingbetter.com.

2. **Arnold Palmer Golf Academy**: With locations in Orlando, Florida, Wesley Chapel, Florida, and Dallas, Texas, Palmer's school offers various packages from $240 to $1,250. Call 800-523-5999 or log onto www.apga.com.

3. **Ben Sutton Golf School**: In Sun City, Florida, Ben Sutton Golf School offers a wide range of packages. Prices vary according to length of course or time of year, but the range is approximately from $425 to $2,035. Call 800-225-8923 or log onto www.golfschool.com.

4. **Mind Under Par Golf Schools**: This Newport Coast, California, school offers half-day, one -, two-, or three-day programs for $295, $495, $995, and $1,365, respectively. Call 888-620-4653 or log onto www.mindunderpar.com.

5. **Classic Swing Golf School**: Based in Myrtle Beach, South Carolina, the Classic Swing Golf School was voted one of the top 25 golf schools by *Golf Magazine* for 2001–2002. Three-day programs run from $369 to $699, depending on the season or whether or not a golf package is included. Call 800-827-2656 or log onto www.classicswing.com.

6. **Summit Golf Academy**: Located in Pt. Orange, Florida, the Summit Golf Academy offers both three- and five-day programs that run from $280 to $1,635. Call 888-563-3152 or log onto www.summitgolfacademy.com.

7. **U.S. Schools of Golf**: The U.S. Schools of Golf currently offers courses in 60 locations nationwide. Prices run from $399 to $2,999. Call 800-354-7415 or log onto www.ussog.com.

8. **FeelGoodGolf Learning Center**: In Florida, Wisconsin, and the Carolinas. Prices vary for the one-, two-, and three-day programs. Call 877-275-GOLF or log onto www.feelgoodgolf.com.

Source: Authors, *The Best and Worst of Golf*

# GOLF SPAS FOR WOMEN

Pampering has been raised to an art form at these luxurious golf spas for women. Offering everything from conditioning classes to improve your swing to skin care and deep-tissue massage, these spas are part of the ever-expanding industry that caters to women golfers, albeit those with enough disposable income to afford such indulgences.

• **The Breakers**: One of the grand old hotels of Palm Beach, the Breakers features the oldest 18-hole golf course in Florida, dating from 1897. There's a second 18-hole course and a golf academy on the lavish grounds, as well as a newly renovated spa where you can relax, soak, and exfoliate to your heart's

*Two golf spa guests wearily prepare for another grueling day of facials, massage, and gourmet meals.*

content. For those guests who want to golf in high style, the Breakers' staff will be happy to deliver a bottle of Veuve Cliquot to your suite. Call 888-273-2537.

• **Nemacolin Woodlands Resort & Spa**: Close to Frank Lloyd Wright's Falling Water house, this southwestern Pennsylvania golf spa features two golf courses: Pete Dye's Mystic Rock and the Links. Of the many services provided, the Mineral Kur is probably the most decadent (in the good sense of the word): a hydromassage in water pulsing with crystals from Hungary's Sarvar Spring is followed by a half hour full-body massage. You'll be so relaxed that it won't matter how you play the next day. Call 800-422-2736.

• **La Quinta Resort & Club**: The desert playground of Hollywood stars since 1926, La Quinta Resort & Club opened a golf spa in 1998. Home to the PGA West Golf Massage, the resort boasts five courses and a state-of-the art fitness center where golfers can tone their muscles and refine their game. If you've strained your back or sprained your wrist, the sports pack body wrap is a must; follow this with the soothing solar wrap for sun-damaged skin and you'll never want to leave this Palm Springs resort. Call 800-598-3828.

• **The Phoenician**: This ornate Scottsdale, Arizona, golf resort may be a little too new-agey for some tastes, what with tarot card readings and meditation, but The Phoenician also offers the usual range of scrubs, wraps, and facials for more earthbound guests. One-on-one sessions with an exercise therapist at the resort's Golf Power Program help guests identify and correct posture problems before they take on the resort's exotically landscaped 27-hole course. Call 800-888-8234.

• **The Resort at Summerlin**: Just minutes from the Las Vegas strip, this spa currently offers hydrotherapy, massage, and fitness classes to rejuvenate weary golfers after a day on the course. Guests can also take advantage of the spa's deluxe skin care treatment, the After Sun Skin Soother, which combines aloe, mud, and lotion to lessen the damage of overexposure to the hot Nevada sun. Although the spa is located on a 54-acre resort, surprisingly, there's no golf course on the property. Spa guests can tee off at TPC at the Canyons across the street, or check out the courses at Paiute, Badlands, Angel Park, and the Painted Desert. Call 877-689-8777 for information and reservations.

Source: *Golf for Women* magazine

# GREENS FEES IN THE U.S.

## Highest and Lowest

Deciding where to go on your golf vacation next summer can be tough. Will it be Hawaii or Iowa? Coconuts or corn? It all depends on your pocketbook and your tastes. The upper Midwest has clearly become the golfing capital of the United States, from the standpoint of offering the most golf for the least money. Within a 30-minute drive of Iowa City, for example, you'll find 11 courses with daily fees ranging from $7 to $50. One of those is Quail Creek, voted as one of the top 50 nine-hole courses in the country by the National Golf Foundation. Fees are $12 weekdays and $14 on weekends, while golf carts are $14 for nine holes or $22 for eighteen holes—a golfing bargain, to be sure.

If your bankroll is bigger, and your appetites tropical, you can always fly to Hawaii where greens fees average $81. On the island of Kapalua, a $180 greens fee entitles you to play the 6,643-yard Village Course designed by Arnold Palmer. Here the fairways are lined with pine and eucalyptus trees, and you'll enjoy a grand view of the mountains and the islands of Maloka'i and Lana'i. Perhaps the next day, for a $220 greens fee, you can play the Plantation Course, ranked by *Golf Digest* as among the top 10 of America's 75 best resort courses. But even in Hawaii you can find golfing bargains, such as the Kukuiolono public course, on Kalaheo, where the greens fee is only $7 for nine holes. That's hard to beat anywhere in the U.S.

Still, if your budget won't take you to paradise, you can always do the next-best thing, which is to play an Iowa course with a Hawaiian-sounding name. That would be the Kalona public course, in Kalona, Iowa, where greens fees are $8.95 weekdays and $12.95 on weekends for nine holes. Just don't expect ocean breezes.

### Highest Average Greens Fees

| | |
|---|---|
| Nevada | $92 |
| Hawaii | $81 |
| Arizona | $54 |
| South Carolina | $51 |
| Georgia | $50 |

### Lowest Average Greens Fees

| | |
|---|---|
| North Dakota | $17 |
| South Dakota | $19 |
| Kansas | $20 |
| Iowa | $22 |
| Nebraska | $23 |

Source: National Golf Foundation; jeonet.com; hawaii.com

# HARLESTON GREEN

## America's First Golf Course

Many golf historians look to the late 1880s as the starting point for American golf, but Scottish immigrants actually introduced golf to the colonies back in 1740. Once they settled in Charleston, South Carolina, the Scots began importing golf clubs and balls from Glasgow. Looking for the best playing field, they decided on Harleston Green, a field along the Ashley River. The game quickly caught on in nearby Charleston and led to the formation of the

*Pebble Beach is one of the world's most beloved and challenging golf courses.*

South Carolina Golf Club in 1786. By the War of 1812, however, golf had virtually disappeared from South Carolina and Harleston Green had become a military base.

Source: *Historic Golf Courses of America* by Pat Seelig

# ORIGINS OF GOLF

## *Where in the World...*

The origins of golf have never been definitively set. The Chinese claim that they played a version of the game back in 300 B.C. And when they weren't throwing Christians to the lions or fending off the barbarians, Roman emperors relaxed playing paganica, in which they used a bent stick to drive a feather-stuffed ball. As the Roman Empire spread across Europe, so did paganica. Variations on the game cropped up in various countries: it was known as cambuca in England, jeu de mail in France, and het kolven in the Netherlands.

Golf as we know it today evolved in 12th century Scotland and gradually became a national obsession. The first formal golf club was established in Edinburgh in 1744; 10 years later, the Royal and Ancient Golf Club

at St. Andrews formed and codified the game's complex rule system.

Source: lag.com.au/guide/history.htm

# PRIVATE GOLF COURSES

What makes a golf course so exalted that its greatness will hold up over time? Well, for starters, a great course should test the skills of a scratch player from the championship tees, challenging him to play all types of shots. It should reward well-placed shots and call on the golfer to blend power and finesse. Each hole should be memorable. There should be a feeling of enticement and a sense of satisfaction in playing the course. The design should offer a balance in both length and configuration, and the course should be properly maintained.

## Best Traditional Private Courses

1. **Cypress Point Club**
   Pebble Beach, CA

2. **Merion Golf Club**
   Ardmore, PA

3. **Oakland Hills Country Club**
   Oakland, CA

4. **Oakmont Country Club**
   Oakmont, PA

5. **Olympic Club (Lake)**
   San Francisco, CA

6. **Pebble Beach Links**
   Pebble Beach, CA

7. **Pine Valley Golf Club**
   Clementon, NJ

8. **Seminole Golf Club**
   N. Palm Beach, FL

9. **Southern Hills Country Club**
   Tulsa, OK

10. **Winged Foot Golf Club**
    Mamaroneck, NY

*Hailed by critics for its dramatic scenery and challenging course design, the Golf Club at Redlands Mesa in Colorado is ideal for golfers on a limited budget.*

## Best New Private Courses

1. **Kinloch Golf Course**
   Manakin-Sabot, VA

2. **Spring Creek Ranch Golf Course**
   Collierville, TN

3. **The Members Club at Aldarra**
   Fall City, WA

4. **The Club at Porto Cima**
   Sunrise Beach, MO

5. **The Club at Las Campanas (Sunset Course)**
   Santa Fe, NM

6. **Isabella Golf Course**
   Hot Springs Village, AR

7. **Eagle Point, Golf Course**
   Wilmington, NC

8. **Iron Horse Golf Course**
   Whitefish, MT

9. **The Stone Canyon Course**
   Oro Valley, AZ

10. **Kiawah Island (Cassique Course)**
    Kiawah Island, SC

Source: *Golf* magazine

# PUBLIC GOLF COURSES

## *Favorite Courses*

Not a member of the country club set? You can still find great courses to play. In fact, some public and municipal courses were conceived by the same designers as the best private courses, such as Robert Trent Jones. Other courses, such as Torrey Pines and the Edgewood Tahoe Golf Course, boast spectacular natural settings.

1. **The Raven at Sabino Springs**
   Tucson, AZ

2. **Brown Deer Park Golf Club**
   Milwaukee, WI

3. **Edgewood Tahoe Golf Club**
   Stateline, NV

4. **Torrey Pines Golf Course (South)**
   La Jolla, CA

5. **Forest Park 18-Hole**
   St. Louis, MO

6. **Otter Creek Golf Club**
   Columbus, IN

7. **Diamondhead Country Club Pine**
   Diamondhead, MS

8. **Tanglewood Golf Club**
   Clemmons, NV

9. **Geneva National**
   Lake Geneva, WI

10. **West Palm Beach Country Club**
    Palm Beach, FL

Source: Authors, *Best and Worst of Golf*

# PUBLIC GOLF COURSES

## *Best New Affordable Courses*

If you're a golfer, you've seen them all—books, magazine articles, and Internet sites all

*Why let a little thing like frostbite get between you and your weekly golf game? See "Snow Golf" on the opposite page.*

highlighting golf courses and resorts around the world. This may sound like a golfer's dream, but how many of us actually get there? It seems the closer the course is to the top of the "best" list, the less likely the average golfer is to be able to afford the green fees. That doesn't even count plane fares, hotel rooms, rental cars, and meals for this little junket.

*Golf Digest* has come to the rescue, however, with this list of affordable courses. To determine the top course, the publication solicited reviews from 700 low-handicap players. They looked at design variety, playability, shot value, and memorability for nominated courses. In this case, all courses also charged green fees of less than $50.

# Top Rated Affordable Courses

**The Golf Course at Redlands Mesa**
Grand Junction, CO
7,007 yds., par 72
970-263-9270
redlandsgolf.com

**The Harvester Golf Course**
Rhodes, IA
7,340 yds., par 72
877-963-4653
harvestergolf.com

**Dacotah Ridge Golf Course**
Morton, MN
7,109 yds., par 72
507-644-4653
dacotahridge.com

**Olympia Hills Golf and Conference Center**
Universal City, TX
6,923 yds., par 72
210-945-4653
olympiahills-golf.com

**Ol' Colony Golf Complex**
Tuscaloosa, AL
7,041 yds., par 72
205-562-3201

**Old Silo Golf Course**
Mount Sterling, KY
6,977 yds., par 72
859-498-4697
oldsilo.com

**Coyote Crossing Golf Course**
West Lafayette, IN
6,839 yds., par 72
765-497-1061
coyotecrossinggolf.com

**Aspen Lakes, Golf Course**
Sisters, OR
7,302 yds., par 72
541-549-4653
aspenlakes.com

**New Albany Links Golf Course**
New Albany, OH
7,004 yds., par 72
614-855-8532
newalbanylinks.com

**Murphy Creek Golf Course**
Aurora, CO
7,456 yds, par 72
303-361-7300
golfaurora.com

Source: *Golf Digest*

# SNOW GOLF

Living in rural Vermont in the 1890s, British author Rudyard Kipling was regarded by the locals as a rich eccentric. His addiction to golf did little to dispel their first impression of the celebrated author of *Captains Courageous* and *The Jungle Book*. No matter what the weather, Kipling played golf—even when snow blanketed the countryside. Undaunted, Kipling would strap on his snow shoes, paint his golf balls a bright red to enhance visibility, and plant tin cans at appropriate distances around his property to serve as holes. He would then fashion a tee out of snow and simply play golf.

Source: *Links Lore* by Peter F. Stevens

# U.S. OPEN

## *Most-Played Courses*

In its 107 year history, the U.S. Open has been played at some of America's most prestigious and challenging courses. Seven courses have been designated "regular" hosts for the U.S. Open: Baltusrol, Oakmont, Oakland Hills, Shinnecock Hills, Pebble Beach, Oak Hill, and Olympic. There are also seven "occasional" courses, five of which appear on the list.

Although Baltusrol is considered less demanding than many of the other courses, the country club's proximity to USGA headquarters has made it the USGA's selection to host the Open seven times since 1903—a record shared with Oakmont, where Jack Nicklaus defeated Arnold Palmer in 1962 to claim the first of his four U.S. Open titles.

Of the other clubs, the Myopia Hunt Club wins hands-down as the most unusually named course to host the U.S. Open.

# WORKPLACE GOLF

## *Best and Worst Offices for Golf*

Salary, benefits, and growth potential—sure, those are all important factors when looking for a job. Now let's talk real "quality of life" issues in the workplace: is your cubicle big enough to practice your golf swing? And what's the office policy on teeing off in the conference room (between meetings, of course)? The unique plight of golfers in the

| Times Hosted Course | U.S. Open | Tournament Years |
|---|---|---|
| 1. Baltusrol Country Club | 7 | 1903, 1915, 1936, 1954, 1967, 1980, 1993 |
| Oakmont Country Club | 7 | 1927, 1935, 1953, 1962, 1973, 1983, 1994 |
| 3. Oakland Hills Country Club | 6 | 1924, 1937, 1951, 1961, 1985, 1996 |
| 4. Winged Foot Country Club | 4 | 1929, 1959, 1974, 1984 |
| Inverness Country Club | 4 | 1920, 1931, 1957, 1979 |
| Myopia Hunt Club | 4 | 1898, 1901, 1905, 1908 |
| Olympic Club | 4 | 1955, 1966, 1987, 1998 |
| Pebble Beach Club | 4 | 1972, 1982, 1992, 2000 |
| 9. Shinnecock Hills | 3 | 1896, 1986, 1995 |
| Oak Hill Country Club | 3 | 1956, 1968, 1989 |
| Southern Hills Country Club | 3 | 1958, 1977, 2001 |
| Medinah Country Club | 3 | 1949, 1975, 1990 |
| The Country Club | 3 | 1913, 1963, 1988 |

Source: sportsillustrated.com

nine-to-five world has largely been ignored—that is, until golf-conscious journalist David Owen blew the lid off the subject in his groundbreaking study *The Complete Office Golf*. Thanks to his efforts, job-seeking golfers everywhere can identify the best and worst industries for playing golf on company time.

## The Best

1. **Golf Equipment Manufacturing**: *'Nuff* said.

2. **Carpet Manufacturing**: All those carpet samples can be turned into your very own course. Shag rug samples make for a good rough.

3. **Aircraft Maintenance**: Once the planes take off, the huge and empty aircraft hangers are a great place to practice driving the ball.

4. **Organized Religion**: OK, maybe golf on Sundays is out of the question, but churches are otherwise pretty good choices. The stained glass, however, makes anything besides putting a little dicey.

## The Worst

1. **Banking**: Corporate focus on the bottom line and the slippery marble floors don't make for a relaxing round of golf.

2. **Antiques**: All those expensive and delicate antiques can really cramp your golf swing.

3. **Medicine**: It's hard to focus on your game with all those sick people around.

4. **Military**: The "down time" necessary for office golf is nonexistent.

Source: *The Complete Office Golf* by David Owen

# WORLD'S BEST GOLF COURSES

Somewhere, Pine Valley Golf Club founder/codesigner George Crump is having the last

laugh. When the wealthy Philadelphia golf lover first broke ground in the New Jersey marshlands, many jeered his choice of location, citing the 22,000 stumps and thick, nearly impenetrable underbrush. When Crump sold his Philadelphia hotel and poured thousands of dollars into the project, critics prematurely dubbed it "Crump's Folly." Despite the odds against success, Crump and design partner H. S. Colt never faltered and within a year they completed the first 11 holes. Sadly, Crump died before Pine Valley Golf Club officially opened in 1922, but his legacy lives on in the course that has been ranked Number 1 in the world by the editors of *Golf Magazine*.

Another course making the top 10 is none other than the Old Course at St. Andrews in Scotland, which dates from 1400 and can be truly considered the mecca of the golf world.

| Course | Year Opened |
|---|---|
| 1. Pine Valley Golf Club | 1922 |
| 2. Cypress Point Club | 1928 |
| 3. Pebble Beach Golf Links | 1919 |
| 4. Augusta National Golf Club | 1933 |
| 5. St. Andrews Old | 1400 |
| 6. Shinnecock Hills Golf Club | 1931 |
| 7. Pinehurst Country Club—No. 2 | 1935 |
| 8. Muirfield | 1744 |
| 9. Royal Melbourne Composite | 1926 |
| 10. Royal County Down | 1898 |

Source: "History of Pine Valley Golf Club" by Doug Gelbert at Pagewise.com

# WORLD COURSES

## *Challenging Holes*

There always seems to be at least one hole per course that strikes fear in the hearts of even the most talented and experienced golfers. Whether it's their sheer distance from the tee or the nearby hazards (both natural and man-made), these golf course holes have been the making and undoing of many players' games.

It was at the Merion Golf Club's fabled 18th hole that Ben Hogan cinched his victory at the 1950 U.S. Open, just one year after he had been critically injured in a car accident. And on Pebble Beach's 18th hole overlooking the Pacific Ocean, the watery grave of many golf balls and players' hopes, Tom Watson shot a birdie that gave him a 2-stroke victory at the 1982 U.S. Open.

| *Most Challenging Golf Holes* | | | | |
|---|---|---|---|---|
| **Course** | **Hole** | **Distance** | **Par** | **Hazards** |
| **Augusta** Augusta, GA | 13th hole | 465 yards | 5 | Trees and water |
| **Merion** Merion, PA | 18th hole | 463 yards | 4 | Quarry between tee and hill. Steep slope and bunkers around the green |
| **Muirfield** Muirfield, Scotland | 9th hole | 495 yards | 5 | Dogleg, bunkers, and out-of-bounds wall |
| **Pebble Beach** Pebble Beach, CA | 18th hole | 548 yards | 5 | Pacific Ocean and gusty winds |
| **Royal Liverpool** Hoylake, England | 16th hole | 560 yards | 5 | Dogleg, practice tee edges onto fairway |
| **Royal Lytham** St. Anne's, England | 18th hole | 412 yards | 4 | 15 bunkers, brush, and shrubs |
| **Royal Troon** Troon, Scotland | 18th hole | 452 yards | 4 | Bunkers |
| **St. Andrews Old Course** St. Andrews, Scotland | 17th hole | 461 yards | 4 | Railroad sheds and deep rough |
| **Turnberry: Ailsa Course** Turnberry, Scotland | 18th hole | 431 yards | 4 | Rough in front of green and gorse bushes |

Source: *Ultimate Golf Techniques* by Malcolm Campbell

# THINGS

America's Top 75 Golf Resorts

The #1 Golf Publication

Golf Digest

www.golfdigest.com

Exclusive by Travel Snead Foldext

5 Keys to
Consistency

by Peter Green
Golf Digest Teaching Professional

Titleist
1

# In This Section

# ADVERTISING

In the scramble for consumer dollars, golf equipment manufacturers spare almost no expense in advertising in all forms of media. Much of these companies' advertising budgets go right into the bank accounts of select PGA and LPGA stars, who've signed multi-million dollar endorsement deals. These deals ultimately generate far more income for the pros than they could ever earn competing, but the big winners are the companies, whose sales continue to skyrocket. Here's a breakdown of how and where golf equipment manufacturers are putting their advertising dollars to work.

- **Television**: 70 percent of the top 20 advertisers say they spend the majority of their budget on TV

- **Magazines**: 60 percent of the top 20 advertisers say they spend at least 40 percent here

- **Largest amount for any one product**: Taylor Made golf clubs: $17.3 million
  Calloway Golf Clubs: $16.5 million
  Cobra Golf Clubs: $12.2 million

- **For golf balls**:
  Titleist: $12.2 million

Source: *American Demographics*

# ANIMALS ON THE COURSE

## *The "Fairway" Bandit*

In 1929 golfers at a New York country club reported that their golf balls were disappearing from the course as fast as they hit them. When police investigated, they arrested a young man and his accomplice, a slobbering bulldog. The young man confessed that he had trained his bulldog to dart from the bushes, grab the balls as they landed, and return them to him for quick sale. Although the young man was sentenced to 10 days in jail, his canine cohort evaded capture and continued to wreak havoc on neighboring courses for months. The wily bulldog's exploits eventually attracted the attention of journalists, who christened him the "fairway bandit." Then, he simply vanished from the courses and was never seen again. What became of the "fairway bandit" remains a mystery, but many speculate that he was taken in by a caddie who put an end to the bandit's life of crime.

Source: *Links Lore*

# BALLS

## *Average Distance for Top Urethane Brands*

Golf ball design has evolved significantly since the game's early days, when enterprising Scots used the roundest stones they could find. From the era of the feathery and the gutta-percha to today's customized, aerodynamically-tested models, sports equipment manufacturers have devoted a lot of time and money to building a better golf ball. Every design facet—the shape, the number of layers, dimples—is scrutinized before it meets that manufacturer's seal of approval. Still, if you were to ask the average golfer why he selects a certain brand of golf ball, most wouldn't care whether it was made of wood or play-dough, as long as it goes the distance. For those discerning consumers, we offer these stats for the top selling urethane golf balls currently on the market.

1. **Calloway Rule 35 Soft Free**   280.3 yards
2. **Wilson Staff Tour**   280.0 yards
3. **Nike Tour Accuracy**   277.1 yards
4. **Titleist Pro VI**   276.9 yards

Source: Wilsonsports.com

# BALLS

## *Specifications*

Whenever companies like Titleist or Wilson introduce the latest in golf ball design, they must submit a sample to the USGA to see if it conforms to the organization's standards. Only if these brands pass muster with "Iron Byron" at the USGA Research Test Center's outdoor range will they be eligible for use in professional competition. The current standards for golf balls arose in 1974, when the R&A finally allowed America's "bigger ball" to be used in the British Open. There are now well over 800 golf ball designs on the USGA list. Although the USGA sets no explicit standards regarding ball color or size, manufacturers adhere to the tried and true.

Golf balls must conform to the following standards for use in professional tournaments.

1. **Weight**: The maximum weight allowed is 1.62 oz. (45.93 g). There is no minimum.

2. **Size**: The minimum size is 1.68 inches (42.67mm) in diameter. There is no maximum.

3. **Initial velocity**: The speed which a ball leaves the club head can be no greater than 250 ft. (76 m) per second. This is roughly 174 mph.

4. **Overall distance standard**: Balls must not go farther than 280 yards (256 m) in carry and roll on the test course.

Source: *Ultimate Golf Techniques* by Malcolm Campbell

# BALLS

## New in 2002

Buying golf balls used to be easy. If you fancied yourself a long hitter, you bought a Titleist. If you wanted to combine distance with durability, you bought a Maxfli. If you had a tendency to cut balls, or hit them into the water, you bought a Top Flite or any of the other cheaper and more durable brands. As the song says, life was oh so simple then.

Buying a golf ball today practically requires a consultant. Titleist, alone, offers six different balls. And there are so many new kids on the block: Calloway, Nike, Taylor Made, and Precept, just to name a few. One Internet seller offers 56 different brands of balls.

But the explosion of choices is more than a marketing bonanza. Technology has truly

changed the ball from the inside out. Now you can select a ball to fit any swing, any game, any conditions. You can even buy golf balls designed for your sex, such as the Precept Lady Distance ball. Today, golf balls can be harder or softer, offer more or less feel, and have a higher or lower spin rate, all depending on the needs of your game.

The old wound golf ball, consisting of a core, the winding, and the cover, has been phased out of production. Most balls today are made with thermo-plastic materials, called isonomers, and employ either two-piece, or multi-layer construction. Two-piece construction generally decreases spin and increases distance, while multi-layer construction generally increases spin and offers more control. Chances are the average weekend golfer will benefit from a two-piece ball to minimize the effects of slice or hook swings. More accomplished golfers may want a ball with greater spin and feel, to improve their irons and short game. So how do you know which ball is best for you? Three little words: experiment, experiment, experiment.

# BALLS

## Preference by Trait

Golf ball manufacturers try to sell their products by appealing to golfers on many levels. But when all is said and done, most golfers will use a ball even if they simply received it as a gift. According to the Darrell Survey of Golf Equipment, here are the traits that golfers say most influence their purchase.

| Trait | Percentage |
|---|---|
| Feel | 25.0 |
| Distance | 18.0 |
| Price | 13.0 |
| Need | 12.0 |
| Gift or prize | 7.0 |
| Brand reputation | 4.0 |
| Recommended by friend | 3.5 |
| Spin | 3.0 |
| Performance | 2.5 |

| Brand Name | Price per Dozen | Description |
|---|---|---|
| Calloway HX | $58 | Unusual dimples provide less drag. |
| Nike Tour Accurate DD | $54 | David Duval's choice for distance. |
| Strata Tour Ultimate 2 | $54 | More distance from harder cover. |
| Maxfli A10 | $52 | An encore to a revolutionary ball. |
| Slazenger Black Label | $52 | Amazing distance. |
| Precept Premium 1.5 | $50 | Made for distance. |
| Taylor Made TP Tour | $35 | Changes make for more control. |
| Titleist NXT Tour | $34 | Soft core covers a great distance. |
| Wilson Staff Tour | $30 | Extra long and extra soft. |
| Top-Flite XL3000 | $25 | New design yields best Top-Flite ever. |

Source: *Golf Tips* February/March 2002; *Golf Illustrated*, Winter 2002

# BALLS

## Pros Using Titleist Pro V1

Titleist has signed a glittering array of stars from the PGA, LPGA, and SPGA Tours to endorse their high-end line of golf balls, such as the Tour Balata, Professional, and Tour Prestige models. The most widely used Titleist golf ball is the Pro VI, which became the hands-down favorite just one week after it was introduced on the PGA Tour. Here are 20 of the hundreds of pro golfers who swear by the Titleist Pro VI, which has been designed to achieve maximum distance and endure wear and tear from frequent use.

Miller Barber

Mark Calcavecchia

Jo Anne Carner

Laura Diaz

Ernie Els

Retief Goosen

Juli Inkster

Hale Irwin

Davis Love III

Bob May

Phil Mickelson

Mark O'Meara

Jose Maria Olazabal

Dottie Pepper

Vijay Singh

Curtis Strange

David Toms

Lanny Wadkins

Karrie Webb

Mike Weir

Source: titleist.com

# BALLS

## Top Balls Used by Pros

It's not uncommon for golf ball manufacturers to pay pro golfers to use their ball on tour. It's a winning situation for the companies, whose product is seen by other players and millions of television viewers.

Free balls may make you suspicious. Who wouldn't use balls provided absolutely free? Well, golf pros, for one. Professionals who make their living playing golf can't afford to choose a ball unless they are confident of its ability. Wound balls, led by Titleist, are still preferred by golfers on all three pro tours. Here's how other brands stack up listed in order of usage by the pros.

| PGA Tour |
|---|
| Titleist |
| Strata |
| Maxfli |
| Bridgestone |
| Nike |

### SPGA Tour

Titleist
Bridgestone
Strata
Maxfli
Taylor Made

### LPGA Tour

Titleist
Bridgestone
Maxfli
Strata
Srixon

Source: Darrell Survey of Golf Equipment

Pinnacle
Maxfli
Bridgestone

Souce: Darrell Survey of Golf Equipment

# BALLS

## Usage by Brand

Once upon a time, all golf balls were wound. That is, they contained a rubber band-like core that was wound tightly together and covered with balata, a rubber derivative. In 1968 Spalding manufactured the first two-part ball. Top-Flite followed with a more refined version in 1971. The two-part balls have a harder cover that resists cuts, allowing a golfer to play more rounds of golf with one ball, no matter how hard it is hit. On the flip side, wound balls offer more control and, some say, a better feel.

As of this writing, wound balls lead all three pro tours, but consumers are buying solid balls by almost two-to-one. Here are the top-selling golf balls by brand.

| Brand | Usage |
| --- | --- |
| Titleist | 39 percent |
| Top-Flite | 23 percent |
| Pinnacle | 9 percent |
| Maxfli | 8 percent |
| Wilson | 6 percent |

Source: *Golf Equipment Almanac 2000*

# BALLS

## Usage by Age of Golfer

Age has very little bearing on golf ball selection, according to the Darrell Survey of Golf Equipment. Golfers may prefer balls that are durable, have a certain feel, or go a long distance. They may choose the brand used by their favorite golf pro, or the golfer who beat them last week in match play. But age? It doesn't mean much. Titleist, Top-Flite, and Maxfli appear among the favorites of every age group. Wilson, Pinnacle, and Bridgestone round out the list, which is shown in order of usage by age groups.

### Under 30

Titleist
Top-Flite
Maxfli
Wilson
Bridgestone

### 31–50

Titleist
Top-Flite
Maxfli
Pinnacle
Wilson

### 51 and over

Titleist
Top-Flite

**Hands down, Titleist's Pro V1 is the most widely used golf ball on the PGA, LPGA and SPGA Tours.**

## BALLS

### Usage by Handicap

Walking into a pro shop or sporting goods store, the golf ball choices are overwhelming. There are wound balls and solid balls, inexpensive balls and balls that are, well, pretty pricey. Most are the traditional white, but there are also balls available in neon orange, lime green, and baby blue. And don't forget the logo balls; you can get one stamped with the name of your favorite team or Disney character. So how is a golfer to choose?

Whether it's a wish to emulate the pros or simply that these balls work well for the serious player, Titleist golf balls are favored by low-handicap golfers. In the higher-handicap range, however, Top-Flite (solid core) balls edge out Titleists by a small margin.

#### 0–10 Handicap

| Ball | Usage |
| --- | --- |
| Titleist | 55 percent |
| Top-Flite | 12 percent |
| Maxfli | 8 percent |
| Bridgestone | 5 percent |
| Wilson | 3 percent |

#### 11–20 Handicap

| Ball | Usage |
| --- | --- |
| Titleist | 20 percent |
| Top-Flite | 8 percent |
| Pinnacle | 6 percent |
| Wilson | 6 percent |
| Maxfli | 5 percent |

#### 21 + Handicap

| Ball | Usage |
| --- | --- |
| Top-Flite | 30 percent |
| Titleist | 27 percent |
| Pinnacle | 18 percent |
| Wilson | 8 percent |
| Maxfli | 6 percent |

Source: *Golf Equipment Almanac 2000*

## BALLS

### Why Do Golf Balls Have Dimples?

If everything else were equal, a smooth golf ball would go about 130 yards. But a dimpled ball travels about 270 yards.

Why? Because at high speeds, the uneven surface causes a layer of air to form around the ball. This forms a "wake," which creates less drag on the moving ball. The natural backspin of a ball, coupled with the rough surface, forces the air to flow faster over the top of the ball and slower underneath, giving the ball a higher lift.

Watch for even more developments in ball covers in the near future. Callaway introduced the first golf ball to sport overlaid ridges rather than the traditional scooped-out dimples. The Callaway HX features 320 hexagons and 12 pentagons on its surface. The ball was developed by the company's senior director of golf ball research, Steve Ogg, who knows his aerodynamics—he once worked for Boeing.

Source: Authors, *The Best and Worst of Golf*

## BOOKS

### Pros in the Pages

In the six years since he turned pro, Tiger Woods has been profiled, dissected, praised, and reviled in countless newspapers, magazines, and television shows. He has also been the subject of nearly 50 books, ranging from biographies to instruction manuals to children's books—all before turning 30.

Here's how many books about some other pros are currently in print, according to the Library of Congress catalogue.

1. **Bobby Jones**: The Georgia-born golfer and founder of the Masters has been the subject of 12 books over the years.

2. **Jack Nicklaus**: The Golden Bear has been written up in 12 books, including 4 children's books.

3. **Arnold Palmer**: Of the 12 books about Palmer, the most unusual has to be the children's book *Arnold Palmer and the Golfin' Dolphin*, by P. Bryon Polakoff.

4. **Ben Hogan**: Hogan has been the subject of nine books, including a "fictionalized biography" by Bob Thomas.

5. **Byron Nelson**: Three books focus on Nelson, including two autobiographies by the player known as Lord Nelson: *How I Played the Game* and *Byron Nelson: The Little Black Book*.

6. **Gary Player**: Player has authored three books, including his 1975 autobiography, *Gary Player, World Golfer*.

7. **Gene Sarazen**: Sarazen's 1990 autobiography and a 1987 biography comprise Sarazen's listing in the Library of Congress catalogue.

8. **Walter Hagen**: Surprisingly, there is only one book about the flamboyant Hagen as of this writing, *Sir Walter and Mr. Jones: Walter Hagen, Bobby Jones, and the Rise of American Golf*, by Stephen R. Lowe.

Source: Authors, *The Best and Worst of Golf*

# BROADCASTERS

## *Golfers Turned Commentators*

Ever since television began broadcasting golf tournaments in the fifties, many professional golfers have moonlighted as on-air commentators. Of course they didn't have much time to practice their delivery in the early days; in 1956 the television networks devoted only five and a half hours of air time to golf for the entire year. Six years later the premiere of *Shell's Wonderful World of Golf* introduced viewers to golfing legends Ben Hogan, Sam Snead, and Arnold Palmer, among others. Created by Gene Sarazen, who also provided on-air commentary, *Shell's Wonderful World of Golf* ran on all three networks from 1962 to 1971. With the launch of The Golf Channel in

the nineties, armchair golfers everywhere can now watch their favorites 24-7.

These golfers have all become fixtures in the broadcast booth during telecasts.

1. **Johnny Miller**: Winner of 24 PGA tournaments, including the 1973 U.S. Open, Miller provides analysis for NBC Sports.

2. **Gary McCord**: The witty SPGA player with the distinctive mustache has been providing on-air commentary for *CBS Sports* since 1986.

3. **Ken Venturi**: The 1964 U.S. Open champion was forced to retire from the PGA because of severe carpal tunnel syndrome. In addition to writing golf instruction books, Venturi has been an analyst for CBS since 1968.

4. **Bobby Clampett**: A member of the PGA Tour from 1980 to 1995, Clampett joined CBS in 1991.

5. **Peter Oosterhuis**: A veteran of the PGA and European tours with 20 victories to his credit, Oosterhuis worked at both the BBC and The Golf Channel before joining CBS.

6. **Ian Baker-Finch**: Winner of the 1991 British Open, Baker-Finch is the lead analyst for the Australian PGA Tour telecasts.

7. **Judy Rankin**: Rankin joined *ABC Sports* in 1984 and has covered all the major LPGA tournaments.

8. **Curtis Strange**: Strange joined ABC Sports as the lead golf analyst in 1997.

9. **Mark Lye**: The lead analyst for The Golf Channel, Lye played on the PGA Tour from 1977 to 1994.

10. **Donna Caponi**: The winner of back-to-back U. S. Women's Open tournaments in 1969 and 1971, Caponi is now The Golf Channel's LPGA analyst and an on-field reporter for PGA tournaments.

Source: *The Golfer's Sourcebook*;
cbsports.com; abcsports.com; golfchannel.com

# CAREERS

## Average Salaries in the Golf Industry

There are almost 17,000 golf courses in the United States. While 60 percent of these employ PGA members, it is possible to get a job in the field without being a member. Among 18-hole courses, however, that figure jumps to 77 percent. For anyone seriously interested in pursuing a career in the golf industry, a PGA membership opens doors and increases the chances of promotion to the head professional spot.

Golf jobs are not without competition. There are currently 16,000 PGA members active in the industry, with another 6,300 apprentices working toward memberships. Don't forget the 1,300 Professional Golf Management (PGM) students earning college degrees along with their PGA memberships. The average age of PGA members is 41; the good news is that the age of retirement is a relatively young 60.

The golf industry believes in the policy of "working your way to the top." And work they do. If you are considering a golf career for the opportunity to play golf on a regular basis, you may want to go into a different line of business. Many golf apprentices and assistant professionals commonly work 50 hours a week, opening pro shops at dawn and closing after dusk. Keep in mind that holidays and weekends are also among the busiest times on the links.

Here is a look at some of the jobs available in the golf profession, along with the average salary for that position.

**Director of Golf Operations**

| | |
|---|---|
| Private facility | $62,100 |
| Municipal | $57,100 |
| Daily fee course | $51,200 |

**Head Golf Professional**

| | |
|---|---|
| Private facility | $42,200 |
| Municipal | $38,900 |
| Daily fee course | $34,800 |

**PGA Apprentice Assistant**

| | |
|---|---|
| Private facility | $26,561 |
| Municipal | $24,391 |
| Daily fee course | $22,793 |

**Course Superintendent**

| | |
|---|---|
| Private facility | $58,100 |
| Municipal | $44,500 |
| Daily fee course | $43,300 |

**Assistant Course Superintendent**

| | |
|---|---|
| Private facility | $24,600 |
| Municipal | $29,600 |
| Daily fee course | $26,700 |

**Food & Beverage Manager**

| | |
|---|---|
| Private facility | $58,100 |
| Municipal | $27,100 |
| Daily fee course | $30,100 |

**General Manager**

| | |
|---|---|
| Private facility | $76,600 |
| Municipal | $52,300 |
| Daily fee course | $52,000 |

**Grounds maintenance worker**
$8.33 per hour

**Landscape architect**
$43,540 per year

**Golf driving range attendant**
$6.63 per hour

Source: Mundus Institute; U.S. Golf Facility Employment Compensation Study; Bureau of Labor Statistics

# CAREERS

## Golf's Playing Ability Test

The first step toward becoming a PGA professional is to pass the PGA's Playing Ability Test (PAT). Offered 600 times per year around the country, the PAT is played from the middle tees with the pin in the center of the green. The PAT is a 36-hole event in which an individual must score no more than 15 strokes higher than twice the course rating. For instance, if the course rating for 18 holes is 74, twice that score would be 148. Add on the 15 additional strokes allowed by the rules, and the player could shoot a 36-hole score of no more than 163.

That may not sound difficult for an accomplished golfer, but consider this: less than 20 percent of those taking the PAT achieve a passing score.

Source: PGA

# CAREERS

## *Top Golf Association Executive Compensation*

If you think that the only people who make money in the golf profession are the top few golfers on the PGA circuit, you're wrong. After all, the PGA Tour wouldn't be able to pay pro golfers those large purses without an awful lot of support from an awful lot of people: fans, media, advertisers, associations, and more. And who is the force behind all this support? Top golf association executives.

These are the men and women that head the organizations that make golf what it is today. Their associations create an interest in the sport, recruit members, educate the public, and educate golfers who want to become pro golfers or teachers. They work with the media, advertisers, product manufacturers, and agents. They raise money, plan tournaments, honor the winners, and compile the statistics.

It may take a staff of hundreds to accomplish all of these tasks, but a strong leader is what keeps the ball rolling. Here are some of the top executives in the golf industry along with their salaries, including benefit package.

**Tim Finchem: $2,119,238**
PGA Tour Commissioner

**Charlie Zink: $736,314**
PGA Tour Exec. VP and CFO

**Ed Moorhouse: $729,504**
PGA Tour Exec. VP and Chief Legal Officer

**Jim Awtrey: $589,962**
PGA of America CEO

**Ron Price: $442,013**
PGA Tour Senior VP/ Finance and Administration

**Donna Orender: $437,229**
PGA Tour Senior VP Productions/New Media

**Bill Calfee: $378,031**
PGA Tour Exec VP COO Buy.com Tour

**Paul Bogin: $376,435**
PGA of America COO

**David B. Frey: $360,042**
USGA Executive Director

**Henry Hughes: $304,676**
PGA Tour Senior VP COO

**Bob Combs: $312,594**
PGA Tour Senior VP Communications and PR

**Joe Beditz: $260,838**
National Golf Foundation president and CEO

**Ty Votaw: $225,651**
LPGA Commissioner

Source: 1999 IRS Form and *Golf Digest*

# CADDIES

It's become a familiar sight at professional tournaments: the victor publicly thanks his caddie for standing by him through triumph and defeat and serving as his toughest critic and biggest champion. Add violins strumming in the background and you have a scene guaranteed to make even the most stoic golfers well up with gratitude for their tireless, reliable caddies.

Yet for every heartwarming story of the enduring bond between a player and his long-time caddie, there's one about a caddie showing up soused (if he shows up at all), or bringing the wrong set of clubs, or second-guessing a player to nervous distraction during a tournament. Where's that legendary Baggar Vance when you need him?

- Of course, being a caddie isn't just a matter of lugging a player's golf bag from one hole to the next—as Jack Nicklaus discovered when he played caddie for his 14-year-old son Gary during a qualifying round at the 1983 U.S. Open. Nicklaus checked the number of clubs at the first tee and it appeared that everything was in order. That's because Nicklaus only counts the numbers on the clubs—not the number *of* clubs. On the third hole, Gary asked for his 4 iron and Jack was surprised to discover two 4 irons in the bag. One belonged to Jack. Gary took a 4-stroke penalty for his father's error.

- Hey, at least Nicklaus doesn't play favorites. A year earlier, he caddied for his son Jack Jr. and lost his son's ball on the first hole.

Hollywood meets the PGA at the Bob Hope Chrysler Classic. Pictured (left to right) are Cary Middlecoff, Danny Thomas, Julius Boros, and Bob Hope.

caddie looked stunned: "Are we in Memphis? I thought we were in Fort Worth."

Source: *The Golf Hall of Shame* by Bruce Nash and Allan Zullo; "Golf's nomad 'silent mules'" by Craig Smith, Seattletimes.com (posted 07/26/98)

- Thanks to his caddie, Dale Douglass recorded the longest (unofficial) putt in the history of the Kemper Open. The caddie got lost, leaving Douglass at the first tee without his bag. With only his putter in hand, he waited for his caddie to appear. When his name was called, he knew had had to tee off or be disqualified. He made the shot with his putter and it went 150 yards down the fairway. Luckily, the caddie found him before he had to play his second shot.

- Another separation between caddie and golfer caused trouble for Raymond Floyd in the 1987 Tournament Players Championship. While Floyd walked to the 10th tee with only his driver, his caddie headed down the fairway with the rest of his bag. Floyd hit a great shot (260 yards) right into his own golf bag. He was assessed two strokes for hitting his own equipment.

- Floyd also had the bad luck of playing with a geographically challenged caddie known as "Golf Ball" at a Memphis tournament. Although Floyd was hitting well, he missed the first four greens. After watching the ball sail 20 yards past the fifth green, Floyd angrily turned to Golf Ball and snatched the yardage book from him. The diagram bore no resemblance to the actual fifth green. When Floyd asked Golf Ball if this was the correct yardage book for Memphis, the

# CELEBRITY NICKNAMES FOR GOLF SHOTS

While it may not have quite the same cachet as getting your footprints cast in cement before Graumann's Chinese Theater, you know you've made it when your name becomes part of the peculiar lingo spoken on golf courses. The following celebrities will live on in the clubhouse long after their stars have faded from the limelight. So check your political correctness meter and read on for the celebrity index of drives, courses, and putts.

1. **Marv Albert**: Ouch! The infamous sportscaster lends his name to an approach shot that bites.

2. **Mario Andretti**: A drive that lands on the cart path and keeps going, much like the veteran Indy driver.

3. **Bo Derek**: There are two definitions referring to the corn-rowed beauty who achieved fame as a perfect "10." 1) a perfect shot, or 2) Scoring 10 on a hole.

4. **Morgan Fairchild**: Gary McCord's term for a shot that's nice but a little thin.

5. **Laurel and Hardy**: "I'm sorry, Ollie," but the classic comedy team is another term for scoring ten on a hole.

6. **Mickey Mouse**: A golf course of questionable design is said to be "Mickey Mouse" (and we don't mean animated!)

7. **Willie**: As in Nelson, the country singer whose hit *On the Road Again* applies to a ball that lands on the road or cart path.

8. **Dolly Parton**: A putt that appears overwhelmed by the size of the cup before going in.

9. **Liz Taylor**: The queen of the gossip columns is another name for a fat shot that somehow remains beautiful.

Source: *Let the Big Dog Eat! A Dictionary of The Secret Language of Golf* by Hubert Pedroli and Mary Tiegreen

# CHARITY GOLF TOURNAMENTS

## *Celebrity-Sponsored*

In 1937 crooner Bing Crosby became the first celebrity to lend his name to a pro-am tournament that was known as the Crosby "clambake." Following his lead, several of Hollywood's big names have established tournaments that have raised millions of dollars for various charities. Here are some of the more notable celebrity sponsored golf tournaments.

1. **The Crosby National Celebrity Golf Tournament**: This final incarnation of Bing Crosby's pro-am tournament was held from 1986 through 2001 in North Carolina under the sponsorship of Sara Lee. The tournament raised over $18 million, which was distributed to such charities as Habitat for Humanity, the Special Olympics, and the United Way.

2. **Bob Hope Chrysler Classic**: After playing in the tournament's pro-am competition, comedian Bob Hope added his name to the Palm Springs Golf Classic in 1965, which became the Bob Hope Desert Classic. Chrysler later came aboard as the title sponsor in 1985. As of this writing, the tournament has donated more than $35 million to over 100 charities.

   Some of Hollywood's biggest names have played in the pro-am competition over the years. Besides Hope, Jackie Gleason, Jack Benny, Sammy Davis Jr., and Andy Williams, recent celebrity golfers include Samuel L. Jackson, Michael Bolton, Clint Eastwood, and rocker Alice Cooper.

3. **Frank Sinatra Celebrity Golf Tournament**: The "Chairman of the Board" launched this two-day tournament in 1988, pairing celebrities and amateurs to raise funds for the Barbara Sinatra Children's Center in Rancho Mirage, California. A nonprofit facility started by the Sinatras in 1986, the Center provides counseling for physically, emotionally, and sexually abused children.

   Celebrity players have included Kirk Douglas, Tony Danza, Robert Wagner, Yogi Berra, and Mike Connors.

Source: bhcc.com; thecrosby.org; sinatracenter.com

# CHEATING

## *Common Ploys in Golf*

The old adage "cheaters never prosper" is apparently lost on some golfers, who place a higher premium on winning than competing fairly. And unless they have friends or competitors watching their every move, these golfers may well get away with bending the rules to their advantage. Yet that goes against the unwritten code of the game, which is played on the honor system, as there are no referees or umpires to catch players cheating. And it's a surefire way to end up playing alone if you consistently resort to any of the following tactics when playing with friends.

1. **Ball bumping**: It's very tempting to ignore the rule of playing the ball where it lies, especially when it's in the middle of nowhere. But it doesn't matter whether you pick it up and hurl the ball towards the green or tap it over with your foot; ball bumping is still considered cheating. The only exception to this rule occurs when you agree to play by "winter rules," which allow you to move your ball to a better lie if fairway conditions warrant it.

2. **Marking a ball closer to the hole**: On the green, watch for players who mark their ball closer to the hole than it actually lies.

3. **Finding a golf ball in the rough**: Much to your chagrin, your last drive disappeared

somewhere in that tangled patch of rough known as the "forbidden zone." Why risk getting exposed to poison ivy or surprising a snake when it's so much easier to fish a new ball out of your pocket and fool everyone by passing it off as the original? It could happen, right?

4. **Whiff or warm up?** There's probably nothing more mortifying than whiffing, especially before onlookers. Rather than admitting this faux pas, some golfers try to pass it off as another practice swing, despite evidence to the contrary.

5. **Misadventures in scorekeeping**: Some players can't resist fudging their score.

Source: *The Complete Idiot's Guide to Golf* by Michelle McGann with Matthew Rudy

# COMPUTER GAMES

## Most Popular Golf Games

Golf games for the computer, like their video game counterparts, have improved significantly since the first ones were introduced a decade ago. They have become more realistic and offer players a wide choice of courses and other options. While you don't have to be a serious golfer to play, computer games more so than video games tend to appeal to people who know their way around the links. Many of these games simulate golf in the real world, making the pace a little slower than the typical video game.

The Links series has led the field since 1996 and has scored another winner with Links 2001, a game that is graphically detailed and offers the choice of many famous courses such as the Old Course at St. Andrews. Many of these games are available in both PC and Macintosh formats.

There are more than 50 electronic golf titles available, but here is a list of some of the most popular games around.

| Title | Maker |
|---|---|
| Golf 2001 | Microsoft |
| Golf Resort Tycoon | Activision |
| Links 2001 | Microsoft |
| Links 2001 Expansion Course | Microsoft |
| Links 2002 Championship Edition | Microsoft |
| Links LS Classic | Microsoft |
| PGA Championship Collector's Edition | Sierra Sports |
| Sid Meier's SimGolf | Electronic Arts |
| Tiger Woods PGA Tour 2000 | EA Sports |
| Tiger Woods PGA Tour 2001 | EA Sports |
| Tiger Woods PGA Tour Collection | EA Sports |

Source: Amazon.com

# CONSUMER SPENDING ON GOLF

## By Category

Twenty-two percent of all golfers are women. Although they spend a whopping $3 billion dollars annually on golf-related products and services, men still outspend them 84 percent to 16 percent.

It follows that those who spend a lot of money on golf do so because they have more money to spend. That's probably why 68 percent of all consumer spending on the sport comes from households with an annual income of more than $50,000. And because higher education leads to better jobs, it's not surprising that college grads account for half of the money spent on golf.

It may take awhile for people to reach that higher income level, though. Younger golfers may start out with second-hand clubs, and get by without a glove or proper shoes. For those reasons, middle-aged players tend to spend more on golf than their younger and older counterparts. Here's a look at consumer spending by gender, age, income, and education.

### Spending by Gender

| | |
|---|---|
| Male: | 84 percent |
| Female: | 16 percent |

### Spending by Age

| | |
|---|---|
| 45–64 years old: | 35 percent |
| 25–34 years old: | 22 percent |
| 35–44 years old: | 17 percent |

*How to lose friends and influence enemies on the golf course.*

| | |
|---|---|
| Over 65 years old: | 12 percent |
| 18–24 years old: | 5 percent |
| 14–17 years old: | 5 percent |
| Under 14 years old: | 4 percent |

## Spending by Education

| | |
|---|---|
| College grad: | 50 percent |
| Some college: | 37 percent |
| High school: | 11 percent |
| Less than high school: | 2 percent |

## Spending by Income

| | |
|---|---|
| $50,000–$74,000: | 37 percent |
| Over $75,000: | 31 percent |
| $35,000–$49,999: | 14 percent |
| $15,000–$24,999: | 9 percent |
| $25,000–$34,999: | 7 percent |
| Under $15,000: | 2 percent |

Source: *Statistical Abstract of the U.S.*

# CONSUMER SPENDING ON GOLF

## By Items

Broken down by age and gender, it seems that middle-aged men spend the most on golf. But what about ability? Do scratch golfers spend the same as duffers? Probably not. Statistics show that golfers who score between 80 and 99 on 18 holes account for 64 percent of all golf expenditures. And those who range between 80 and 89 spend an average of $1,182 annually on golf merchandise. It's still unclear which came first: the fancy golf equipment or the lower scores.

Here's where the money goes.

| | |
|---|---|
| Private fees and dues: | 40 percent |
| Public fees: | 34 percent |
| Golf clubs: | 11 percent |
| Soft goods (bags, gloves and shoes): | 4 percent |
| Golf balls: | 4 percent |
| Range balls on golf course: | 4 percent |
| Range balls at range: | 3 percent |

Source: National Golf Foundation

# COURSE CARE

Golf course etiquette is not something to be taken lightly or worse, ignored. That is, unless you want to be banned from a golf course for life or incur the wrath of the greenskeepers! Nothing betrays a novice on the golf course more than his or her ignorance of the game's hallowed standards of courtesy. Luckily, it doesn't require a finishing school degree to conduct yourself appropriately on the green.

**More than 4,000 golfers from around the world belong to the National Amputee Golf Association.**

golfer Casey Martin took the PGA to court over its ban of the use of golf carts in tournaments—and won. His Supreme Court victory drew attention to the thousands of disabled golfers nationwide. The following organizations sponsor tournaments for their members and offer everything from moral support to putting advice.

1. **National Amputee Golf Association**: Started by a World War II veteran who had lost his leg below the knee, the National Amputee Golf Association was incorporated in 1954 and now boasts over 4,000 members across the country and from 17 countries. In addition to hosting tournaments, the NAGA also sponsors clinics for golfers with physical disabilities. Website: www.nagagolf.org

2. **United States Blind Golf Association**: A blind lawyer and golf enthusiast started the United States Blind Golf Association in 1953. USBGA sponsors both national and statewide tournaments yearly. Website: www.blindgolf.com

3. **Physically Challenged Golf Association**: A nonprofit organization founded in 1995, the Physically Challenged Golf Association sponsors both tournaments and workshops for golfers and healthcare professionals alike. Website: www.town usa.com/pcga

4. **FORE ALL!**: This organization holds clinics nationwide to teach people with disabilities how to play golf. Christopher Reeve and Bob Dole are among this organization's many supporters. Website: www.foreall.org

Source: Authors, *The Best and Worst of Golf*

You may not play like a pro, but at least you can behave like one—and we don't mean throwing your clubs like an enraged Tommy Bolt. Here are nine "do's and don'ts" of golf course etiquette:

1. Replace divots carefully.

2. Rake bunkers after use.

3. Don't leave your bag or cart in front of the green while putting.

4. Don't leave your bag or cart and walk ahead to hit your ball, having to go back for it.

5. Repair pitch marks on the green.

6. Use care when removing the pin and setting it on the green.

7. Be quiet while your fellow golfers take their shots.

8. Never mark the scorecard until you leave the green.

9. Be careful of scuffmarks on the green.

Source: *Ultimate Golf Techniques* by Malcolm Campbell

# DISABLED GOLFERS

## *Player Organizations*

Born with a rare circulatory disorder that makes it difficult to walk long distances, pro

# DRIVING DISTANCE

## *Pros, 1980 vs. 2001*

In just 21 years, the average driving distance of PGA Tour pros has increased nearly 23 feet. What accounts for this dramatic jump? Primarily better equipment, which has come a

*Cobra is one of the most preferred brands of all drivers.*

long way since the days of hickory shafts and feather balls. With companies like Callaway and Ping constantly unveiling "new and improved" versions of golf clubs that look like props from *The Jetsons*, who knows how far the pros will be able to drive in the next few years?

### Average Driving Distance

| | |
|---|---|
| 1980: | 256.9 yards |
| 2001: | 279.4 yards |

### Top-Ranked Players' Average Driving Distance

| | |
|---|---|
| 1980: | 274.3 yards |
| 2001: | 306.7 yards |

### PGA Rank of Player Hitting 270-Yard Average

| | |
|---|---|
| 1980: | 7th place |
| 2001: | 178th place |

Source: February 2002 *Golf Magazine*

Drivers have changed more than any other club in the last 20 years. They have moved away from the steel shaft and wooden head common in the seventies. Now, thanks to Taylor Made Golf's 1979 introduction of "metal woods," most drivers are graphite and titanium.

Callaway leads the way in new clubs with the popular Big Bertha and Great Big Bertha. Here are the top five bestselling *used* drivers, along with the list price for a club in very good condition

1. **Titleist 975D**
   Graphite shaft: $212.97
   Steel shaft: $220.18

2. **Callaway Hawkeye VFT**
   Graphite shaft: $245.32

3. **Ping ISI Ti**
   Graphite shaft: $233.74

4. **Taylor Made 320**
   Graphite shaft: $251.91

5. **Callaway Biggest Big Bertha**
   Graphite shaft: $207.23
   Steel shaft: $148.57

Source: golfclubexchange.com

# DRIVERS

## Most Popular Used

The price of new golf clubs can be staggering for top quality equipment. It's not uncommon to pay $400 for a new driver. And that's only one of the 14 clubs found in a typical golf bag.

# DRIVERS

## Preferred Brands

A born entrepreneur who introduced the Big Bertha in 1991, Ely Callaway died in 2001 at the age of 82. Nineteen years ago, he bought a small, mom and pop company that made reproductions of hickory-shafted clubs for collectors and transformed it into a major player generating millions in sales worldwide. How did Callaway, a former textiles executive and winemaker, manage this feat? By aiming his product directly at the weekend golfers, albeit those with enough disposable income to buy Big Bertha or any of the other high tech drivers, putters, and golf balls that his design team could produce. Callaway's products didn't always go over well with the USGA. One of his later brainstorms, the ERC II driver, was dismissed by the USGA for its "trampoline effect." The club face features a metal that recoils and instantly springs forward upon impact with the ball to give it more momentum. According to the USGA, the ERC II driver gives golfers an unfair advantage. Callaway's loyal customers at driving ranges and golf clubs everywhere would undoubtedly disagree.

Here are the top brands used by the average Joe.

| Brand | Usage |
| --- | --- |
| 1. Callaway | 29 percent |
| 2. Taylor Made | 17 percent |
| 3. Cobra | 8 percent |
| 4. Titleist | 7 percent |
| 5. Ping | 5 percent |

Source: "Power to the Duffers" by Charles McGrath in the *New York Times Sunday Magazine* 12/30/01.

## PGA Tour

1. **Titleist**
2. **Callaway**
3. **Ping**
4. **Taylor Made**
5. **Kasco**

## SPGA Tour

1. **Callaway**
2. **McHenry metals**
3. **Titleist**
4. **Kasco**
5. **Orlimar**

## LPGA Tour

1. **Callaway**
2. **Ping**
3. **Titleist**
4. **Orlimar**
5. **Taylor Made**

Source: *Golf Equipment Almanac 2000*; titleist.com

## DRIVERS

### Top Tour Usage by Brand

Of all the golf equipment manufacturers, Titleist and Callaway are probably the best known and most widely used, particularly among tour professionals. Titleist drivers, like the Titleist Pro Titanium 975J, which is designed to increase speed and distance, are the No. 1 choice of PGA Tour players. For the LPGA and SPGA pros, however, Callaway drivers rule the tee. Titleist is the third favorite, coming in behind McHenry metals and Ping for SPGA and LPGA players, respectively.

## DRIVERS

### Why Golfers Select Certain Drivers

Every year, golf equipment manufacturers spend a fortune hawking their clubs in glossy ads featuring endorsements from pro golfers. Yet for all the media buzz generated by these expensive pitchmen, they ultimately figure littler in golfers' choice of drivers. According to golfers surveyed, only 4 percent of the respondents said that they bought a specific driver because of advertising. The top reason for buying a driver? Distance, hands down.

| Reason purchased | Percentage |
|---|---|
| 1. Distance | 17 |
| 2. Feel | 13 |
| 3. Tried a demo | 11 |
| 4. Price | 10 |
| 5. Gift/Prize | 9 |
| 6. Recommended by a friend | 7 |
| 7. Need | 6 |
| 8. Brand reputation | 5 |
| 9. Advertising | 4 |
| 10. Recommended by pro shop | 3 |

Source: *Golf Equipment Almanac 2000*

**A golfer with a cell phone is persona non grata on the course.**

# ETIQUETTE

Who are the real slobs when it comes to offending their fellow golfers? They're the ones who breach golf etiquette, of course. These jerks, according to golf course superintendents, are the ones who make the following faux pas on the links. At right is the percentage who screw up when playing. They are in order of the proportions of offense.

### *Golf Faux Pas*

| Transgression | Percent Doing |
|---|---|
| 1. Not fixing ball marks | 60 |
| 2. Not raking bunkers | 18 |
| 3. Not replacing divots | 8 |
| 4. Lack of golf rule knowledge | 8 |
| 5. Using cell phones | 2 |
| 6. Walking in a player's line | 2 |

Source: *USA Today*

# FREE GOLF STUFF

Golf is not the cheapest sport. It seems like there's a charge for everything: golf clubs, golf bag, golf balls, tees, ball markers, golf shoes, and socks. For the well dressed, there's the expense of that clean-cut preppy outfit of matching collared shirts and shorts that are not too long and not too short. Don't forget a hat or visor, sunglasses, bug spray, and sunscreen. Once you get to the course, you've got the green fees and, often, the cost for either a cart or a caddy. Golf vacations including airfare, food, and lodging are expenses of an entirely different class.

So golfers, take heart. Finally, here is a list of "stuff" for golfers that will cost you nothing. Some items are absolutely free to use here and now. Some require downloading or signing up. A few are contests that award free items to weekly (lucky) winners. Enjoy!

- **Daily golf jokes**: If golf makes you smile, sign up to get a golf joke every day from www.bettergolf.net.

- **Screen savers**: Pretend you're golfing all year round with these golf screen savers from www.golfathalfprice.com.

- **Clip Art**: Find over 1000 pieces of golf clip art at www.golfathalfprice. com.

- **Handicap calculator**: Log on to this free online service and figure your handicap in minutes. www.worldgolf. com

- **Handicapper software**: Calculate your handicap from home using your computer and this free software from www.golfat halfprice.com.

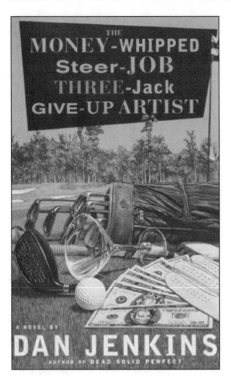

*Dan Jenkins strikes comic gold again in his latest novel about professional golf.*

- **Ball and caps**: Enter to win a free Slazenger cap or a dozen Slazenger golf balls at www.golfballs.com.

- **College scholarships for women golfers**: Check out the colleges that offer golf scholarships to girls who can break 100. Go to www.womensgolf.about.com and click on Freebies/college scholarships.

- **Free email**: This site offers a free email service to all golfers at www.golfmail.com.

- **Golf fitness analysis**: Complete a questionnaire and discover your physical limitations and recommendations for a better game from www.golf-trainer.com.

- **Golf jobs**: If you want to make a living from golf, check out these job listings at www.usgolfjobs.com.

- **Greeting Cards**: Send free golf-themed cards by email at www.golfat halfprice.com or www.american greetings.com.

Source: Authors, *The Best and Worst of Golf*

# FUNNY GOLF NOVELS

Golf has long inspired writers to wax poetic about the glories of the game. Then there's Dan Jenkins, the sportswriter/novelist who gleefully skewers the PGA in his hilarious satire, *Dead Solid Perfect*. Published in 1974, the book depicts the raucous and raunchy misadventures of good ol' boy Kenny Lee Puckett on the PGA Tour. Following Jenkins' lead, other writers have mined comic gold from the colorful personalities, botched shots, and petty rivalries that are part of the game's lore. The following novels, in no particular order, capture golf in all its wonder and absurdity.

1. *Missing Links* by Rick Reilly: Sick and tired of playing on a course littered with abandoned cars and shopping carts, four working class golfers scheme to crash the nearby Mayflower Club, Boston's most exclusive golf course. What begins as a friendly bet, however, soon spirals into comic disaster once they get a look at how the other half golfs.

2. *The Green* by Troon McAllister: Two-bit Florida golf hustler Eddie Caminetti hits the jackpot when desperate pro Al Bellamy drafts him for the United States Ryder Cup team. The proverbial odd man out, the fast-talking con artist ultimately proves invaluable to the team in this good-natured send-up of the biennial competition.

3. *The Foursome* by Troon McAllister: The adage "A fool and his money shall soon part" comes true for four incredibly rich and arrogant golfers in this darkly comic novel. Arriving at the luxurious golf resort Swithen Bairn, they meet their undoing in the form of Eddie Caminetti, who's both the resort's proprietor and resident hustler.

4. *The Money-Whipped Steer-Job Three-Jack Give-Up Artist* by Dan Jenkins: Jenkins takes fresh aim at the PGA Tour with his

**Will they still be friends when they settle up their bets?**

latest novel. Near the very bottom of the PGA money list, Bobby Joe "Spin" Grooves has never won a major tournament in his sixteen year career. In a final bid for credibility, he sets his sights on making the U.S. Ryder team, a goal that will probably be a lot easier than keeping his ex-wives and a jealous girlfriend at bay.

Source: Authors, *The Best and Worst of Golf*

# GAMBLING AT GOLF

## *Betting Games*

Whether it's simply a friendly wager or six figures per hole, betting games in golf are extremely popular. The PGA Tour's Skins Game draws huge audiences yearly to watch four top pros play one of the oldest betting games in golf. Novice golfers are advised to steer clear of playing these games for money, unless they're feeling particularly lucky or generous. You never know when one of your friends may turn out to be another Titanic Thompson, the legendary golf hustler.

1. **Nassau**: The most popular golf bet, this game can be separated into three categories—front 9, back 9, and the total 18-hole score. The winner is the player with the lowest score for each 9- or 18-hole round.

2. **Low Ball**: This bet breaks the score down to each hole. The player with the lowest score for a given hole, wins that hole, no matter what the total score for the round may be.

3. **Low Ball/Low Total**: This is a variation of low ball played with foursomes, where both the lowest score and the pair's total score for a hole are taken into account. A golfer can win low score, low total, both, or neither for each hole.

4. **Robins**: A popular game with foursomes, each player is partnered with a different member for 6 of the 18 holes. This divides the talent fairly and gives each player a better chance to win some of the low ball holes. Low total can also be played in a round robin.

5. **Press**: A new bet is a secondary wager, put on the table by a losing player. Generally, the player must be 2 down before a press is accepted.

6. **Skins**: This is an exciting variation on low ball where each hole is assigned a value (such as $2 or $5). The player who wins that hole with the lowest score wins that amount from each player for that hole. If two players tie, all are considered tied and the cash value carries on to the next hole. This game is called Cats or Skats in some parts of the country.

7. **Bingo Bango Bongo**: One of the oldest golf betting games, Bingo Bango Bongo consists of three points awarded per hole. One point (Bingo) goes to the first player to reach the green, another point (Bango)

*You could be the first on your block to have a golfer/caddy weather vane.*

is awarded to the player whose ball is closest to the cup after all golfers are on the green, and the last point (Bongo) goes to the first player to hole out

Source: Authors, *The Best and Worst of Golf*

# GAMBLING AT GOLF

## Side Bets

Want to jazz up your weekly golf date with friends? Then why not throw any of the following side bets into the mix—for penny ante stakes, of course.

1. **Longest drive in the fairway**: A no-brainer: the player with the longest drive that remains in the fairway wins.

2. **Longest putt**: The putt that is farthest away from the cup, and which goes in.

3. **Do/Don't**: A bet between a player and any number of the other golfers. One golfer who finds himself with an especially good lie—or a disastrous one—may offer to bet that they "do" make a certain shot. For instance, a golfer in the middle of the fairway may bet that he makes the green on his next shot. In another instance, a golfer in the woods may bet that he makes it over the trees and onto the fairway with his shot. Other players can accept or reject the bet for any value they choose.

4. **Disaster**: Some players who have a low score may simply be skilled at getting out

of trouble. This game penalizes players for each "disaster" they encounter or mistake that they make, such as landing in a sand trap, whiffing, losing a ball, or 3-putting a hole. Each disaster is assigned a certain number of penalty points and players keep track of their penalties. These are added up at the end and the player with the lowest number wins.

5. **Humility**: This is low ball with severe consequences. When a player loses a hole to his opponent, he must carry that golfer's bag. Not recommended for novices or those who "choke" under pressure.

6. **Gimme the Putt**: In this game 2- to 5-foot-putts rule. When a player has a putt in this range, he can ask his opponent to let him concede the putt (allow him to take just one stroke without actually putting the ball). If the request is denied, the first player must putt, but now the bet for this hole is doubled. If the putt is made, the player takes double the value. If he misses, the other player wins the doubled pot.

Source: *Action on the First Tee* by Doug Sanders

# GIFTS

For birthdays, Christmas, or even Valentine's Day, it's easy to find the perfect gift for a golfer. The popularity of this sport has inspired an abundance of items to choose from. And the gifts aren't specific to one certain age or gender. There's something for everyone.

Some golf gifts are practical—gadgets and equipment that players can actually use out on the links. Give something the recipient has never tried before, or go with a gift that may be a little too pricey for them to buy themselves.

If you don't want to go practical, try a golf-themed gift. These are ordinary products, such as picture frames and keychains, made or decorated with the golf-lover in mind. Whatever you choose, your golfer will know that you put some thought into getting a gift they'll really like.

Here are some golf gifts listed according to price range. Some of these gifts can span several price ranges. When that's the case, they're listed in the lower end of the range.

## $10–$20

Earrings: $10
Club cleanser: $15
Ball washer: $15
Money clip: $15
*USGA Rules of Golf*: $15
Golf calendar: $15
Picture frame: $15
Golf head covers: $20
Ball monogrammer: $20
Golf video: $20

## $25–$50

Golf Scrabble/Golf Monopoly: $30
Golf balls: $20–$35 (dozen)
Golf mousepad: $25
Tumblers (four): $25
Golf shorts: $25–$50
Ball retriever: $35
Golf scope: $35
Golf pen set: $35
Nylon rain suit: $50
Watch: $50 –$75

## $50–$75

Golf bookends: $50
Golf-topped wine corks: $50
Pull cart: $60
Golf shirt: $60
Throw blanket: $65
Golf umbrella: $65
Sweater: $75
Golf bags: $75–$100
Framed golf course print: $75
Golf cargo locker: $75

## $100 +

Clock: $100
Waterford club and ball: $100
USGA luggage: $100
Golf travel bag: $125
Golf figurine chess set: $150
Bag storage caddy: $170
New driver: $400

Framed Ryder Cup collage: $500
Cadillac golf cart : $10,675

Source: Authors, *The Best and Worst of Golf*

# GIFTS

## *Humorous Gifts*

It's usually easy to buy gifts for a golfer because there are so many products to choose from. But what about the man or woman who has everything? And while you're at it, how about gifts for your Saturday morning golf buddies? You know, the guys who laugh at your every mishap and the ones who brag about their straight drives and long putts.

A novelty golf gift may be just the ticket. You can find these items at most golf retail stores (not pro shops) or on the Internet at www.golfun.net. Here are a few fun gifts that are guaranteed to bring a smile—maybe yours, maybe theirs.

Wacky golf clubs (that break or bend)
Singing golf bags (break into song at the
    sound of a clap)
Digital scorecards (keeps track of scores,
    putts, and more)
Personalized golf signs
Golf joke books
Goofy golf balls (exploding, never straight,
    ribbon trailing, floating)

Source: Golfun.net

# GLOVES

## *Preferences*

Wearing a glove on the golf course serves a dual purpose: it prevents blistering and helps golfers grip the club better. The leather golf glove is both the softest and most attractive, but doesn't hold up to the elements or keep its shape as well as the synthetic brands, which are waterproof and far more durable.

When selecting a glove, golfers take utility over fashion by a sizable margin: 37 percent choose a glove based on its fit, while only 2 percent consider the glove's appearance.

Footjoy is the top-selling brand of golf glove for both consumers and pros alike.

| Trait | Usage |
|---|---|
| Fit | 37.0 percent |
| Price | 18.0 percent |
| Feel | 17.5 percent |
| Need | 11.0 percent |
| Quality | 4.0 percent |
| Durability | 4.0 percent |
| Gift | 3.5 percent |
| Comfort | 3.0 percent |
| Appearance | 2.0 percent |

Source: *Golf Equipment Almanac 2000*

# GOLF CARTS

## *Top Manufacturers*

Known primarily for hosting The Masters, the town of Augusta, Georgia, can also lay claim to being the golf cart manufacturing capital of the world. The top two companies, E-Z-Go Textron and Club Car, are based in Augusta; their nearest competitor, Yamaha, has a plant in Newnan, Georgia, in the western central region of the state.

The Number 1 manufacturer of golf carts in the world, E-Z-Go Textron opened its doors for business in 1954 in Augusta. A one-room machine shop, E-Z-Go merged with the corporate giant Textron in 1961 and steadily grew to have the top sales and service network in the golf cart manufacturing industry. The company's Freedom and TXT models seat two comfortably and average 12–15 mph. All the E-Z-Go golf carts are designed according to the company's patented Precision Drive System, which enables drivers to pick a golf cart suited to a golf course's particular terrain.

A division of Ingersoll Rand, Club Car has over 600 distributor, dealer, and factory branch locations worldwide. Recently Club Car introduced an electric vehicle power and operating system in its golf cart models. Club Car and E-Z-Go Textron currently sell more publicly used golf carts than any other company in the world.

The Yamaha Company dates back to 1887, when founder Torakusu Yamaha built his first organ. Yamaha Motors began operations in 1955 and eventually moved into golf cart manufacturing. The company's top model is the Ultima, which is designed and assembled according to some of the strictest quality control standards in the industry.

Source: acegolfcar.com; ezgotextron.com; yamahagolfcar.com; clubcar.com

# GOLF CHAIRS

While football and baseball stadiums are being renovated for more space, more luxury, and climate control, golf fans are an entirely different breed. Not only do they miss out on the sky-boxes and retractable roof, many follow their idols from hole to hole, either standing or providing their own chair. Fortunately, some savvy companies have designed chairs with the golf fan in mind—chairs that are easy to carry yet comfy to sit on. Here is a sampling of seating available for golf fans.

**Health Umbrella**                                    $112
www.britishaccents.com
The umbrella is a great add-on, but the metal seat could be more comfortable.

**Packaway Folding Elite Seat**                  $82
www.britishaccents.com
Folds up with ease. The seat is soft and works on all ground types.

**Special Wader**                                        $40
www.elkcreeksports.com
The leather seat and carrying strap make this the perfect golf chair. The low price is a bonus.

**Super Crook**                                           $100
www.britishaccents.com
Great portability and for use as a walking stick. The chair is less comfortable than some.

**Trio/Linden Seat Stick**                          $55
www.britishaccents.com
This is a good combination of walking stick and folding chair, with a great price to boot.

Source: *Equipment Digest*

# GOLF CLUB NICKNAMES

Long gone from the current vernacular, these nicknames for golf clubs harken to the game's early days, when hickory, not steel, was the preferred material for golf club shafts.

| Club | Nickname | Meaning |
|---|---|---|
| 1. | "Baffy" | 4-wood |
| 2. | "Brassie" | like a 2-wood |
| 3. | "Jigger" | like a 4-iron |
| 4. | "Mashie" | like a 5-iron |
| 5. | "Mashie-Niblick" | like a 6 or 7-iron |
| 6. | "Mashie-Iron" | 4-iron |
| 7. | "Niblick" | 9-iron |
| 8. | "Pitcher" | light iron club with a broad face |
| 9. | "Pitching Niblick" | like an 8-iron |
| 10. | "Spade Mashie" | like a 6-iron |
| 11. | "Spoon" | woods with concave faces |

Source: *Why Do They Call It a Birdie?* by Frank Coffey

# GOLF CLUBS

## *Average Driving Distances*

When it comes to achieving maximum driving distance, Duke Ellington put it best: "It don't mean a thing if it ain't got that swing." Unless you work on your swing, including stance, weight distribution, and follow-through, you'll be relying on karma and a good wind to drive the ball the desired distance down the fairway. Driving distance is also predicated by which club you use—and as the following stats bear out, your status as a player. The difference between pro and amateur golfers is considerable—as if amateurs need any further reminder why they're not PGA Tour stars!

| Golf Club | Pro Golfer | Amateur Golfer |
|---|---|---|
| 1. Driver | 260 yards | 210–240 yards |
| 2. 3-wood | 240 yards | 195–205 yards |
| 3. 3-iron | 210 yards | 180–190 yards |
| 4. 4-iron | 200 yards | 165–175 yards |

*Karsten Solheim introduced the Ping line of putters in the 1950s.*

| 5. 5-iron | 185 yards | 150–160 yards |
|---|---|---|
| 6. 6-iron | 175 yards | 135–145 yards |
| 7. 7-iron | 160 yards | 120–130 yards |
| 8. 8-iron | 150 yards | 105–115 yards |
| 9. 9-iron | 135 yards | 90–100 yards |
| 10. Pitching wedge | 120 yards | 75–85 yards |
| 11. Sand wedge | 105 yards | 60–70 yards |

Source: *Amazing But True Golf Facts* by Allan Zullo and Bruce Nash; *Complete Idiot's Guide to Golf* by Michelle McGann & Matthew Rudy

# GOLF CLUBS

## *Innovative Clubs*

The game of golf has been around for a couple of hundred years. As far as rules, the sport has seen very few changes in that time. When it comes to equipment, however, it's an entirely different story. Clubs that were popular when Jack Nicklaus ruled the links wouldn't sell for 25 cents at a garage sale today.

Club shafts have evolved from ash to hickory to steel, aluminum, and finally, to today's popular graphite. Introduced in the seventies, graphite was both lighter and stronger than steel. This was a welcome innovation for women, kids, and older golfers, for whom the heavier clubs began to wear on their game—and their bodies—somewhere on the second nine.

*An ill-fitting grip can undermine your swing, so choose one carefully.*

Remember these clubs?

| Club | Year | Originator |
|------|------|------------|
| Sarazen Sand Wedge | 1937 | Gene Sarazen |
| Graphite shafts | 1972 | Jim Flood |
| Ping Putters | 1950s | Karsten Solheim |
| The Jumbo | 1991 | Bridgestone Sports |
| Big Bertha | 1991 | Callaway Golf |
| The Adjustable Superstick (17 clubs in one) | 1927 | Joe Novak |

Source: Authors, *The Best and Worst of Golf*

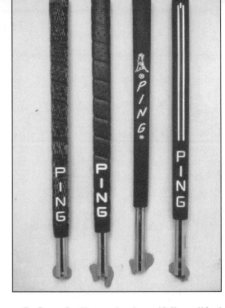

# GOLF CLUBS

## *Variables that Affect a Golfer's Swing*

Several factors related to a golfer's club could affect their swing and the outcome of the shot. Pros, of course, are aware of every aspect relating to their clubs, but many casual golfers just assume that any clubs will work. Here are five equipment factors to keep in mind before hitting the first tee.

- **Grip size**: Grips are made in different sizes and the upper end of the club also comes in different diameters, so it's easy to find one that fits the hand. Grips that don't fit properly cause a golfer to compensate in other ways, making the swing less accurate.

- **Length**: Both height and arm length factor into the length of a golfer's clubs. Ones that are too long or too short cause poor posture, and again, the golfer needs to compensate to make them work.

- **Shaft length**: The club's shaft vibrates and flexes with each shot and it's the length of the shaft that causes that flex. The goal is to get the same feel from each club whether it is a 9 iron or a 3 iron. Length may need to be added or removed from a club to create consistency between shots.

- **Lie angle**: Even with all those considerations, it's still possible for a club's toe to be too high or too low. Check the angle of the club to improve the contact on the shot.

- **Loft angle**: To get that beautifully uplifted shot, make sure to have the proper loft angle. There should be a 4-degree difference between each club to attain the most accuracy, loft, and consistency with each shot.

The cost to make these adjustments is not as high as you might think. Here's a look at typical prices for these services.

| Adjustment | Price Per Club |
|------------|----------------|
| Loft adjustment | $5 |
| Lie adjustment | $5 |
| Regripping | $5–$12 |
| Reshafting | $20–$100 |

Source: *Golf Illustrated* Winter 2002

# GOLF COURSE DEATHS

For a sport that seems so casual and relaxing, golf can sometimes take a grisly turn. Freak accidents have taken the lives of quite a few golfers over the years. For example, a Canadian golfer died in 1963 while trying to play out of a bunker. His golf club shaft broke against a tree and gashed his throat. And in 1951 a Seattle golfer broke the shaft of his driver, piercing his groin in the process. Bleeding profusely, he struggled to make it back to the clubhouse, but collapsed and died 100 yards from the ninth tee.

Source: *Astonishing But True Golf Facts* by Bruce Nash and Allan Zullo

# GOLF COURSE MARKERS

Depending on where your golf ball lies, the course markers can either boost your confidence or underscore your miserable failings as a golfer. Who hasn't sent the ball soaring past the white stakes into another zip code? Or watched a drive become a "worm burner" that rolls to a halt well short of the blue marker (and your friends' drives further down the fairway?) However you "read" these markers, they are an integral part of both the course landscape and the sport's complex rules of etiquette. For all those golf novices or anyone who needs a refresher, here's a lexicon of golf course markers.

1. **White stakes**: out of bounds

2. **Red stakes**: lateral hazards

3. **Yellow stakes**: hazards

4. **Red markers in fairway**: 100 yards to center of green

5. **White markers in fairway**: 150 yards to center of green

6. **Blue markers in fairway**: 200 yards to center of green

7. **Broken white lines on grass**: ground under repair

Source: *The Complete Idiot's Guide to Golf*

*A few unfortunate golfers have paid the ultimate price for a round of golf.*

# GOLF COURSES

## *Golf Course Maintenance Costs*

The upkeep of our golf courses is something that most golfers take for granted. Sure, we occasionally run into someone mowing, or get soaked by sprinklers that turn on when they aren't supposed to. Generally, however, we don't notice all the work—or expense—involved unless something goes wrong. Here's a look at what the average course superintendent spends on golf course maintenance over a year's time, according to *Golfdom* magazine. It's not easy staying green.

| Expense | Average Price tag |
|---|---|
| New irrigation system | $97,000 |
| Fertilizer/plant nutrition products | $21,600 |
| Fungicides | $20,100 |
| Fairway or other mowers | $16,500 |
| Greens mowers | $15,200 |
| Utility vehicles | $12,500 |
| Irrigation parts and other supplies | $9,900 |
| Turf seed | $9,600 |
| Herbicides | $8,460 |
| Insecticides | $7,090 |
| Aeration or cultivation equipment | $5,240 |
| Growth regulators | $3,090 |
| Total | $226,360 |

Source: *Golfdom* magazine

# GOLF EQUIPMENT

## *Best-Selling Items for Women*

Want to spend more time on the course and less in the pro shop? In the October 2001 issue of *Golf For Women*, the editors polled pro

*Callaway Big Bertha Steelhead X14: the club of choice among women golfers.*

shops nationwide to determine which brands of the following items are the best-sellers among women.

1. **Club**: Callaway's Big Bertha Steelhead X-14 irons with Ladies' Gems Shafts

2. **Ball**: Precept's MC Lady

3. **Shoe**: Footjoy's Soft Joys Terrains

4. **Apparel**: Tommy Bahama's Itsy-Bitsy flat-front shorts

5. **Bag**: Ogio's Big stand bag for women

Source: *Golf for Women*

# GOLF ON TELEVISION

## Ratings

Golf, as a sport, has grown over the last decade. Maybe it's this personal involvement in the game that has boosted interest in watching the sport on TV. Whatever the reason, golf viewership has gained in popularity over the last few years. Not since the days of Arnies's Army, when Palmer and Nicklaus faced off each week, has golf attracted so much attention. Much of the credit, of course, goes to Tiger Woods, who took the golf world by storm. The good news for advertisers is that golf is now attracting people who don't typically watch sports. The bad news is that viewership drops drastically if Tiger is out of the running.

According to Nielsen Media Research, programs which have larger audiences are, by definition, the successful ones. Ratings numbers are the average audience rating, or the percentage of people tuned in to a particular program during a specific time period. Here, then, are a few facts pertaining to the television ratings for golf.

- The final round of the PGA Championship got an 8.8 rating versus only 3.7 in 1995.

- The last day of the British Open attracted a 6.4 rating versus 3.0 in 1996.

- On the last day of the U.S. Open, ratings reached a 20-year high of 8.1.

- The Masters has reached a 10+ rating for each of the last four years.

| *Growth of Golf, 1970–2000* | | | | |
|---|---|---|---|---|
| | **1970** | **1980** | **1990** | **2000** |
| Golfers (in millions) | 11.2 | 15.1 | 27.8 | 26.7 |
| Rounds Played (millions) | 266 | 358 | 502 | 586 |
| Golf Facilities | 10,188 | 12,005 | 12,658 | 15,487 |
|    Daily Fee | 4,248 | 5,372 | 6,024 | 8,759 |
|    Municipal | 1,321 | 1,794 | 2,012 | 2,438 |
|    Private | 4,619 | 4,872 | 4,810 | 4,290 |
| Golf Courses | 10,848 | 12,849 | 13,951 | 17,108 |
|    Daily Fee | 4,513 | 5,741 | 6,497 | 9,637 |
|    Municipal | 1,461 | 1,957 | 2,222 | 2,698 |
|    Private | 4,874 | 5,151 | 5,232 | 4,773 |
| Source: NGF | | | | |

- In the last half hour of Tiger Woods' Grand Slam win, the tournament drew a 17.5 rating.

- Over 13 telecasts, CBS drew a 5.3 rating average if Tiger Woods won or was in contention.

- Over those same 13 weeks, CBS got only a 2.5 rating when Woods was out of the top money.

- Among African-American viewers, golf earns a 3.9 rating with Tiger Woods playing, but only a 1.5 rating without him.

- A 30-second spot on one Grand Slam tournament telecast costs $150,000.

Source: *Broadcasting and Cable*

# GOLF ON TELEVISION

## Senior PGA Tour Viewership

The number of senior golfers and tournaments has risen steadily since the SPGA Tour began in 1980. Back then, there were only two tournaments, with a total purse of $250,000. By 2001, the tour boasted 38 events with a total purse of $59 million.

With seasoned veterans losing to the younger guys in the PGA, some of the more experienced golfers are looking to the day when they can join the SPGA tour. In response to that, and as another hook to create interest in the tour, the SPGA is considering lowering the entry age from 50 to 45 to attract pros still in their prime.

A tour favorite, Arnold Palmer has retired his golf clubs (professionally, that is) and Jack Nicklaus has been playing less since undergoing hip replacement surgery. With some of the most beloved names in golf leaving the tour, this would be the perfect time to attract some new (but familiar) faces. In the meantime, the SPGA management has planned changes for 2002, hoping to increase interest in the pros of the past. Here are some of the changes that will be taking place.

- SPGA telecasts will be moving to earlier airtimes.

- Some of the players will be wearing mikes to converse with commentators during the round.

- Spectators will be allowed to follow behind the last group on the course.

- On-course interviews will be encouraged.

- Post-round clinics will be hosted by the pros.

- Senior Pros will field questions and offer instructional advice on-line.

Source: SPGA

# GOLF PLAY

## Rounds Played Compared to Previous Year

While the golf industry has seen growth over the last decade, leisure activities throughout the nation have taken a hit since the terrorist attacks on the World Trade Center in September of 2001. Golf is no exception, with fewer people playing at the end of 2001 compared to one year ago.

Initially, some people may have felt it was inappropriate to enjoy leisure activities and play games while others were suffering. Many travelers developed a newfound fear of flying, causing those with planned vacations to cancel them, and others to hold off on making new travel plans. Still other Americans, worried about the economy, chose not to spend money on vacations or golf green fees.

Here is the percentage of change for rounds played from the fall of 2000 through fall, 2001, by region.

| Geographical Area | Percent Change |
|---|---|
| New England | − 1.4 |
| Middle Atlantic | − 7.2 |
| East North Central | + 2.3 |
| West North Central | − 4.1 |
| South Atlantic | + 1.7 |
| Florida | − 8.4 |
| East South Central | + 1.4 |
| West South Central | + 3.1 |
| Texas | − 10 |
| Mountain | − 2.9 |

tinues to skyrocket in popularity, due in no small part to the emergence of Tiger Woods as a genuine cultural phenomenon in the late nineties.

| | |
|---|---|
| Pacific | – 1.8 |
| California | – 0.9 |
| **Total** | **– 1.5** |

Source: Golf Datatech

# GROWTH OF GOLF

## *1970–2000*

Just how popular is golf in the United States? Thanks to the numbers crunchers at The National Golf Foundation, we now have a good idea. In 30 years' time, the number of golfers in this country has more than doubled, from just over 11 million in 1970 to nearly 27 million in 2000. What's even more remarkable about these numbers is that from 1970 to 1986, the NWF statisticians included golfers five years of age and higher in their estimates. From 1986 to 2000, the numbers only include golfers at least 12 years old.

Golf facilities (defined as having at least one nine-hole course) in addition to other courses—and golf courses have also spread, primarily in the public sector (the number of private golf courses actually declined slightly from 1970 to 2000). With dozens of new courses added since this data shown in the table on page 106 was compiled, golf facilities and courses will soon top 20,000 each in the United States. While golf may never displace baseball as the great American pastime, it con-

# HAZARDS

Chances are, amateur golfers encounter more hazards than pros. But even professionals aren't immune; the cost is just greater for those pros that fall victim.

Tim Weiskopf, for instance, probably has an aversion to water after his encounter with Rae's Creek in the 1980 Masters. On the 12th hole, he hit five straight balls into the water, causing his score for the hole to skyrocket to a whopping 10-over-par 13.

Thirty years before that, hazard trouble earned Hermann Tissies an incredible 15 on a par 3 at the British Open. The 127-yard eighth hole was what caused the crisis for Tissies, who jumped back and forth from one sand trap to another before finding the green, where the stressed-out player preceded to 3-putt the hole.

PGA caddie Michael Carrick has seen many a pro player plunge on the leader board due to an encounter with a hazard. Here's his take on which hazards to avoid at all costs. They are ranked by severity of penalty as well as difficulty in getting out.

1. **Out of bounds**

2. **Water**

3. **High grass or rocks**

4. **Trees**

5. **Rough**

6. **Sand**

7. **Downhill or side hill lie**

Source: Michael Carrick

# HOLE-IN-ONE RECORDS

Even though the odds against an amateur scoring a hole-in-one hover around 12,000-to-1, players of all ages and abilities have pulled off some spectacular aces over the years.

1. **Longest hole-in-one by a man**: Bob Mitera hit a ball a staggering 447 yards to make a hole-in-one on the 10th hole at an Omaha golf course in 1965.

2. **Longest hole-in-one by a woman**: Marie Robie drove a golf ball 393 yards on the first hole at a Wollaston, Massachusetts, course in 1949.

3. **Oldest man to hit a hole-in-one**: 101-year-old Harold Stilson pulled off this remarkable feat on the 16th hole at a Deerfield Beach, Florida, golf course in 2001.

4. **Oldest woman to hit a hole-in-one**: Spry 96-year-old Rose Montgomery made a hole-in-one on the seventh hole at Palm Springs golf course in 1992.

5. **Youngest boy**: Precocious five-year-old Keith Long drove a golf ball 140 yards to ace the fourth hole at a Jackson, Michigan golf course in 1998.

6. **Youngest girl**: six-year-old Brittney Andreas watched her ball sail 100 yards into the second hole at an Austin, Texas, golf course in 1991.

7. **Amateur with most aces overall**: Norman Manley of Long Beach, California, has hit 59 holes-in-one.

So much for those odds, huh?

Source: March 2001 *Golf Digest*

# Holes-in-One

## *Same Day, Same Hole*

The Professional Golfers Association (PGA) put the odds of a professional golfer sinking a hole-in-one in a single round of a PGA event at 3,708-to-1. In other words, for every 3,709 rounds of golf played, one of them will contain a hole in one. On the average PGA course containing four par-3 holes, the odds of a player sinking the tee shot on any particular par-3 hole are approximately 15,000-to-1.

From the Believe-It-Or-Not Department: Even in the pro ranks, a hole-in-one is a rarity. But even more rare are multiple holes-in-one during the same round of a PGA event. But, how about multiple holes-in-one on the same hole by separate golfers on the same day, within a matter of hours? Amazingly, on June 16, 1989, at the U.S. Open at Oak Hill Country Club in Pittsford, New York, not one, but four, golfers each aced the par-3, 167-yard sixth hole.

The PGA calculates the odds of any four golfers acing the same hole on the same day as 332,000-to-1. Actually, in the U.S. Open, one would expect the odds to be slightly lower, since it is a premier event that attracts only the top golfers on the tour. Though the hole-in-one may seem like pure luck, pro golfers, who consistently hit the green on par-3 holes have much better odds of sinking an ace. Indeed, the four who hit the holes-in-one that lucky day had 16 other aces between them in professional play prior to the fluke at the U.S. Open. Here's how the day went:

10:23 A.M.: Doug Weaver, a pro from Hilton Head, South Carolina, was the first player to shoot at the hole that day. His 7-iron shot landed 15 feet beyond the cup. The backspin of the ball gently took it down a slope toward the cup, and as the roar of the crowd grew, the ball rolled in the cup for a hole in one. But that simply set the stage for the dramatics to follow.

11:38 A.M.: A threesome including 31-year-old Coloradoan Mark Wiebe stepped up to the tee. Wiebe promptly dropped his 7-iron tee shot in the cup for the second ace on the hole that day.

12:19 P.M.: Jerry Pate put in his 7-iron shot on the same hole. By that time, word had spread throughout the gallery, and the crowd all around the course was abuzz.

12:26 P.M.: In the threesome immediately following Pate's, one can imagine the golfers each grabbing anxiously for their own 7-irons. Sure enough, Zimbabwean Nick Price nailed his tee shot onto the crest of the green about 20 feet from the hole, and the ball spun right back into the hole.

Source: *New York Times*, June 17, 1989

# INJURIES

## ER Visits

According to a 1996 survey conducted by the National Safety Council of emergency room visits for 10 different sports-related injuries, golf came in seventh overall, with 36,480 ER visits recorded for that year. Surprisingly, golfers reported more injuries than skateboarders, who came in eighth with 35,751 ER visits. But before you start strapping on elbow and kneepads to tee off, you need to place these numbers in the proper context. As of 1996, the National Safety Council put the number of golfers nationwide at approximately 23 million; skateboard enthusiasts hovered just below 5 million. The ratio of injury to overall participants is thus significantly lower for golf than skateboarding. And coming in at Number 1? Basketball, with 653,676 ER visits for an estimated 33 million hoopsters.

Source: National Safety Council 1996 survey

# INJURIES

## Gender Differences

Even if the "men are from Mars, women are from Venus" spiel explains many of the differences between the sexes, the planets are pretty much in alignment when it comes to golf injuries on the PGA and LPGA circuits. According to a study of professional golfers in

the July 1999 issue of *The Physician and Sports Medicine*, men and women players both cite hand and wrist injuries as the most common. Although the percentage ratios for specific injuries often vary greatly between the sexes, here are the four most commonly reported golf injuries among pro golfers, in descending order.

### Percent of Pro Players Reporting Injuries

| Injury | Men | Women |
|---|---|---|
| Hands and wrists | 29.6 | 44.8 |
| Lower back | 25.0 | 22.4 |
| Shoulder | 11.4 | 7.5 |
| Elbow | 7.3 | 6.0 |

For amateurs, the percentages vary according to the following chart.

### Percent of Amateur Players Reporting Injuries

| Injury | Men | Women |
|---|---|---|
| Lower back | 36.0 | 27.4 |
| Elbow | 32.5 | 35.5 |
| Hands and wrists | 21.2 | 14.5 |
| Shoulders | 11.0 | 16.1 |

Source: physssportsmed.com

# INJURIES

## Medical Emergencies in Tournaments

It's a good thing so many doctors reportedly like to play golf, because their services have often been needed on the course over the years. Freak accidents have forced many pros to withdraw from tournaments, often with life-threatening injuries; some have had to endure a lengthy convalescence before returning to competitive play. Fortunately, such incidents are comparatively rare. Of course, that's scant consolation to the unlucky golfers whose stories are listed below.

1. **Bobby Cruickshank** was knocked unconscious when the golf club he threw high in the air landed square on his head at the 1934 U.S. Open.

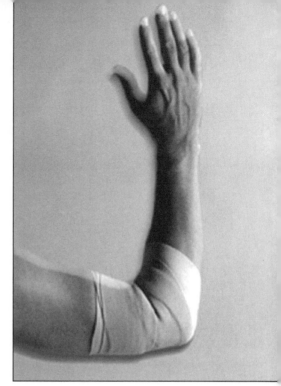

*A weak grip can lead to right elbow injuries.*

2. **Richard Baxall** broke his leg while teeing off during the third round at the 1991 British Open.

3. **Cathy Gerring** was badly burned in a hospitality tent fire at the 1993 Sara Lee Classic.

4. **Lee Trevino** was struck by lightening at the 1975 Western Open. It took Trevino quite a while to recover from the injuries he sustained.

5. **"Champagne" Tony Lema** jumped for joy at the 1957 Bing Crosby National Pro-Am and fell down an 18-foot cliff before horrified onlookers. Fortunately, Lema sustained only bruises to his shins and elbows.

Source: *Guiness Book of Golf Facts and Feats*; golfeurope.com; *Golf Hall of Shame*; *Astonishing But True Golf Facts*

# INJURIES

## *Causes and Preventions*

Golf is often considered a relaxed sport. There's no physical contact among players, no running, pavement pounding, or even jumping. The reasons why golf is a game that can be played even by octogenarians are also the reasons why golf is sometimes taken for granted—resulting in injury.

The good news is that golf is easier on your body than football, or even tennis. But here's the catch. Few people would think of playing those sports without warming up, stretching, or maintaining an overall level of physical fitness. Except for a token stretch on the first tee, few casual golfers take the steps they should to stay injury free.

Here are a few of the most common injuries incurred by the average golfer, along with tips to prevent them.

### Left Elbow

- **Cause of injury**: The right arm pushes while the left arm pulls during the downswing, stretching the tendons.

- **Prevention**: Be sure that you are gripping the club correctly and that the grip is the right size. Do arm exercises. Squeeze a tennis ball to strengthen forearm muscles.

### Right Elbow

- **Cause of injury**: A weak grip.

- **Prevention**: Check your grip. Do strengthening exercises.

### Wrists

- **Cause of injury**: Trauma from hitting the ground with the club.

- **Prevention**: Invest in vibration-absorbing clubs. Strengthen forearm and shoulder muscles. Squeeze a tennis ball to build strength.

### Shoulders

- **Cause of injury**: Raising arms for the backswing leads to pinching and inflammation of the joint.

- **Prevention**: Build up shoulder muscles with strengthening exercises. Also, try limiting shoulder movement in your backswing.

*Only 20 percent of golfers reportedly use some form of sunscreen. At left is another way to protect yourself.*

showed that only 20 percent of golfers regularly use sunscreen. Here are some tips for avoiding skin cancer—so you'll still be around to golf in your retirement years.

- **Use a sunscreen** with an SPF of at least 15 (even on cloudy days.)

- **Cover your head** with some type of hat.

- **Wear good sunglasses** that protect your eyes from UV and UVB rays.

- **Wear long sleeves** and long pants when possible.

- **Choose clothes** with a tight weave, a loose fit. and darker colors for the most protection.

- **Perform skin self-exams** every three months, looking for any changes.

- **See a dermatologist** once a year or sooner if you notice any changes or see something that looks suspicious.

- **Look for these warning signs** including a change in a mole, a sore that does not heal, a skin growth that has increased in size, and a spot that continues to itch, hurt or scab.

Source: American Cancer Society

## Lower Back

- **Cause of injury**: The extreme twisting motion of a golf swing can irritate the lower back. Other contributors include improper swing, poor flexibility, and insufficient warm-ups.

- **Prevention**: Warm up and stretch your muscles before each round of golf. Don't forget to stretch your hamstring muscles, since tight hamstrings can cause low back pain. Strengthening abdominal muscles will also work to support your lower back. Do knee raises and crunches daily.

Source: Authors, *The Best and Worst of Golf*

## INJURIES

### *Protecting Against Skin Cancer*

Exercise and fresh air go almost hand-in-hand with golfing. Unfortunately, so does skin cancer. According to the American Cancer Society, skin cancer affects one in five Americans, with 1.3 million curable cancers discovered each year. The more serious melanoma is expected to hit 51,400 this year. Even though this type accounts for 79 percent of all skin cancer deaths, it also offers a five-year survival rate of 88 percent if caught in the early stages. A 1999 study by USA Today

## INJURIES

### *Top Dangers on the Course*

For a sport that's a favorite among retirees, golf is surprisingly fraught with potential injuries—and not just to your pride, either. As the following list demonstrates, a leisurely game of golf with friends can end with the players in the emergency room rather than in the clubhouse bar.

- **Golf balls**: Flying golf balls can easily hit other golfers quite hard. In fact, players have been killed by errant balls hitting their heads. Lesser problems are concussions and broken or sprained bones.

- **Golf clubs**: Wild swings can result in loose flying clubs that could injure another player. Worse yet, is getting too close to a club when a golfer is in his backswing or follow

*The last thing you want to be holding is a metal golf club when lightning strikes.*

*Callaway's Steelhead X-14: the best-selling used iron on the market.*

through. When a club is still attached to the player, there's a lot more force behind it.

- **Heatstroke**: Golfers should drink fluids and hit the shade whenever possible.

- **Sunburn**: Golfers tend to forget that they are in the sun longer than most sunbathers. Unless you want to resemble shoe leather, don't forget to use a sunscreen with a minimum SPF of 15.

- **Golf carts**: Carts can shoot forward, tip over, and do funny things when in reverse.

- **Lightning**: Those sirens are sounded for a reason. When lightning has been sighted, it's time to get off the course. Stay away from trees, open spaces, hills, water hazards, and never hold a club in the air, like the ill-fated priest in Caddyshack.

- **Plants**: The woods can be prime places to run into poison ivy and poison oak.

- **Trees**: These aren't dangerous by themselves, of course, but golfers should be careful with golf shots near trees. Balls can ricochet off the trunk and hit someone. The force of a club hitting a tree can stun or injure a player. And watch out for those evergreens; playing a ball too close to the prickly branches can be a danger to eyes.

Source: Authors, *The Best and Worst of Golf*

# IRONS

## *Most Popular Used*

Pros on the PGA Tour are allowed 14 clubs in their golf bag. Amateur golfers often carry fewer clubs, choosing a driver, a putter, at least two woods, and eight irons.

For retail purposes, a set of irons usually consists of eight clubs, which includes a 3, 4, 5, 6, 7, 8, and 9 iron, plus a wedge. Each iron is designed to hit the ball a certain distance, with about 10 yards difference between each numbered club. Consumers report that the most important factor in choosing a set of irons is the feel of the clubs, followed by their price and how they enhance the player's game.

Buying used clubs is one way to reduce the price concern and look for irons that fit other important criteria. Here are the top five best-selling used irons sets along with the list price for a set of clubs in very good condition.

1. **Callaway Steelhead X-14**
   Graphite shaft    $556.44
   Steel shaft       $474.78

2. **Callaway Steelhead X-14 Pro series**
   Graphite shaft    $540.26
   Steel shaft       $532.90

**Over 1.5 million readers subscribe to or buy Golf Digest.**

3. **Callaway Hawkeye**
   Graphite shaft    $748.37
   Steel shaft        $610.86

4. **Ping i3 O Size**
   Graphite shaft    $520.73
   Steel shaft        $467.44

5. **Callaway Big Bertha X-12**
   Graphite shaft    $434.06
   Steel shaft        $367.68

Source: golfclubexchange.com

# MAGAZINES

## *By Circulation*

What is the world's best golf magazine? That question is best answered not by a panel of judges, but by individual readers exercising their discretion as consumers. And more people buy *Golf Digest* than any other golf magazine, making it the Number 1 publication of its genre.

With a circulation of just over 1.5 million, the Digest boasts about 165,000 more readers than its closest competitor, *Golf Magazine*. These monthly publications have been battling each other for nearly half a century, with *Golf Digest*, founded in 1950, enjoying a head start over *Golf Magazine*, which began in 1958. Each is a general interest golf magazine with tips on improving your game, interesting golf courses, advances in golf equipment, and features about leading golf pros. Because both magazines have large subscriptions, they also carry a wealth of slick advertising for equipment, courses, and golfing peripherals such as cars and liquor.

Other golf magazines cater to more specialized audiences. *Golf For Women*, founded in 1988, includes articles about golf fashions, vacation suggestions, and, of course, the women's professional golf tour. *Links Magazine* aims at an upscale audience of avid golfers who have a desire to play at outstanding golf courses in the U.S and around the world. *Golf Tips*, as the title suggests, caters to enthusiasts intent on improving their games. And *Golf Illustrated*, founded in 1914, also emphasizes tips and equipment that can shave strokes off a golfer's score.

*Golf World*, published 40 times a year, caters primarily to fans of professional golf. It publishes extensive information about professional and amateur tournament results, enabling readers to keep up with who won; who lost; who shot what; who is playing where; and what can be seen on television. Here are some popular golf magazines, listed by circulation.

| Magazine | Circulation |
| --- | --- |
| *Golf Digest* | 1,567,604 |
| *Golf Magazine* | 1,403,074 |
| *Golf for Women* | 380,120 |
| *Links Magazine* | 254,595 |
| *Golf Tips* | 247,224 |
| *Golf World* | 152,778 |
| *Golf Illustrated* | 145,047 |
| *Golf Today* | 96,000 |
| *Golfweek* | 78,654 |

Source: Authors, *The Best and Worst of Golf*

# MENTAL STRATEGIES

Best known for his books *Self-Hypnosis for Better Golf* and *The One-Minute Golfer*, noted sports psychologist Chuck Hogan has helped many golfers overcome the mental blocks undermining their game. Although his language may be a little too academic for some, Hogan's reasoning is sound and evidently produces results. Based at The Raven Golf Club in Phoenix, he was named Arizona's best golf teacher by *The Arizona Republic*.

*Focus and follow-through are key to improving your golf game.*

Here are some of Hogan's mental strategies to help the golf swing.

1. Accelerate the learning process.

2. Make learning personal for each individual rather than generic.

3. Keep mechanics short-term in the learning sequence.

4. Assure the conceptual imprint of "why" to the "hows" of learning.

5. Assure rapid habituation of fundamentals.

6. Permit the graduation from intellectualizing of golf swing to the creativity of playing golf and becoming "target integrated."

7. Allow the golfer to enjoy the game.

Source: *A Tribute to Golf: A Celebration in Art, Photography and Literature*—Compiled/Edited by Thomas P. Stewart

# MISTAKES

## *Butch Harmon's Top Eight*

Want to work with one of the world's best golf teachers but can't afford his fee without taking out a second mortgage? Then this is the list for you—from the man who's coached Tiger Woods since 1996. Here is Butch Harmon's list of golf "don'ts" that can undermine even the best players.

1. Putting your ball too far forward or back, instead of even with your heart.

2. Picking up the club or pulling the club inside in your takeaway.

3. Keeping your knee straight or locked at the start of the backswing.

4. Starting your downswing with your upper body.

5. Hitting the "ego shot," i.e., going for the sucker pin or taking too little club for the shot.

6. Laying up too close.

7. Keeping all your weight on your back foot when chipping.

8. Taking the putter blade back too far and then decelerating coming into the ball.

Source: "The Eight Stupid Mistakes Every Golfer Makes—And How You Can Avoid Them," by Butch Harmon with Ed Weathers. *Golf Digest*, December 1999.

# MOVIES

Ask your average movie fan to name a movie about golf and he'll usually mention *Caddyshack*. The 1980 country club farce starring Chevy Chase, Rodney Dangerfield, and Bill Murray as a groundskeeper waging war against a stubborn gopher has become a classic gross-out comedy and features this inestimable bit of wisdom for would-be golfers: "Be the ball, Billy."

*Caddyshack* is one of a handful of movies about golf. As the following list demonstrates, these films run the gamut from slapstick comedy to mystical drama.

1. *The Golf Specialist* (1930): This comedy short features W. C. Fields reprising one of his classic vaudeville routines.

*Gophers rule and greenskeepers drool: Bill Murray meets his furry nemesis in the 1980 comedy hit* **Caddyshack.**

2.  *Follow the Sun* (1951): An earnest, sentimental biography of Ben Hogan, released just two years after the devastating car accident that nearly ended his career. Glenn Ford portrays Hogan while Donna Reed is his supportive wife Valerie.

3.  *Pat and Mike* (1952): In this breezy Tracy and Hepburn romantic comedy, Hepburn plays a golf pro loosely based on Babe Didrikson Zaharias. Zaharias herself has a cameo in the film.

4.  *The Caddy* (1953): Martin and Lewis wreak their usual comic havoc in this comedy which also features Donna Reed. Ben Hogan, Sam Snead, and Julius Boros appear in cameos.

5.  *Banning* (1967): Robert Wagner portrays a country club golf pro in a steamy melodrama co-starring Jill St. John.

6.  *Babe* (1975): This television movie brought actress Susan Clark an Emmy for her performance as Babe Didrikson Zaharias. Clark's real-life husband Alex Karras costars as wrestler George Zaharias.

7.  *Caddyshack* (1980): Golf, gophers, and Bill Murray; what more could you want in a movie?

8.  *Caddyshack 2* (1988): Vastly inferior sequel that has its moments, but Jackie Mason and Dan Aykroyd are no substitute for Dangerfield and Murray.

9.  *Dead Solid Perfect* (1988): HBO adaptation of Dan Jenkins' hilarious novel features Randy Quaid as the hard-drinking pro Kenny Lee.

10. *Happy Gilmore* (1996): Adam Sandler stars as a hockey player turned pro golfer in this silly farce, which is chiefly memorable for Sandler's brawl with game show host Bob Barker.

11. *Tin Cup* (1996): Director/writer Ron Shelton reteams with his *Bull Durham* star Kevin Costner for a romantic comedy about a small town Texas golf pro who attempts to qualify for the U.S. Open.

12. *The Tiger Woods Story* (1998): Television movie biography of the golf prodigy.

13. *The Legend of Baggar Vance* (2000): Robert Redford directed this big-budget adaptation of the Stephen Greenfield novel about a battle-scarred golf pro's bond with his mystical caddie.

Source: imdb.com; amazon.com

# NEWS

## Top-10 Golf Stories of 2001

If you follow pro golf, you know that nothing is ever a given. Just when you think one golfer has a tournament locked up, someone comes along with a fabulous final round and takes the prize. Just when you think pros can't get any younger, a 17-year-old qualifies for tournament play. And just when you think pro golf is as reliable as the post office, where nothing can prevent a tournament from going on, it is canceled due to a national tragedy.

ESPN golf analyst Karl Ravech not only follows golf, he analyzes the ins and out for broadcast. Here are his votes for the top 10 golf stories of 2001.

1.  Tiger Woods wins his second Masters and sixth major championship, making

him the only golfer with four PGA major titles at one time.

2.  Pro tours are canceled the week after the September 11 terrorist attacks.

3.  Karrie Webb, 26, becomes the youngest golfer in LPGA history to win the Grand Slam.

4.  David Duval wins his first major tournament, the British Open.

5.  Annika Sorenstam comes from 10 strokes behind to win the Office Depot Tournament, making it the biggest comeback in LPGA history.

6.  The PGA Tour agrees to an $850 million deal with five networks through 2003.

7.  The Supreme Court makes an unprecedented ruling: golfer Casey Martin, who suffers from a circulatory disease, may use a cart in tournament play.

8.  Retief Goosen bests Mark Brooks to win the U.S. Open after a series of putting mishaps.

9.  Tiger Woods and Jim Furyk play seven sudden-death holes in the NEC Invitational making it the longest PGA playoffs in 10 years. Woods wins.

10. David Toms wins his first major title when he sinks a 15-foot putt to beat Phil Mickelson by one stroke in the PGA Championship.

Source: ESPN.com

# Penalties

If you decide to play golf strictly according to the venerable rules of the game, be forewarned: this is not a game for the ultra-sensitive or sore losers. Penalties can accumulate quickly for even the most seemingly minor of infractions, and each can add one or two strokes to your score. Hitting your ball into a water hazard or out of bounds also earns additional penalty strokes.

Although the USGA Rules Committee gathers annually to address situations not covered in *The Rules of Golf*, their rulings

sometimes raise more questions rather than providing clear-cut answers. Unless you're a stickler for the rules, it might be easier (and a lot less stressful for all concerned) to confine penalty strokes to the following golf course incidents.

1.  Once a player retrieves a ball from a water hazard, he must drop it at the point of entry and add one penalty stroke to his score.

2.  When a player hits a ball out of bounds, he must rehit it from the same spot and add one penalty stroke to his score.

3.  An unplayable lie brings a player two clublengths relief from the spot and one penalty stroke.

4.  Once a player finds a lost ball, he must drop it at the nearest point and take two penalty strokes.

5.  Grounding a club in a hazard earns two penalty strokes.

6.  If a player hits a flagstick while putting on the green, he must add two penalty strokes to his score.

Source: *The Complete Idiot's Guide To Golf* by Michelle McGann & Matthew Rudy

# Pet Peeves

## *On the Course*

While most golfers enjoy the two to four hours they spend out on the links, there are always a few things that can put a damper on the fun.

Your chronic slice and those water hazards are only part of the problem. Most complaints are actually about other golfers.

One survey recently reported that the vast majority of golfers feel that their rate of play is fast while groups in front of them are moving at a snail's pace. A group of women golfers took that a step further and complained about slow male golfers who refuse to let faster women play through, as a result of the mistaken theory that all men play faster than women. Don't they?

Here is a list of the most frequently sited pet peeves on the golf course.

- Golfers who are not ready to play when it's their turn.

- Players who take several practice swings.

- Players who search too long for a ball that went deep into the woods.

- People who ask other players what club they should use.

- Players who swear over every mistake.

- Golfers who insist on waiting to hit to the green, when their past shots indicate they are not likely to hit the ball that far.

- Cart golfers who park in front of the green rather than to the side or back.

- Amateur golfers who offer their comrades unsolicited advice.

- Golfers who don't replace divots or ball marks.

- Players who record their scores on the green.

- Golfers who don't play by the USGA Rules of Golf.

Source: *Golf for Women*

# PGA TOUR RECORDS

Contrary to popular belief, there are still a few PGA Tour records that Tiger Woods has *not* set or broken since 1997, though he certainly has a share under his belt. Besides Woods, a name that keeps popping up in the PGA Tour record books is Mark Calcavecchia. A member of the tour since 1982, Calcavecchia has won 10 PGA tournaments, most notably the 2001 Phoenix Open, where he set or tied many of the records listed below.

- **Lowest 72-Hole Score**: Mark Calcavecchia scored 256 at the 2001 Phoenix Open. Woods' all-time low is 259 at the 2000 WGC NEC Invitational.

- **Lowest 72-Hole Score in Relation to Par**: Calcavecchia was 28-under-par at the 2001 Phoenix Open. He shares the record with John Huston. who shot 28-under-par for a final score of 260 at the1998 United Airlines Hawaiian Open.

- **Lowest First 36-Holes**: Woods and Calcavecchia are tied with a score of 125 at the 2000 WGC NEC Invitational and 2001 Phoenix Open, respectively.

- **Lowest First 54-Holes**: John Cook shot 189 at the 1996 FedEx St. Jude Classic. Calcavecchia tied this record at the 2001 Phoenix Open.

- **Lowest 18-Hole Score**: Al Geiberger scored 59 at the 1977 Memphis Classic. Since that time, Chip Beck and David Duval have tied his record at the 1991 Las Vegas Invitational and 1999 Bob Hope Chrysler Classic, respectively.

- **Largest Margin of Victory**: J. D. Edgar won by 16 strokes at the 1919 Canadian Open. His record has since been equaled by two other players: Joe Kirkwood Sr. in the 1924 Corpus Christi Open and Bobby Locke in the 1948 Chicago Victory Championship.

- **Most Consecutive Events Making the Cut**: Byron Nelson holds the record here, with 113 events. As of this writing, Woods has made the cut 78 consecutive times.

- **Lowest Adjusted Scoring Average**: Woods is the current record holder, with an adjusted score of 67.79 for the 2000 season.

- **Lowest Actual Scoring Average**: Tiger strikes again, with an actual scoring average of 68.17 for the 2000 PGA Tour, breaking Byron Nelson's 1945 scoring average of 68.33.

- **Lowest Consecutive Rounds**: Calca-vecchia scored 60–64 in the second and third rounds of the 2001 Phoenix Open.

- **Most Consecutive Rounds at Par or Better**: Woods has played 52 consecutive rounds at par or better, starting with the second round of the 2000 GTE Byron Nelson Classic and ending with the first round of the 2001 Phoenix Open.

- **Most Consecutive Events at Par or Better**: Woods has played 35 consecutive events at par or better. All the events, from the 1999 PGA Championship through the 2001 Memorial Tournament, are stroke-play events.

- **Most Consecutive Victories in a Single Event**: The champ here is Walter Hagen, who won four consecutive PGA Championships from 1924–1927.

- **Most Prize Money in One Year**: No surprises here—Woods earned more than $9 million on the 2000 PGA Tour.

- **Most USGA National Championships**: Robert T. Jones Jr., better known as Bobby Jones, won nine USGA National Championships.

Source: PGAtour.com; tigerwoods.com

*Golfers use the Ping putter more than any other brand on the market.*

## The Golfer's Prayer

*I do not ask for strength to drive*
*Three hundred yards and straight;*
*I do not ask to make in five*
*A hole that's bogey eight.*

*I do not want a skill in play*
*Which others can't attain;*
*I plead but for one Saturday*
*On which it doesn't rain.*

Source: Ring Lardner, Jr.

# POETRY

## *The Golfer's Prayer*

The exhilarating, maddening game of golf has captured the imagination of writers ranging from P.G. Wodehouse to John Updike. William Faulkner's epic novel *The Sound and The Fury* begins with a golf game seen through the eyes of a mentally retarded young man; and F. Scott Fitzgerald's short story "Winter Dreams" depicts the experiences of a caddie who marries into society.

Add to this list of golf-minded writers the late Ring Lardner Jr., who was an Oscar-winning screenwriter, a satirist, newspaper columnist, and poet. His poem, below, wittily evokes the feelings of weekend golfers everywhere.

# PUTTERS

## *Brand Usage*

Some golfers use the same putter for years on end, while others display no such loyalty, switching putters faster than they change clothes. This "putter du jour" mentality stems from the club's many design variables, like shape, weight, and shaft length, to name a few. For example, does a mallet or blade-style putter better suit your game? And will the extended shaft length putter compensate when you suffer a flare-up of the dreaded yips?

Perhaps the most delicate of golf clubs, the putter can literally get bent out of shape. A bent putter makes it extremely difficult to line up the clubface perpendicular to the target. Because pro golfers average nearly 30 putts per round, it's no wonder that many alternate between several putters in a tournament. Fortunately, putters are relatively inexpensive, so buying one or two of the most popular brands, either new or used, won't wipe out your savings.

| Brand | Usage |
|---|---|
| 1. Ping | 28 percent |
| 2. Odyssey | 18 percent |
| 3. Titleist | 10 percent |
| 4. Tear Drop | 7 percent |
| 5. Callaway | 3 percent |

Source: *Golf Equipment Almanac 2000; The Complete Idiot's Guide to Golf*

# PUTTERS

## *Most Popular Brands on Tour*

All golfers approach putting differently: some strike quickly, while others gently stroke the putt. Whatever your putting style, it's key to find a putter that suits your grip, is a comfortable length, and most of all, helps you aim the ball. This can take time, since there are five putter shapes to test on the market: the blade, the mallet, the heel-and-toe balanced putter, the center-shafted putter, and the broomhandle, which is a long-handled putter used by players suffering from the yips. As for specific brands, here are the putters that the pros use the most on the PGA, LPGA, and SPGA Tours.

### PGA Tour

1. Titleist

2. Odyssey

3. Ping

4. Tear Drop

5. Never Compromise

### SPGA Tour

1. Odyssey

2. Never Compromise

3. Ping

4. Titleist

5. Dogleg Right

### LPGA Tour

1. Odyssey

2. Never Compromise

3. Ping

4. Titleist

5. Cobra

Source: *Golf Equipment Almanac 2000*

# PUTTERS

## *Preferences*

For die-hard golfers, it's only a slight exaggeration to compare selecting the right putter to finding your soulmate. Alternately a golfer's best friend and worst enemy, sometimes in the same round of play, the putter is used more than any other club in the golfer's bag. Amateurs reportedly average 30–35 putts while playing an 18-hole round of golf, so a lot can ride on finding a putter that works for you consistently—or maybe a few putters that do the trick. Arnold Palmer went through so many putters that he eventually donated over a thousand to charity.

Among golfers surveyed, 37 percent stated that they used a certain putter because of its "feel," far and away the number-one factor in putter selection.

| Trait | Usage |
|---|---|
| 1. Feel | 37 percent |
| 2. Gift/prize | 13 percent |
| 3. Need | 8 percent |
| 4. Price | 7.5 percent |
| 5. Tried demo | 5 percent |
| 6. Appearance | 5 percent |
| 7. Recommendation | 4.5 percent |
| 8. Design | 3 percent |

Source: *The Complete Idiot's Guide to Golf* by Michelle McGann & Matthew Rudy; *Golf Equipment Almanac 2000*

# PUTTERS

## Used, Top Five Best-Selling Brands

Whenever you purchase used golf clubs, remember the phrase "caveat emptor," meaning let the buyer beware. The last thing you want to do is make a rash, possibly expensive purchase of clubs that undermines, rather than enhances, your golf game. This is particularly true of putters, which you'll probably use more than any other club in your bag.

Finding just the right putter can take time, especially if you're going the "used" route. There are several factors to consider, such as if the putter has a face insert, which became common in the mid-nineties, when Callaway introduced their trademark Stronomic insert. These inserts have a softer "feel," to help the golfer control his putt. Some putters also have a milled face, which makes it flatter, or a larger head, which supposedly help more erratic putters. With all these variables to consider, it's easy to feel overwhelmed. Perhaps the easiest way to start your search is by reviewing the top five selling used putters currently available.

| Brand | Price of Used Putter |
|---|---|
| 1. Titleist Cameron Newport | $182.31 |
| 2. Odyssey Golf Tri Force 2 | $105.71 |
| 3. Ping Anser 2 | $76.53 |
| 4. Odyssey Golf DF Rossie 2 | $55.87 |
| 5. Ping Scottsdale Anser | $86.22 |

Source: golfclubexchange.com; swingweight.com/putter_fitting.htm; "Putter Fitting: Factors for a Best Fit, Part 1" by Jeff Jackson

# PUTTING FACTS

## How the Pros Putt

Every golfer has had their share of putting trials and tribulations. Three-putts have been the undoing of many a killer round. For the casual golfer, putting is often that convenient excuse for not breaking 100, or 90, or 80.

But what about the pros? When you make your living on the golf course, you have to be a little more consistent on the green than the amateur golfer. It's no surprise, then, that pros usually take no more than two putts per hole. When the hole is on the line, however, pros can fall victim to pressure just like the rest of us. In fact, they are significantly more likely to make their putt when it's for par than when putting for a birdie. The distance doesn't even matter.

If you've ever felt like a lifetime passed while you waited for a ball to drop, you might be interested to know that a golf ball rolls 13.6 times before dropping for a six-foot putt. Here is a look at how often pros make their putts.

| Distance | Percentage of Putts Made |
|---|---|
| 6 feet | 54.87 |
| 10 feet | 33.5 |
| 15 feet | 16.8 |
| 25 feet | 10.2 |

Source: Authors, *The Best and Worst of Golf*

# QUOTES

## To Make You Smile

Has any sport inspired as much self-deprecating humor as golf? The beauty of the game is that it's truly the great equalizer, no one, not even golf pros, always plays at the top of his or her game. While some wax philosophical about the game and its spiritual underpinnings, we'll take those golfers who prefer to see the humor in the situation any day. Most golfers can identify with quite a few of the observations below.

"I'm hitting the woods just great, but I'm having a terrible time getting out of them."
—Henry Toscano

"I don't say my golf is bad, but if I grew tomatoes, they'd come up sliced."
—Miller Barber

"The reason the pro tells you to keep your head down is so you can't see him laughing."
—Phyllis Diller

"Always throw clubs ahead of you. That way you don't have to waste energy going back to pick them up."
—Tommy Bolt

"Golf's three ugliest words: still your shot."
—Dave Marr

"Golf combines two favorite American pastimes: taking long walks and hitting things with a stick."
—P. J. O'Rourke

"President Eisenhower has given up golf for painting. It takes fewer strokes."
—Bob Hope

"I know I'm getting better at golf because I'm hitting fewer spectators."
—Gerald R. Ford

"It took me 17 years to get 3,000 hits in baseball. I did it in one afternoon on the golf course."
—Hank Aaron

"Pebble Beach is Alcatraz with grass."
—Bob Hope

Source: Authors, *The Best and Worst of Golf*

# QUOTES

## *To Make You Better at Golf*

In no-nonsense, often terse language, these golf pros demonstrate wisdom born of much experience on the course. Although every pro has something worthwhile to share, Julius Boros stands out by virtue of his sheer brevity. His "Swing easy, hit hard" should become the mantra of struggling golfers everywhere.

"The only thing you should force in a golf swing is the club back into the bag."
—Byron Nelson

"The biggest thing is to have the mind-set and the belief you can win every tournament going in."
—Tiger Woods

"A bad attitude is worse than a bad swing."
—Payne Stewart

"The toughest thing for people to learn in golf is to accept bad holes—and then forget about them."
—Gary Player

"One bad shot does not make a losing score."
—Gay Brewer

"If there is one thing I've learned during my years as a professional, it's that the only thing constant about golf is inconsistency."
—Jack Nicklaus

"Golf is a game in which perfection stays just out of reach."
—Betsy Rawls

"Swing easy, hit hard."
—Julius Boros

Source: Authors, *The Best and Worst of Golf*

# SHOES

## *Preferences for Golf Shoes*

Necessity has been the mother of much invention in golf. Prior to the introduction of spiked shoes, many golfers simply pounded nails and tacks into regular shoes and boots for better traction.

Today, golf shoes come with alternative, nonmetal spikes, that are plastic and less likely to damage the green. Companies still makes shoes with metal spikes, but many courses in the United States and abroad ban their use to keep maintenance costs low.

When shoe shopping, golfers cite these factors in selecting a brand. Incidentally, Footjoy is the top seller for both consumers and professional golfers.

| Trait | | Percent |
|---|---|---|
| 1. | Comfort | 22 |
| 2. | Fit | 17 |
| 3. | Appearance | 16 |
| 4. | Price | 13 |
| 5. | Need | 7 |
| 6. | Gift/prize | 7 |

7. Feel 4
8. Durability 3.5

Source: Darrell Survey of Golf Equipment

# SHOES

## Terminology of Golf Shoes

Sam Snead may have been on to something when he used to practice golf barefoot. Planting your feet on the ground gives you a traction and play that no golf shoe can match. Unfortunately, the "no shoes, no service" policy rules on most golf courses, so finding the right shoes are a must, particularly with so many brands on the market. As this short list of design options and materials reveals, the golf shoe of the 21st century is a mix of high tech innovations and old standards.

1. **Bal opening**: A V-shaped lace opening gives the golfer several styling options.

2. **Blucher opening**: This style of opening is recommended for golfers with high insteps, since it enables the wearer to lace it tighter than the Bal.

3. **Calfskin**: The absolute top of the line in shoe leather.

4. **Cleat receptacle system**: Available on shoes with nonmetal spikes, the cleat receptacle system enables the wearer to replace worn-down spikes.

5. **Forefront cushioning**: Pads in the shoe's forefront provided added comfort.

6. **Full grain leather**: Waterproof leather that is the select, top layer of the cowhide.

7. **Heel cushioning**: Pads in the shoe's heel area for extra comfort.

8. **Intelligel**: This temperature-sensitive gel insert provides customized fit and support.

9. **Intellishield**: A waterproof, breathable membrane.

10. **Last**: A form in the shape of a foot. Once a golfer determines his proper shoe size, he uses a last to find just the right shoe.

11. **Membrane**: The membrane manages moisture level in the shoe.

12. **Midsole**: A lightweight, flexible cushioning material that is molded to high-performance TPU outsoles.

13. **Nubuc**: A waterproof leather with a soft nap that is made from fine grain leather.

14. **Outsole**: Either rubber or thermoplastic urethane, the outsole provides a solid hitting platform.

15. **Upper**: The upper is made of calfskin or full grain or synthetic leather.

Source: *Golf Digest Equipment Planner 2002*; www.golfshoesplus.com

# SLANG

For the uninitiated, the colorful and highly idiosyncratic golfer's vernacular makes about as much sense as Egyptian hieroglyphics. Distinguishing between a birdie and a bogey is proverbial child's play compared to understanding what it means to "hood the club face" or be "on the bubble." But don't despair; in *Let the Big Dog Eat! A Dictionary of the Secret Language of Golf*, authors Hubert Pedroli and Mary Tiegreen painstakingly define these and other terms so even the most clueless of golfers can talk like a pro. Here are a few to get you started.

1. **Angel Gooser**: A drive that flies extremely high.

2. **Barkie**: Making par after hitting a tree.

3. **Boss of the Moss**: Compliment given to a skilled putter.

4. **Cabbage Pounder**: A player who spends a lot of time in the rough, or cabbage.

5. **Captain Kirk**: A shot that goes "where no man has gone before."

6. **Divorce Court**: When couples play together in the same match.

7. **Emergency Room**: Either the locker room or the bar.

*To* **Star Trek** *fans he's Captain Kirk, but to a golfer a "Captain Kirk" is a shot that goes "where no man has gone before."*

8. **Fried Egg**: A golf ball half-buried in the sand.

9. **Gopher-Killer**: Not a reference to Bill Murray's character in Caddyshack. A drive that flies along about six inches above the ground.

10. **Hospital Zone**: Where you can practice your swing. A kinder, gentler term than Murderer's Row.

11. **Jamalies**: To be avoided at all costs. Resort golfers with a bad swing and worse attitude.

12. **Leaking Oil**: When a player's game is beginning to collapse.

13. **Lorena Bobbit**: A particularly cruel slice.

14. **Marquis de Sod**: Nickname for the greenskeeper who handles pin placement.

15. **Philips Petroleum**: A score of 66.

16. **Roodle**: A player who doesn't win a single hole in match play.

17. **Solitaire**: A hole in one.

18. **Stretcher-Bearer**: Another name for a caddie.

19. **Toilet Flusher**: A putt that swirls around the rim of the hole before going down the drain.

20. **Yard Sale**: When a player's bags and clubs fall out of the cart.

Source: *Let the Big Dog Eat! A Dictionary of the Secret Language of Golf*

# SONGS

## To Golf by

Does your golf game make you want to sing? Country singer and songwriter Brad Belt found that's what happened to him, so he wrote and recorded a CD devoted to the game. "I love golf. I love music, and I love writing humorous songs," Belt explained. Released in April of 2001, *Golf is a Cussin' Game* is available to order at www.bradbelt.com.

One review gave it four stars, saying, "Folksy charm is the best way to describe these 10 easygoing odes to life on the links…the songs are sugared with gentle humor and spiced with touches of raciness." Another recent purchaser said, "When me and my buddies go on a golf trip, I put Brad's tape in and we listen to it." What better recommendation is there than that?

Here's a rundown of the songs on this golf CD.

1. "Golf Scramble-it is"

2. "Golf Is a Cussin' Game"

3. "Smart Aleck Caddie"

4. "I Don't Go Golfin' With My Wife"

5. "Golf Is Best"

6. "That's Not Why I Play With Lovely Sharlene"

7. "Never Up, Never In"

8. "It Don't Take Brains to Play this Game"

9. "Dick Hits It Long"

10. "Double Bogey Blues"

Source: bradbelt.com

# SPORTS MANAGEMENT COMPANIES

The 1996 movie *Jerry Maguire* sheds a humorous light on the manic, go-for-broke world of sports agents, who come across as alternately nurturing and ruthless. Whether or not this depiction of sports agents is realistic or stereotypical, the film dramatizes the unique bond that professional athletes share with their agents or managers.

**International Management Group:** according to golf lore, Arnold Palmer and manager Mark McCormack formalized their business relationship in 1960 with a handshake. With that handshake, IMG was born. Over 40 years later, the company that first signed Arnold Palmer is now the world's largest sports management group. In fact, IMG has diversified into scores of other areas, from representing writers and models to golf course design, to name a few of the company's divisions. IMG's client roster currently includes Tiger Woods, David Duval, Vijay Singh, Karrie Webb, and Annika Sorenstam. And as for company founder Mark McCormack, he's now IMG's chairman and a best-selling author. Website: www.imgworld.com

**SFX Sports** probably the second biggest sports management firm is SFX, which is a division of the SFX Group. SFX Sport's golf client roster, which includes Greg Norman, John Daly, and Scott Hoch, grew even more impressive with the company's 2001 acquisition of the Signature Sports Group. Now SFX Golf also represents Tom Lehman, Larry Mize, and Scott Simpson. Website: http://sfx.com/

**Octagon** launched in 1997 by The Interpublic Group of Companies, one of the world's top advertising and marketing communications companies, Octagon has rapidly become a force in sports management. A global enterprise since 1999, Octagon currently represents such PGA and LPGA stars as Davis Love III, Tom Kite, and Meg Mallon. Website: www.octagon.com

**Gaylord Sports Management** of these four sports management companies, only this one focuses exclusively on golfers. Based in Scottsdale, Arizona, the company's management division is headed by Steve Loy and David Yates, who groom many young players for stardom (and hopefully lucrative endorsement contracts). Gaylord Sports Management currently reps players from the Japan Golf Tour, the PGA Australasia Tour, and the Buy.Com Tour, as well as such PGA and LPGA stars as Phil Mickelson, Mark Calcavecchia, and Kelli Kuehne. Website: www.gaylordsports.com

Source: Authors, *The Best and Worst of Golf*

# TIPS

## *Avoiding Common Problems*

Avoiding golf's most common pitfalls is easier said than done. In fact, if a few words of advice could eliminate those problems, all duffers would golf like the pros. Many golfers, however, continue to collect golf tips, hoping to find the one that will make the big difference in their game. Maybe that's why Barnes and Noble Booksellers stocks as many as 15 golf magazines on their shelves. And the Internet is overflowing with the names of golf schools offering instruction for a few hours or a few weeks.

If you are looking for something a little less expensive, however, try these tips suggested by golf professionals, designed to improve just one area of your game at a time.

- **Practice with purpose**: Know what you want to accomplish during a practice session and aim at a specific target, as if you were on an actual course. Work on one skill at a time. —*Lynn Marriott, golf educator, The Legacy Golf Resort, Phoenix*

- **Beach balls**: The beach is a kind way to describe the sand trap. But even from the sand you can save strokes by aiming for the middle of the green and going for a two-putt. Aiming for the pin is difficult and often results in more strokes rather than less.— *Jackie Kaufman, Nicklaus/Flick Golf Schools*

- **Short putts**: Don't play with a putter that's too long. A putter that allows you to leave your arms extended gives you better shoulder and wrist control, which promotes consistency in putting. —*Karen Palacios, Jim McLean Golf School, Miami*

- **Teed off**: In order to avoid hazards from the tee box, tee the ball on the side closest to the problem (out-of-bounds areas, trees, water, or other hazards) and aim away from them.—*Nancy Quarcelino, The Legends Club of Tennessee*

- **Abandon your backswing**: Concentrate on your downswing and follow-through to get your shot on target. Your backswing will take care of itself.—*Debbie Steinbach, The Reserve, Indian Wells, CA*

- **Get a grip**: The most important thing about a good grip is holding the club handle more in the fingers of both hands, rather than in the palms.—*Rebecca Dengler, Ed Oliver Golf Course, Wilmington, DE*

- **Putting pointers**: When faced with a breaking putt, don't follow through toward the hole. Instead, follow through to your target, which factors in the break and sends the ball along the right path.—*Nancy Lopez, LPGA Hall of Famer*

- **Heads!** Instead of keeping your head (totally) down, keep your eyes parallel to the ground during your backswing. That allows your head to move a few inches laterally, which helps keeps it behind the ball at impact resulting in fewer "topped" shots.—*Krista Dunton, Forsgate CC, Jamesburg, N.J.*

Source: *Golf for Women*

# TIPS FOR THE GOLFER'S MENTAL HEALTH

If you were to ask golfers what they've learned from playing the game, their answers would probably run the gamut from "humility" to "grace." One day they're kissing a championship trophy before adoring spectators; the next they're stuck in some bunker or rolling up their trousers to fish a ball from the water. Whether you double-bogey or double-eagle, golf forces you to rally from disappointment, narrow your focus and keep a sense of humor. Of course, you can swear, toss your clubs into the rough, and storm off the course; just don't expect to be invited back to play anytime soon. But if you take the higher road, golf can provide invaluable training for dealing with everything from petty frustrations to major life changes.

A professor of educational psychology at the University of North Carolina at Chapel Hill, Dr. Richard Coop has written several books on golf psychology, including *Mind Over Golf*. In addition to his books and columns for *Golf Magazine*, Coop has worked with such PGA stars as Ben Crenshaw and Mark O'Meara on their golf game. He has distilled golf's mental health benefits in seven skills and strategies, which first appeared in a 1989 article entitled "Golf as Therapy."

1. Live in the present tense.

2. Develop a realistic focus of control.

3. Adapt your behavior to fit the situation you're in.

4. Develop the skill of self-analysis and self-understanding.

5. Develop the skill of cognitive restructuring.

6. Learn to accept yourself.

7. Develop the wisdom to value the basics.

Source: "Golf as Therapy" by Dr. Richard H. Coop, 1989 (Original Source pending). This was reprinted in *A Tribute to Golf: A Celebration in Art, Photography and Literature* —compiled/edited by Thomas P. Stewart. http://www.tourprostats.com/coop.html

# TIPS

## *Sam Snead's Tips on Match Play*

A prolific writer as well as a champion golfer, veteran Sam Snead has penned everything from instructional manuals to an autobiography, *Slammin' Sam*. Drawing upon his years of experience on both the PGA and SPGA tours, Snead offers golfers concise, practical information that steers clear of any new agey golf psychobabble. Here are Snead's thoughts on match play, taken from his 1986 book *Pigeons, Marks, Hustlers and Other Golf Bettors You Can Beat.*

1. Play more conservatively early in the match.

2. When in doubt, check your opponent's lie.

3. After winning a hole, concentrate on hitting a solid drive.

4. When the momentum is going against you, change the pace of the match.

5. Always figure your opponent will make a long putt.

6. Never give up on yourself.

7. Don't get mad, get even.

8. When you decide to gamble, "Katy bar the door."

9. Know the rule differences for match play.

10. Always keep the pressure on your opponent.

Source: *Pigeons, Marks and Hustlers* by Sam Snead and Jerry Tarde

# Tips

## Top Things that Hurt Your Golf Game

You can buy the latest set of high tech clubs, you can read every instruction book written by the pros, and you can meditate until you achieve zenlike calm; but at the end of the day, if you haven't practiced enough at the local course or driving range, your game simply won't improve. As any golf teacher will tell you, practice may not make perfect, but it can help many golfers fully realize their potential, whether they are strictly amateurs playing for fun or budding professionals trying to qualify for the PGA Tour. Skipping or cutting practice is only one of the many elements that golf teachers cite as damaging to your game. The majority of golf teachers, however, feel that a poor short game is the one factor hampering most people from golf success.

- not enough practice
- not enough distance
- poor attitude
- poor chipping
- poor putting
- poor distance control
- poor approach shots
- slicing
- hooking
- lack of accuracy
- sand play

Source: Authors, *The Best and Worst of Golf*

# Toys

## Children, 3–10 Years Old

Providing invaluable hand-eye coordination training, these toys are a safe, fun, and relatively inexpensive way to introduce children to golf. And you never know when your toddler might turn out to be another Tiger Woods or Karrie Webb.

1. **Easy Hit Golf Set** by Little Tikes: Recommended for ages three to six years old, the Easy Hit Golf Set is made of durable plastic and comes with a putter and driver, three oversize golf balls and a practice hole.

2. **Golf Set** by International Playthings: For ages three to six, this set features a mini-plastic course and golf bag containing three clubs and two oversize golf balls. Children can change the course by adding plastic obstacles and a hole with its own flag.

3. **Grow to Pro Golf** by Fisher-Price: For ages three to six years old, this plastic golf bag comes with a driver, putter, tee and five oversize golf balls, that roll into position when the child depresses a lever on the golf bag.

4. **Junior Sport Golf Set** by Stats: For ages three to six, this lightweight plastic set can be used indoors or outdoors. The three clubs are different colors to help the child differentiate between the blue driver, red iron, and yellow putter.

5. **Frog Golf** by Swimways: Recommended for ages five and up, Frog Golf is a favorite with young golfers and swimmers alike. Standing on the pool's edge, kids try to hit fly balls into the gaping mouths of three foam frogs floating in the shallow end of the pool. Adult supervision is strongly suggested.

6. **Lil' Driver 6-Volt Golf Cart with Clubs** by Lerado: For ages five to six, this miniature electric golf cart hits a top speed of 2.5 miles per hour (don't worry, there's a safety brake too.) The cart comes with a musical horn and a canopy to protect children from the sun.

7. **Splash Bombs Golf Challenge** by Prime Time Toys: For ages five to ten, this colorful toy set builds visual and motor skills.

Source: amazon.com

# TRIVIA

1. Former Speaker of the House Thomas "Tip" O'Neill caddied for the great Bobby Jones when the Georgia-born golfer attended Harvard.

2. Golfer Ken Venturi turned to golf instead of baseball because of his stutter.

3. Nick Faldo once climbed 25 feet up an oak tree to retrieve a golf ball at the 1992 U.S. Open.

4. Best-selling novelist James Ellroy (*LA Confidential, The Black Dahlia*) once worked as a caddie at a Los Angeles country club.

5. Gary McCord once appeared on LawrenceWelk's television show to hit a golf ball at an archery target 35 feet away.

6. Jimmy Demaret once appeared on the popular game show *What's My Line.*

7. Legendary architect Stanford White designed America's first clubhouse, Shinnecock Hills in Southampton, New York, in 1892.

8. Mark Calcavecchia caddied for Ken Green at the 1986 Honda Classic, and then returned the following year to win the trophy.

9. Gardner Dickinson once gave Ben Hogan an IQ test on the sly, and then pronounced Hogan a genius after reviewing the results.

10. Byron Nelson was paid $500 in 1936 to endorse a brand of cigarette that he didn't even like.

11. Fred Astaire actually hit 12 golf balls in rapid succession while tap dancing, and all the balls landed on the green. Check out his 1938 film *Carefree.*

12. Andy Bean once stopped playing on the PGA Tour Qualifying School to grab a six-foot alligator by the tail and flip it over.

13. Legally blind golfer Margaret Walden scored holes in one two days in a row at

the Long Point Golf Course's 87-yard seventh hole in 1990.

14. PGA Tour pro Howard Twitty agreed to display the Burger King logo on his bag in exchange for 500 free whoppers in 1977.

15. Paul Azinger once caddied for LPGA Hall-of-Famer Mickey Wright.

16. Dinah Shore is a member of the World Golf Hall of Fame.

17. Gary Player recorded an album called, aptly enough, *Gary Player Sings*.

18. Sam Snead learned to play golf barefoot in the Virginia mountains.

19. Golfer Lefty Stackhouse once got so angry that he burned his entire set of hickory golf clubs.

20. A British golfer reportedly took 156 putts on a single hole in 1890.

21. Tommy Armour was nearly blind in one eye after getting gassed in World War I.

22. Tomboy Patty Berg turned to golf after her mother forbid her to play football.

23. The 1995 comedy *To Wong Foo, Thanks For Everything, Julie Newmar* features actor John Leguizamo playing a drag queen named Chi Chi Rodriguez. The real-life golfer was not amused and sued Universal Pictures.

24. Fifty-one-year-old Ray Floyd is the old-est golfer ever to play for the United States in the Ryder Cup.

25. Dave Eichelberger has the most starts on the PGA Tour with a grand total of 783.

Source: *The Ultimate Golf Trivia Book* by Mike Towle; triviagolf.com

*Between 1970 and 1980, Lee Trevino won the Vardon Trophy five times.*

lowest stroke average in tour events. Among Vardon Trophy recipients, however, these golfers have the *highest* stroke average in the award's history.

| | Golfer | Year | Score |
|---|---|---|---|
| 1. | Lee Trevino | 1972 | 70.89 |
| 2. | Billy Casper | 1965 | 70.85 |
| 3. | Lee Trevino | 1970 | 70.64 |
| 4. | Ray Floyd | 1983 | 70.61 |
| 5. | Billy Casper | 1963 | 70.58 |
| 6. | Bruce Crampton | 1973 | 70.57 |
| 7. | Calvin Peete | 1984 | 70.56 |
| | Don January | 1970 | 70.56 |
| 8. | Jack Burke | 1952 | 70.54 |
| 9. | Lee Trevino | 1974 | 70.53 |
| 10. | Bruce Crampton | 1975 | 70.51 |

Source: infoplease.com; espn.com

# VARDON TROPHY

## All-Time Highest Stroke Averages

Since 1947 the Vardon Trophy has been awarded each year to the player who has the

# VARDON TROPHY

## All-Time Lowest Stroke Averages

If you *still* need additional proof that Tiger Woods is one of the all-time great golfers, then simply look to his three consecutive Vardon Trophy wins. Not only did Woods average the lowest number of strokes on the PGA tour from 1999 to 2001, but he also set a new record low with his 67.79 average for the 2000 season. As of this writing, Woods' dominance of the game shows no sign of abating.

Here are the Vardon Trophy recipients with the 10 lowest stroke averages since 1947.

| Golfer | | Year | Score |
|---|---|---|---|
| 1. | Tiger Woods | 2000 | 67.79 |
| 2. | Tiger Woods | 1999 | 68.43 |
| 3. | Tiger Woods | 2001 | 68.81 |
| | Greg Norman | 1994 | 68.81 |
| 4. | Nick Price | 1997 | 68.98 |
| 5. | Greg Norman | 1990 | 69.10 |
| 6. | Nick Price | 1993 | 69.11 |
| 7. | David Duval | 1998 | 69.13 |
| 8. | Sam Snead | 1950 | 69.23 |
| 9. | Ben Hogan | 1948 | 69.30 |
| 10. | Sam Snead | 1949 | 69.37 |

Source: hickoksports.com

# VARDON TROPHY

## Multiple Winners

A member of golf's "Great Triumvirate" along with James Braid and J. H. Taylor, Englishman Harry Vardon is generally acknowledged as the golf world's first international celebrity. In addition to winning the British Open a record six times, Vardon also popularized the overlapping grip. In recognition of his achievements, the PGA created the Vardon Trophy in 1937. From 1937 through 1941, this trophy was given to the player who had the best overall record on the PGA tour via a point system. The PGA did not present the Vardon Trophy from 1942 through 1946, during the height of World War II. Reinstated in 1947, the Vardon has since been given to the player with the lowest stroke average in tour events. Only golfers who play at least 80 official tournament rounds are eligible for consideration.

The following players have won the Vardon Trophy multiple times.

| Golfer | Victories |
|---|---|
| Billy Casper | 5 |
| Lee Trevino | 5 |
| Arnold Palmer | 4 |
| Sam Snead | 4 |
| Ben Hogan | 3 |

| Greg Norman | 3 |
|---|---|
| Tom Watson | 3 |
| Tiger Woods | 3 |
| Fred Couples | 2 |
| Bruce Crampton | 2 |
| Tom Kite | 2 |
| Lloyd Mangrum | 2 |
| Nick Price | 2 |

Source: .hickoksports.com; msnbc.com

# VARE TROPHY WINNERS

## Highest Stroke Averages

Back in the era when Babe, Berg, and Suggs dominated the LPGA, averaging 74 or more strokes per tournament round brought them the Vare Trophy. By today's standards, these pros probably wouldn't even be in the running. These six Vare Trophy winners, all from the fifties and early sixties, have the 10 highest stroke averages in the award's history.

| Player | | Year | Score |
|---|---|---|---|
| 1. | Babe Zaharias | 1954 | 75.48 |
| 2. | Patty Berg | 1953 | 75.00 |
| 3. | Beverly Hanson | 1958 | 74.92 |
| 4. | Louise Suggs | 1957 | 74.64 |
| 5. | Patty Berg | 1956 | 74.57 |
| 6. | Patty Berg | 1955 | 74.47 |
| 7. | Betsy Rawls | 1959 | 74.03 |
| 8. | Mickey Wright | 1962 | 73.67 |
| 9. | Mickey Wright | 1961 | 73.55 |
| 10. | Mickey Wright | 1960 | 73.25 |

Source: hickoksports.com

# VARE TROPHY

## Lowest Averages

When Patty Berg took home the first Vare Trophy in 1953 for the lowest average number of strokes per tournament round, her winning average was an even 75. Nearly 50 years later, Berg's average pales in comparison to the record 69.43 low set by Annika Sorenstam and

Karrie Webb in 2001 and 1999, respectively. These LPGA players have the 10 lowest stroke averages in the award's history.

| Player | Year | Score |
| --- | --- | --- |
| 1. Annika Sorenstam | 2001 | 69.43 |
| Karrie Webb | 1999 | 69.43 |
| 2. Annika Sorenstam | 1998 | 69.99 |
| 3. Karrie Webb | 1997 | 70.00 |
| 4. Beth Daniel | 1989 | 70.38 |
| 5. Annika Sorenstam | 1996 | 70.47 |
| 6. Beth Daniel | 1990 | 70.54 |
| 7. Pat Bradley | 1991 | 70.66 |
| 8. Nancy Lopez | 1985 | 70.73 |
| 9. Dottie Pepper | 1992 | 70.80 |
| 10. Betsy King | 1993 | 70.85 |

Source: hickoksports.com

# VARE TROPHY

## Multiple Winners

A fierce competitor on the amateur golf circuit in the twenties and thirties, Glenna Collett Vare won six U.S. Amateur titles between 1922 and 1935. Her legacy lives on with the LPGA's Vare Trophy, which is presented each year to the female golfer who has the lowest average number of strokes per round in professional tour events. Only those players who have competed in at least 70 official tournament rounds are eligible.

First presented to Patty Berg in 1953, the Vare Trophy has been given to the following LPGA players multiple times over the years.

| Player | Number of Trophy Wins |
| --- | --- |
| 1. Kathy Whitworth | 7 |
| 2. JoAnne Carner | 5 |
| Mickey Wright | 5 |
| 4. Annika Sorenstam | 4 |
| 5. Patty Berg | 3 |
| Beth Daniel | 3 |
| Nancy Lopez | 3 |
| Judy Rankin | 3 |
| Karrie Webb | 3 |
| 10. Pat Bradley | 2 |
| Betsy King | 2 |

Source: hickoksports.com

# VIDEO GAMES

## Most Popular Golf Games

When Nintendo burst onto the scene, introducing us to "realistic" video games, old-timers couldn't believe the advances that had been made since the days of Atari in the eighties. But the few golf titles available didn't have enough pizzazz to attract much interest.

Now, between N64, Sega Dreamcast, and Playstation 1 and 2, games have had to become more exciting, more realistic, and more appealing to compete in the market. The games have gone mainstream, attracting golfers and video game enthusiasts alike. Realism is available for those players dreaming of the PGA Tour. Players can choose not only the club they want to play, but the course as well. Ball spin, uneven lies and wind direction can all be factored into the mix.

But for those more attuned to the video arcade aspect of the game, there's still Mario, a Nintendo tradition. Mario Golf is a faster paced golf game with options such as speed golf. In addition to the regular TV hook-up, many of these games are also available in hand-held versions. In the table atop the next page are some of the best-selling titles out there.

# VOCABULARY

## A Golfer's Basic Primer

Want to appear less like the novice you are when playing golf for the first time? Then stop practicing your swing and start learning the basic jargon (etiquette's another lesson.) Golfers have their own verbal shorthand— terms that spring from the sport's rich history, larger-than-life characters, and pop culture, to name just a few of the sources. While we're not suggesting that you memorize every term coined since the Scots took up the game in the 15th century, it's important to know the basics, some of which are listed below. It may not improve your game, but you'll probably feel a little less overwhelmed if you can at least "talk the talk."

### Most Popular Video Golf Games

| Title | Maker | Player |
|---|---|---|
| Cyber Tiger | Electronic Arts | Playstation |
| Cyber Tiger | Electronic Arts | Nintendo 64 |
| Cyber Tiger Golf | Electronic Arts | Game Boy Color |
| ESPN Final Round Golf 2002 | Konami | Game Boy Advance |
| GolfTrac Pro | Handmark, Inc. | PDA |
| Hot Shots Golf 2 | Electronic Arts | Sony Playstation |
| Mario Golf | Nintendo | Nintendo 64 |
| Swing Away Golf | Camelot | Playstation 2 |
| Tiger Woods PGA Tour 2000 | Electronic Arts | Playstation |
| Tee-Off | Acclaim | Sega Dreamcast |

Source: Amazon.com

*In golf, an "eagle" is no ordinary old birdie.*

1. **Birdie**: One stroke less than par.

2. **Bogey**: One stroke over par.

3. **Bunker**: A mound or indentation created as an intentional hazard. Sometimes filled with sand.

4. **Chip**: A short shot unto the green.

5. **Divot**: A clump of grass dug out with the club during a shot.

6. **Double bogey**: 2 over par.

7. **Draw**: A shot that is curved from right to left.

8. **Eagle**: 2 less than par.

9. **Fade**: A shot that curves from left to right.

10. **Fairway**: The center "lane" of a golf hole, characterized by closely cut grass.

11. **Fore!**: A shout or cry that is used to warn other golfers of a ball coming their way.

12. **Gimme**: A short putt that a player may count as just one stroke rather than putt it out.

13. **Hook**: A shot that curves severely to the left.

14. **Par**: The number of strokes a player is expected to get when a hole is played perfectly.

15. **Penalty**: A stroke added to a players score due to a rule violation.

16. **Putt**: A stroke taken on the green with a short club called a putter.

17. **Rough**: An area of tall grass bordering the fairway.

18. **Scratch player**: A player who regularly shoots par.

19. **Slice**: A shot that curves severely from left to right.

20. **Tee shot**: First shot of any hole, taken on the tee box, usually with the ball positioned on a wooden tee.

21. **Waggle**: A slight movement of the body or club as the golfer addresses the ball before a shot.

22. **Whiff**: Missing the ball entirely with a swing.

Source: Authors, *The Best and Worst of Golf*

# WEBSITES

## *For Golfers*

Anyone who has surfed the Internet knows that there is information to be had on practically any subject. Golf is no exception. In fact, the topic of golf may well be one of the most prolific. There are websites of interest to pros and duffers alike. On the World Wide Web you can follow the pros and get the latest tour results as soon as they become available. You can get tips from the experts on how to improve your own golf game. You can buy golf equipment at discount prices and research which pros use what products and why. And of course, you can find—and book—the perfect golf vacation.

Other sites provide the names of books or videos about golf. Don't forget golf magazines. And then there's eBay, the place for everything golf, secondhand! Most of the sites listed below also provide links to other sites. If not, try a golf search engine, the ultimate guide to other golf websites.

- **Golf** at www.golf.com. A plethora of golf articles compiled from a variety of source.

- **The Professional Golf Association** at www.pgatour.com. A site with everything for the golf fans. You can follow the pros (men, women, and seniors), plan your next golfing vacation, or gets tips on correcting your slice.

- **Professional Golf Association** at www.pga.com. This is the site for golf pros and people who want information on becoming one. But it's also for the average golfer who wants to keep up with what's new in golf.

- **United States Golf Association** at www.usga.com. Need to refresh your memory on the rules of golf? The USGA has it all, from rules to etiquette. Also learn about USGA members, equipment, and other things of interest to golfers.

- **Golf Digest** at www.golfdigest.com. Here's the online connection to golf's most popular magazine.

- **World Golf** at www.worldgolf.com. Looking for a vacation site or just golf news? Look no further.

- **The 19th Hole** at www.golfball.com. Your store for golf equipment, gifts, and supplies.

- **Ladies Golf** at www.lpga.com. Fans of women's pro golf will delight in this website which feature everything from pro stats to tips for the amateur woman golfer.

- **National Golf Foundation** at www.ngf.org. Provides golfing facts and market research to foundation members. Also offers publications for sale to the general public.

- **Golf Judge** at www.golfjudge.com. The standard in golf testing and review, this website reviews all brands of golf balls and equipment.

- **Senior Golf** at www.seniorgolf.com. Here's a website with the older golfer in mind. Tips, equipment, and SPGA stats.

- **Golf Help** at www.golfhelp.com. This is a search engine just for golf! When all else fails, this will take you where you want to go.

Source: Authors, *The Best and Worst of Golf*

# WEDGES

## *Best-Selling Used*

Several factors must be weighed when buying a wedge. Is the clubface soft enough to give it sufficient spin? Does the wedge have enough "bounce," or appropriate width of the sole plate, to enable you to play on hard and soft surfaces? And how does the shaft flex compare to the other clubs in your bag? Once you review all these variables, then it's time to price shop. Bear in mind that new wedges are not cheap and can cost upwards of $100 apiece.

*A used Cleveland Golf 588 RTG costs around $65.*

Buying three or four of these can set you back, so if you don't want to fork over that kind of cash, consider going the used golf club route—carefully. Do your homework and inspect the clubs before making any purchase, particularly if you're not familiar with the seller. These are the five best-selling used wedges, per latest sales figures.

1. **Cleveland Golf 588 RTG**
   Graphite shaft—N/A
   Steel shaft—$66.38

2. **Cleveland Golf 588**
   Graphite shaft—$55.00
   Steel shaft—$57.52

3. **Callaway Big Bertha X-12**
   Graphite shaft—$71.63
   Steel shaft—$79.80

4. **Ping ISI N**
   Graphite shaft—$77.56
   Steel shaft—$70.13

5. **Cleveland Golf 588 Gun Metal**
   Graphite shaft—$55.56
   Steel shaft—$63.65

Source: golfclubexchange.com; eopinions.com: "Wedges A Lot to Consider" posted 09/03/01

# WOODS

## New for 2002

Novice golfers, equipped with today's state-of-the-art equipment, probably wonder why drivers and a select group of other clubs are known as woods. Long-time golfers, however, have the answer on the tip of their tongues. They used these clubs back in the days when the club heads were actually made from wood. In fact, some old-timers or golfing die-hards still use wooden woods.

These older woods did the job just fine until manufacturers started experimenting with other shapes and materials. Since then, club heads have grown larger and more forgiving. And they are made from increasingly lighter-weight materials for an easier swing.

The newest offerings are both lighter and thinner than ever before. Surprisingly, they are also stronger. And best of all, manufacturers are experimenting with a variety of metals in an effort to create a high-end product with a low-cost price. Here are some of today's top woods.

**Cleveland Launcher**: $399
   Gets you off to a good start.

**Kosco K2K0**: $480
   Club head forgives easily.

**Orlimar HIP Steel**: $240
   Titanium feel from steel.

**Taylor Made 200 Series**: $330
   Successor to last year's hit driver.

**Srixon XXIO**: $600
   Power-driven.

**Tour Edge Bazooka F4**: $300
   Forged titanium for ultimate performance.

**Cobra King Cobra S5350**: $369
   Forgiveness is king.

**Callaway C4**: $540
   Goes a long way.

**The Cleveland Launcher: lighter, thinner, and stronger.**

**PING TiS1 Tec**: $515
   Light club's not lightweight on distance.

**Wilson Deep Red 365**: $500
   In a word, sweet (spot.)

Source: *Golf Tips* February/March 2002

# WORST SCORES ON ONE HOLE OF PLAY

We've all had days on the golf course we'd rather forget; whiffing on the first tee, losing a ball to the rough, shanking repeatedly. To paraphrase Thomas Paine, these are the times that try golfers' souls. At least when we have an off day, it's not a matter of public record, friends' teasing aside. Unfortunately, the same cannot be said for these following players, pros and amateurs alike, who've persisted in the face of disaster, probably to their lasting regret.

- **161**: Mrs. J. F. Meechan reached this incredible score in the 1913 Shawnee Invitational for Ladies in Pennsylvania. Mrs. Meechan's ball landed in the water and instead of taking the penalty and dropping a new ball, she chose to play it. Unfortunately, the ball moved downstream, costing her 40 strokes before the ball reached dry land. By then there was a thick wooded area between the ball and the green. It took a half an hour for Mrs. Meechan to put the ball in the hole.

- **20**: A new pro, Philippe Porquier made the history books by hitting the worst score in the history of the European Tour, on the par-5 13th hole at the 1978 French Open. He was doing fine until he neared the green, where he began to shank the ball. He finally completed the hole by compensating for the problem. He aimed his 18th shot at the next tee—and landed the ball 10 feet from the cup of the correct green.

- **18**: Willie Chisholm refused to take a penalty stroke in the 1919 U.S. Open when his shot landed on the rocks. He played the practically unplayable lie. With rock chips flying crazily, he pounded the ball 13 times to no avail before he changed tactics. He finally decided to chip the shot the other direction, landing on the green, where he proceeded to 3-putt for an 18.

- **15**: The shortest hole on the course stymied Hermann Tissies as he tallied the worst score in the modern history of the British Open. It was in 1950 that he hit his tee shot into a bunker, shanked the ball, and tried again and again to hit out of the sand for a mortifying 3-putt finish.

- **15**: The total wasn't too bad compared to the number of putts by Brian Barnes in the 1968 French Open. He wasn't able to sink his first few putts, so he turned to his hockey training and slapped and swatted the ball toward the hole. Twelve putts later he was relieved to hear the ball drop into the hole.

- **13**: This is a tie for the worst one-hole score in the Masters. Tommy Nakijima shot this on hole 13. He incurred penalty strokes for hitting both his tee and second shots into water hazards and got still more when he dropped his club into the water.

- **12**: Arnold Palmer was the defending U.S. Open Champion when he managed to get this high score on one hole of the Los Angeles Open in 1961, after hitting four balls out of bounds.

• **9**: The number isn't as bad as the three whiffs by pro golfer Al Chandler in the 1986 Senior Tournament Players Championship. The poor hole cost him between $5,000 and $6,000 in prize money in this close tournament, when he dropped from the top 10 to 32nd place.

Source: *The Golf Hall of Shame* by Bruce Nash and Allan Zullo

# YIPS

## *Pro Golfers Afflicted*

The 10th edition of *Merriam Webster's Collegiate Dictionary* defines *yips* as "a state of nervous tension affecting an athlete (such as a golfer) in the performance of a crucial action." While accurate, this overly generic definition fails to convey the sheer dread surrounding this mysterious ailment, which typically afflicts veteran golfers with a low handicap. Although the exact cause of the yips remains unknown, its symptoms are immediately recognizable on the putting green. Some golfers will literally jump back from the ball while putting; others suffer from a sudden, jerky twitch in the wrist that ruins their swing and undermines their confidence. The game that once brought them so much pleasure becomes a grim endurance test for golfers suffering a case of the yips.

Over time, many of golf's most celebrated players have endured their bouts with the yips. Some have attempted to overcome this condition by changing their grip or trying to reduce performance anxiety. Unfortunately, these remedies often provide only temporary relief from the yips. As Tommy Armour once quipped about this baffling condition, "Once you've had 'em, you've got 'em." He heads the alphabetical list of golfers who've reportedly suffered from the yips.

1. Tommy Armour

2. Ben Hogan

3. Bobby Jones

4. Bernhard Langer

5. Johnny Miller

6. Arnold Palmer

7. Sam Snead

8. Harry Vardon

9. Tom Watson

Source: dummies.com; *Merriam-Webster Collegiate Dictionary* (10th edition); from the Wednesday, February 25, 1998 issue of the Los Angeles Times. Used with permission.; *Dreaded words to golfers' ears: The Yips* by Thomas Bonk

# TOURNAMENTS

# In This Section

# AT&T PEBBLE BEACH NATIONAL PRO-AM

## All-Time Highest Winning Scores

With his 1964 victory at what was then known as the Bing Crosby National Pro-Am, Tony Lema made a triumphant return to form in the tournament. His prior claim to fame at Pebble Beach had been both painful and humiliating; in 1957, Lema had fallen down an 18-foot cliff during the competition. Winning the 1964 tournament was therefore all the sweeter for Lema, who finished second to Bruce Crampton the following year. Tragically, that would be Lema's swan song at the Crosby pro-am tournament. He and his young wife would die in a 1966 plane crash. Remembered today as "Champagne" Tony Lema (his drink of choice in victory), he ties for fifth place with Crampton, Jack Nicklaus, and Lon Hinkle on the list of highest winning scores since 1958.

| Player | Year | Score |
|---|---|---|
| 1. Doug Ford | 1962 | 286 |
| Ken Venturi | 1960 | 286 |
| 3. Billy Casper | 1963 | 285 |
| Johnny Pott | 1968 | 285 |
| 5. Bruce Crampton | 1965 | 284 |
| Lon Hinkle | 1979 | 284 |
| Tony Lema | 1964 | 284 |
| Jack Nicklaus | 1967 | 284 |
| Jack Nicklaus | 1972 | 284 |
| 10. George Archer | 1969 | 283 |
| Don Massengale | 1966 | 283 |
| Mark O'Meara | 1985 | 283 |

Source: http://golfonline.comfluent.net/cgi.pan?golfstats

# AT&T PEBBLE BEACH NATIONAL PRO-AM

## All-Time Lowest Winning Scores

One of the more star-studded events on the PGA Tour, the AT&T Pebble Beach National

Pro-Am is the latest incarnation of Bing Crosby's famed "clambake," which the Hollywood crooner launched in 1937. Sam Snead won that year and walked away with $500 for his efforts. By 2002, the total cash purse had crossed the $4 million mark; winner Matt Gogel, who had been the runner-up to Tiger Woods in 2000, pocketed $720,000.

While the AT&T Pebble Beach National Pro-Am has become one of the most popular and glitziest events on the tour, it remains an informal, friendly gathering where the pros share both the spotlight and the occasional umbrella with Hollywood stars. Heavy rains have cut the tournament short several times over the last few years. In fact the 1996 competition was canceled altogether because of the rain damage to the course. Weather permitting, these players have notched the lowest winning scores since the tournament was expanded to four rounds in 1958.

| Player | Year | Par | Final Score |
|---|---|---|---|
| 1. Mark O'Meara | 1997 | −20 | 268 |
| 2. Peter Jacobsen | 1995 | −17 | 271 |
| 3. Davis Love III | 2000 | −16 | 272 |
| 4. Tom Watson | 1977 | −14 | 273 |
| Tiger Woods | 2000 | −15 | 273 |
| 6. Paul Azinger | 1991 | −14 | 274 |
| Matt Gogel | 2002 | −14 | 274 |
| Jim Simons | 1982 | −14 | 274 |
| 9. Mark O'Meara | 1992 | −13 | 275 |
| 10. Brett Ogle | 1993 | −12 | 276 |

Source: golfonline.comfluent.net/cgi.pan?golfstats

# AT&T PEBBLE BEACH NATIONAL PRO-AM

## Most Victories

From the mid-eighties to the late nineties, Mark O'Meara all but owned the AT&T Pebble Beach National Pro-Am. In addition to winning the event five times in 12 years, O'Meara also set the record for the all-time lowest winning score with 268 in 1997; even more remarkably, he achieved that by shooting 67 all four rounds.

*Two-time winner of the AT&T Pebble Beach National Pro-Am Tom Watson.*

Another golfer whose record at the AT&T Pebble Beach National Pro-Am deserves mention is Johnny Miller, who has won the tournament three times, each time in a different decade.

Finally, the perseverance award goes to Dutch Harrison, whose double victories came 15 years apart, in 1939 and 1954.

| | Player | Number of Victories | Years |
|---|---|---|---|
| 1. | Mark O'Meara | 5 | 1985, 1989–1990, 1992, 1997 |
| 2. | Sam Snead | 4 | 1937-1938, 1941, 1950 |
| 3. | Johnny Miller | 3 | 1974, 1987, 1994 |
| | Jack Nicklaus | 3 | 1967, 1972–1973 |
| 5. | Dutch Harrison | 2 | 1939, 1954 |
| | Lloyd Mangrum | 2 | 1948, 1953 |
| | Cary Middlecoff | 2 | 1955–1956 |
| | Tom Watson | 2 | 1977–1978 |

Source: pgatour.com

# BOB HOPE CHRYSLER CLASSIC

## All-Time Lowest Winning Scores

At the 1960 Palm Springs Golf Classic (the precursor to the Bob Hope Chrysler Classic) Arnold Palmer took first place with a score of 338 in 90 holes of play. Palmer went on to win this tournament four times, more than any other player, and this remains his lowest winning score. Twenty-one years later, Bruce Lietzke broke Palmer's record with a score of 335. Since that tournament, players have set new scoring records at a breakneck pace. For the time being, here are the lowest winning scores in Bob Hope Chrysler Classic history.

| | Player | Score | Year |
|---|---|---|---|
| 1. | Joe Durant | 324 | 2001 |
| 2. | Tom Kite | 325 | 1993 |
| 3. | Jesper Parnevik | 331 | 2000 |
| | Corey Pavin | 331 | 1991 |
| 5. | Fred Couples | 332 | 1998 |
| 6. | Lanny Wadkins | 333 | 1985 |
| 7. | David Duval | 334 | 1999 |
| 8. | Scott Hoch | 334 | 1994 |
| 9. | Keith Fergus | 335 | 1983 |
| | Ed Fiori | 335 | 1982 |
| | Donnie Hammond | 335 | 1986 |
| | Bruce Lietzke | 335 | 1981 |
| | Kenny Perry | 335 | 1995 |

Source: bhcc.com

*In 1968, Arnold Palmer defeated Deane Beman in a sudden-death play-off to take the third of his four Bob Hope Chrysler Classic victories.*

# BOB HOPE CHRYSLER CLASSIC

## Sudden-Death Playoffs

In its 42-year history, the Bob Hope Chrysler Classic has been the scene for some of the most dramatic finishes on the PGA Tour. No less than 14 times, the most in PGA history, the tournament has gone into a sudden-death playoff to decide the winner. Although the Bob Hope Chrysler Classic isn't considered one of the more demanding PGA tournaments, it is one of the more lucrative: 2002 winner Phil Mickelson took home $720,000 from a total cash purse of $4 million.

**Tournament**

| Year | Players |
|------|---------|
| 1963 | Jack Nicklaus defeated Gary Player (18-hole playoff) |
| 1964 | Tommy Jacobs defeated Jimmy Demaret |
| 1966 | Doug Sanders defeated Arnold Palmer |
| 1968 | Arnold Palmer defeated Deane Beman |
| 1971 | Jack Nicklaus defeated Ray Floyd |
| 1982 | Ed Fiori defeated Tom Kite |
| 1983 | Keith Fergus defeated Rex Caldwell |
| 1984 | John Mahaffey defeated Jim Simons |
| 1985 | Lanny Wadkins defeated John Cook |
| 1989 | Steve Jones defeated Sandy Lyle and Paul Azinger |
| 1991 | Cory Pavin defeated Mark O'Meara |
| 1992 | John Cook defeated Gene Sauers, Mark O'Meara, Rick Fehr, and Tom Kite |
| 1998 | Fred Couples defeated Bruce Lietzke |
| 2002 | Phil Mickelson defeated David Berganio Jr. |

Source: bhcc.com

# BRITISH OPEN

## American Winners

With his victory at the 1922 British Open, American golfer Walter Hagen effectively ended the British golfers' domination of the tournament. The sun had finally set on the British Empire—at least temporarily, on the golf course at Sandwich anyway. Although Englishman A. G. Havers won the following year, Hagen and fellow American Bobby Jones owned the tournament for the rest of the decade. From 1926 to 1930, either Jones or Hagen took the winner's claret jug; their five-year winning streak stands as both an inspiration and challenge to all the American golfers who have since won the British Open.

In the 79 years since Hagen's victory, 20 American golfers have won 33 British Open titles. Here are all 20, in chronological order of victory.

1. **Walter Hagen**: 1922, 1924, 1928, 1929
2. **Bobby Jones**: 1926, 1927, 1930
3. **Gene Sarazen**: 1932
4. **Denny Shute**: 1933
5. **Sam Snead**: 1946
6. **Ben Hogan**: 1953
7. **Arnold Palmer**: 1961, 1962
8. **Tony Lema**: 1964
9. **Jack Nicklaus**: 1966, 1970, 1978
10. **Lee Trevino**: 1971, 1972
11. **Tom Weiskopf**: 1973
12. **Tom Watson**: 1975, 1977, 1980, 1982, 1983
13. **Johnny Miller**: 1976
14. **Bill Rogers**: 1981
15. **Mark Calcavecchia**: 1989
16. **John Daly**: 1995
17. **Justin Leonard**: 1997
18. **Mark O'Meara**: 1998
19. **Tiger Woods**: 2000
20. **David Duval**: 2001

Source: sportsillustrated.com

# BRITISH OPEN

## *The Courses*

Since the first British Open was held at Prestwick in 1860, fourteen of Great Britain's most venerable and challenging courses have hosted the tournament. Here are the courses, listed according to the number of times each has held this Grand Slam event.

| | | |
|---|---|---|
| 1. | St. Andrews | 26 times |
| 2. | Prestwick | 24 times |
| 3. | Muirfield | 14 times |
| 4. | Royal St. George's | 12 times |
| 5. | Hoylake | 10 times |
| 6. | Royal Lytham | 10 times |
| 7. | Royal Birkdale | 8 times |
| 8. | Royal Troon | 7 times |
| 9. | Musselbaugh | 6 times |
| 10. | Carnoustie | 6 times |
| 11. | Turnberry | 3 times |
| 12. | Royal Cinque Ports | 2 times |
| 13. | Royal Portrush | 1 time |
| | Princes | 1 time |

Source: opengolf.com

# BRITISH OPEN

## *First and Last Place Finishes, 1991–2001*

Of the 155 golfers eligible to compete in the 2001 British Open at Royal Lytham and St. Annes, only 70 survived the cut to compete for the coveted Claret Jug. When it was all over, David Duval emerged victorious, while his

**Seve Ballesteros (right, with Bernhard Langer) won the 1984 British Open at St. Andrews.**

predecessor, Tiger Woods, languished in a four-way tie for 25th place. Like all the majors, the British Open has been the scene of astonishing upsets, stunning defeats, and surprise turnarounds. Take the case of embattled pro John Daly. After finishing dead last in the 1992 and 1994 British Opens, Daly came back to win the 1995 Open. Daly's mercurial track record at the British Open is hardly unique; after all, this is a tournament where past champions have often failed to make the cut.

---

### First- and Last-Place Finishes, 1991–2001

1991: First Place:     Ian Baker-Finch. Score: 272 Par: –8
       Last Place:     Neal Briggs. Score: 300 Par: +20

1992: First Place:     Nick Faldo. Score: 272 Par: –12
       Last Place:     John Daly. Score: 298 Par: +14

1993: First Place:     Greg Norman. Score: 267 Par: –13
       Last Place:     Ricky Willison. Score: 293 Par: +13

1994: First Place:     Nick Price. Score: 268 Par: –12
       Last Place:     John Daly. Score: 292 Par: +12

1995: First Place:     John Daly. Score: 282 Par: –6
       Last Place:     Pedro Linhart. Score: 303 Par: +15

1996: First Place:     Tom Lehman. Score: 271 Par: –13
       Last Place:     Arnaud Langenaeken. Score: 298 Par: +14

1997: First Place:     Justin Leonard. Score: 272 Par: –12
       Last Place:     Billy Andrade. Score: 298 Par: +14

1998: First Place:     Mark O'Meara. Score: 280 Par: 0
       Last Place:     Dudley Hart. Score: 310 Par: +30

1999: First Place:     Paul Lawrie. Score: 290 Par: +6
       Last Place: (tie):   Martyn Thompson and Derrick Cooper. Score: 313 Par: +29

2000: First Place:     Tiger Woods. Score: 269 Par: –19
       Last Place: (tie):   Lionel Alexandre and Peter Senior. Score: 295 Par: +7

2001: First Place:     David Duval. Score: 274 Par: –10
       Last Place: (tie):   Sandy Lyle and Scott Henderson. Score: 301 Par: +17

Source: opengolf.com

---

# BRITISH OPEN

## *Highest Winning Scores*

Once a fourth round of play was introduced at the 1892 British Open, the winners' final scores regularly topped 300 for the next few years. J. H. Taylor, one of golf's "Great Triumvirate," won the 1894 tournament with a whopping final score of 326. That's 25 points higher than the last-place finishers in the 2001 Open, Sandy Lyle, and Scott Henderson. Ten

years would pass before 1904 champion Jack White became the first winner to score below 300, with a final score of 296 bringing him the silver Claret Jug.

Taylor's all-time highest winning score at the British Open further demonstrates how much the game has changed over the years.

| Player | Year | Score |
|---|---|---|
| 1.   J. H. Taylor | 1894 | 326 |
| 2.   W. Auchterlonie | 1893 | 322 |
|     J. H. Taylor | 1895 | 322 |
| 4.   James Braid | 1905 | 318 |
| 5.   Harry Vardon | 1896 | 316 |

| | | | |
|---|---|---|---|
| 6. | Harold Hilton | 1897 | 314 |
| 7. | Arnaud Massey | 1907 | 312 |
| 8. | Harry Vardon | 1899 | 310 |
| 9. | James Braid | 1901 | 309 |
| | J. H. Taylor | 1900 | 309 |

# BRITISH OPEN

## *Lowest Winning Scores*

For the first 32 years of the British Open, competitors played only three rounds of golf for the title. Beginning in 1892, a fourth round was added at Muirfield, which saw English amateur Harold Hilton win the Open with a final score of 305—a far cry from Greg Norman's all-time lowest score of 267 in the 1993 tournament. "The Shark" heads the list of British Open champions with the all-time lowest scores since 1892.

| Player | | Year | Score |
|---|---|---|---|
| 1. | Greg Norman | 1993 | 267 |
| 2. | Tom Watson | 1977 | 268 |
| | Nick Price | 1994 | 268 |
| 4. | Tiger Woods | 2000 | 269 |
| 5. | Nick Faldo | 1990 | 270 |
| 6. | Tom Lehman | 1996 | 271 |
| | Tom Watson | 1980 | 271 |
| 8. | Ian Baker-Finch | 1991 | 272 |
| | Nick Faldo | 1992 | 272 |
| | Justin Leonard | 1997 | 272 |

Source: opengolf.com

# BRITISH OPEN

## *Most Wins*

The oldest of the Grand Slam Tournaments, the British Open was first played at Prestwick on Scotland's west coast in 1860. Willie Park Sr. beat seven other local professionals in three rounds of golf on this 12-hole course to walk away with the red Moroccan leather Championship Belt. The silver Claret Jug wouldn't be given to the winner until 1872.

With four British Open victories, Park joins an elite group of golfers who've won the tournament multiple times. The list is headed by the game's "Great Triumvirate," who dominated golf from the turn of the century to the years preceding World War I. Only two Americans, Tom Watson and Walter Hagen, make the list with five and four victories, respectively.

1. **Harry Vardon**—6 wins: 1896, 1898 1899, 1903, 1911, 1914
2. **J. H. Taylor**—5 wins: 1894, 1895, 1900, 1909, 1913
   **James Braid**—5 wins: 1901, 1905, 1906, 1908, 1910
   **Peter Thomson**—5 wins: 1954, 1955, 1956, 1958, 1965
   **Tom Watson**—5 wins: 1975, 1977, 1980, 1982, 1983
6. **Willie Park Sr.**—4 wins: 1860, 1863, 866, 1875
   **Tom Morris Sr.**—4 wins: 1861, 1862, 1864, 1867
   **Tom Morris Jr.**—4 wins: 1868, 1869, 1870, 1872
   **Walter Hagen**—4 wins: 1922, 1924, 1928, 1929
   **Bobby Locke**—4 wins: 1949, 1950, 1952, 1957

Source: worldgolf.com; *The British Open: A History of Golf's Greatest Championship* by Francis Murray

# BRITISH OPEN

## *Playoffs, 1876–Present*

In the annals of golf, David Strath must qualify as one of the unluckiest. At the 1876 British Open at St. Andrews, Strath adamantly refused to face Bob Martin in a playoff for the title. While Martin's name was added to the famed Claret Jug, Strath retreated from golf and died three years later in Australia.

Since that controversial tournament, 15 British Opens have been decided in playoffs. One of the more dramatic moments occurred in 1970, when a bad putt forced Doug Sanders into an 18-hole playoff against Jack Nicklaus. Sanders more than held his own, only to watch Nicklaus hit his ball from the rough to within eight feet of the hole on the final green. The

Golden Bear sunk that final putt to win the British Open, his second of three victories.

1. **1883:** Willie Fernie defeats Bob Ferguson in 36 holes.

2. **1889:** Willie Park Jr. defeats Andrew Kirkaldy in 36 holes.

3. **1896:** Harry Vardon defeats J. H. Taylor in 36 holes.

4. **1911:** Harry Vardon wins by Arnaud Massy's concession at the 35th hole.

5. **1921:** Jack Hutchison defeats Roger Wethered in 36 holes.

6. **1933:** Denny Shute defeats Craig Wood in 36 holes.

7. **1949:** Bobby Locke defeats Harry Bradshaw in 36 holes.

8. **1958:** Peter Thomson defeats Dave Thomas in 36 holes.

9. **1963:** Bob Charles defeats Phil Rodgers in 36 holes.

10. **1970:** Jack Nicklaus defeats Doug Sanders in 18 holes.

11. **1975:** Tom Watson defeats Jack Newton in 18 holes.

12. **1989:** Mark Calcavecchia defeats Wayne Grady and Greg Norman in 4 holes.

13. **1995:** John Daly defeats Costantino Rocca in 4 holes.

14. **1998:** Mark O'Meara defeats Brian Watts in 4 holes.

15. **1999:** Paul Lawrie defeats Justin Leonard and Jean Van de Velde in 4 holes.

Source: opengolf.com

# CURTIS CUP

## Winners, 1980–2000

An enduring tribute to Harriot and Margaret Curtis, champion amateur golfers who donated the Paul Revere–designed silver championship bowl, the Curtis Cup was first played in 1932 at the Wentworth Golf Club in England. Eight amateur American women golfers, selected by the United States Golf Association faced their British counterparts in a two-day competition that consisted of three 36-hole foursomes and six 36-hole singles. Although the British team was led by Joyce Wethered, then widely considered the greatest woman golfer, the Americans triumphed, with a final score of 5 to the British team's 3.

Except for the years 1940–1946, the Curtis Cup has been held every two years since 1932. In 1964 the teams began playing three 18-hole foursomes and six 18-hole singles matches twice in two days. Several of the LPGA's leading players, including Louise Suggs, Nancy Lopez, Hollis Stacy, and Patty Sheehan, competed in the Curtis Cup before turning professional.

In terms of overall victories, the United States leads with 24 victories to Great Britain's 6. Here are the results of the Curtis Cup tournaments for the last 20 years:

**1980:** United States defeated Great Britain 13–5

**1982:** United States defeated Great Britain 14–3

**1984:** United States defeated Great Britain 9–8

**1986:** Great Britain defeated United States 13–5

**1988:** Great Britain defeated United States 11–7

**1990:** United States defeated Great Britain 14–4

**1992:** Great Britain defeated United States 10–8

**1994:** No winner; a draw at 9–9

**1996:** Great Britain defeated United States 11–6

**1998:** United States defeated Great Britain 10–8

**2000:** United States defeated Great Britain 10–8

Source: curtiscup.org

# EUROPEAN PGA TOUR

## All-Time Career Earnings

Although Colin Montgomerie has twice been the runner-up in the U.S. Open and once in the PGA Championship, the Scottish golfer has fared considerably better on the PGA European Tour, with 33 wins and five Ryder Cup appearances since 1987. This impressive string of victories, including three Volvo Scandinavian Masters, secures Montgomerie the number one position in all-time career earnings on the European PGA Tour. Spain's Seve Ballesteros and Fiji's Vijay Singh come in 13th and 14th, respectively.

Only one American golfer makes the top 100. Bob May, who lost the 2000 PGA Championship to Tiger Woods in a dramatic three-hole playoff, comes in 70th with 1,921,213 euros in earnings, which translates to approximately $1,659,351 by current exchange rates. All the earnings below have been converted from euros to dollars according to the 01/30/02 official rates published by the European Central Bank.

| Player | Country | Earnings |
|---|---|---|
| 1. Colin Montgomerie | Scotland | $11,686,962 |
| 2. Bernhard Langer | Germany | $8,664,495 |
| 3. Darren Clarke | Northern Ireland | $7,942,599 |
| 4. Ian Woosnam | Wales | $6,890,950 |
| 5. Lee Westwood | England | $6,640,954 |
| 6. Jose Maria Olazabal | Spain | $6,411,054 |
| 7. Retief Goosen | South Africa | $5,843,159 |
| 8. Ernie Els | South Africa | $5,797,869 |
| 9. Nick Faldo | England | $5,475,176 |
| 10. Miguel Angel Jimenez | Spain | $5,141,881 |

Source: http://fxtop.com, europeantour.com

# EUROPEAN PGA TOUR

## Most Career Starts

Still going strong on the European PGA Tour, Scottish golfer Sam Torrance turned pro at 16 in 1970. Ranked second by the European Tour Order of Merit in 1984 and 1995, Torrance has made the Ryder Cup team eight times and won the Scottish PGA Championship four times. He also holds the record for the most career starts on the European PGA Tour, with 655 as of this writing. He's trailed by Eamonn Darcy, who's probably best known here for ending the American team's chances for victory at the 1987 Ryder Cup.

| Player | Country | Career Starts |
|---|---|---|
| 1. Sam Torrance | Scotland | 655 |
| 2. Eamonn Darcy | Ireland | 598 |
| 3. Des Smyth | Ireland | 566 |
| 4. Carl Mason | England | 540 |
| 5. Mark James | England | 518 |
| 6. Roger Chapman | England | 512 |

Source: *Golf Magazine*, November 2001. Stats through 09/01/01

# GRAND SLAMS

## All-Time Victories

In his six years on the PGA Tour, Tiger Woods has blazed through an impressive number of long-standing records and become one of five career Grand Slam winners. Not only is he the youngest player to achieve a career Grand Slam, with all four majors under his belt by age 24, but Woods also pulled this off in just three years. To date, he has six victories at the majors. Whether or not he'll match or surpass Jack Nicklaus's record of 18 Grand Slam titles is a question best left to golf pundits and Las Vegas oddsmakers. Inevitably, another prodigy will emerge from the pack of contenders to topple Woods from his current place atop the world rankings. Yet even if Woods were to crash and burn in the coming years, his place alongside these golfing legends is already assured.

| *All-Time Grand Slam Victories* | | |
|---|---|---|
| **Player** | **Wins** | **Time Span** |
| **Jack Nicklaus** | **18 victories** | **24 years** |
| British Open | 3 titles | 1966, 1970, 1978 |
| Masters | 6 titles | 1963, 1965, 1966, 1972, 1975, 1986 |
| PGA Championship | 5 titles | 1963, 1971, 1973, 1975, 1980 |
| U.S. Open | 4 titles | 1962, 1967, 1972, 1980 |
| **Ben Hogan** | **9 victories** | **7 years** |
| British Open | 1 title | 1953 |
| Masters | 2 titles | 1951, 1953 |
| PGA Championship | 2 titles | 1946, 1948 |
| U.S. Open | 4 titles | 1948, 1950, 1951, 1953 |
| **Gary Player** | **9 victories** | **19 years** |
| British Open | 3 titles | 1959, 1968, 1974 |
| Masters | 3 titles | 1961, 1974, 1978 |
| PGA Championship | 2 titles | 1962, 1972 |
| U.S. Open | 1 title | 1965 |
| **Gene Sarazen** | **7 victories** | **13 years** |
| British Open | 1 title | 1932 |
| Masters | 1 title | 1935 |
| PGA Championship | 3 titles | 1922, 1923, 1933 |
| U.S. Open | 2 titles | 1922, 1932 |
| **Tiger Woods** | **6 victories** | **3 years** |
| British Open | 1 title | 2000 |
| Masters | 2 titles | 1997, 2001 |
| PGA Championship | 2 titles | 1999, 2000 |
| U.S. Open | 1 title | 2000 |

Source: *Philadelphia Inquirer* website: http://philainq.infi.net/

# GRAND SLAM

## *Pros Who Are One Victory Short of a Grand Slam*

To date, only five golfers—Ben Hogan, Jack Nicklaus, Gary Player, Gene Sarazen, and Tiger Woods—have completed a career grand slam by winning all four major tournaments. Some of the sport's all-time greats are conspicuously missing from that elite group, though it's certainly not for lack of trying. Although he numbers three Masters, three PGA Championships, and one British Open among his many victories, Sam Snead never won the U.S. Open during his lengthy career. The all-time leader in PGA victories, Snead came in second at the U.S. Open four times before retiring from the tour in 1965.

As the following list demonstrates, "Slammin' Sam" is one of a handful of golfers who are one victory shy of a career grand slam.

1. **Walter Hagen**: One of the sport's earliest celebrities, Hagen won the U.S. Open twice, the British Open four times and the PGA Championship five times. He ruled the sport during the twenties, but was past his prime when The Masters was launched in 1934 and never won that tournament.

2. **Byron Nelson**: Lord Byron has many victories to his credit, including the U.S. Open, and double wins at The Masters and PGA Championship. Victory at the British Open, however, eluded him during his career.

3. **Arnold Palmer**: The first golfer to cross the million dollar mark in earnings, Palmer was selected by the Associated Press as one of the greatest golfers of the 20th century. He won The Masters four times, the British Open twice, and the U.S. Open once. Unfortunately, he never hoisted the winner's trophy at the PGA Championship.

4. **Lee Trevino**: One of the great characters of golf, Trevino won three of the majors twice: the U.S. Open, the British Open, and the PGA Championship. He never had the chance to don the green winner's jacket at The Masters, however.

5. **Tom Watson**: A five-time winner of the British Open, Watson was hailed as the heir apparent to Nicklaus in the late seventies. While he also won The Masters twice and the U.S. Open once, Watson failed to win the PGA Championship before joining the SPGA in 1999.

Source: golfeurope.com; sandhillsonline.com

**Tom Watson has won all of the majors except for the PGA Championship.**

# GRAND SLAM

## *Purses and Prizes, Then and Now*

Willie Park Sr. must be spinning in his grave. The winner of the first British Open, Park earned *nothing* for his efforts at Prestwick. One hundred forty-one years later, 2001 British Open winner David Duval walked away with $858,000 from a total purse of $4.62 million; that translates to $214,500 for each round of golf.

The purses and the prize money in the Grand Slam tournaments have increased exponentially over the years, as the following comparisons demonstrate.

## British Open

**1860:** Willie Park Sr. was presented with the red Moroccan leather championship belt. There was no purse and no prize money at the first British Open.

**2001:** David Duval received $858,000 from a total purse of $4.62 million.

## U.S. Open

**1895:** Horace Rawlins received $150 from a total purse of $335. Rawlins also took home a gold medal for his first victory.

**2001:** Retief Goosen earned $900,000 from a total purse of $5 million.

## Masters

1934: Horton Smith won $1,500 of total purse of $5,000.

2001: Tiger Woods took home $1,008,000 from a total purse of $5.6 million, the richest of all the Grand Slam tournaments.

## PGA Championship

1916: Englishman Jim Barnes received $500 and a diamond medal from the $2,580 purse donated by Rodman Wanamaker.

2001: David Toms received $936,000 from a total purse of $5.2 million.

Source: opengolf.com; usopen.com; masters.org; pga.com

# GRAND SLAM

## Winners

It is golf's Holy Grail: the Grand Slam. In the history of professional golf, only five players

*Nicknamed the "Squire," Gene Sarazen was the first golfer to win all four major tournaments.*

have ever won the British Open, The Masters, the U.S. Open, and the PGA Championship. With his sweeping victory at the 2000 British Open, wunderkind Tiger Woods joined this elite circle of golfing greats:

1. **Gene Sarazen**: The first golfer to win golf's Grand Slam, Sarazen began in 1922, winning both the U.S. Open and the PGA Championship. Only 20 years old, he was the first golfer to take both titles in the same year. He won the British Open in 1932 and followed it with his legendary victory at the 1935 Masters, where Sarazen defied the odds to make a double-eagle on the 15th hole.

2. **Ben Hogan**: He may not have been known for his charm, but the taciturn Hogan won three of golf's Grand Slam tournaments in 1953: the U.S. Open, the British Open, and the PGA Championship. These victories, along with his win at the 1951 Masters, are all the more remarkable, since Hogan had nearly died in a devastating 1949 car accident and suffered chronic pain for the rest of his life.

3. **Gary Player**: The third golfer to win golf's Grand Slam, the South African–born Player won the 1959 British Open when he was 23—the tournament's youngest winner until 22-year-old Seve Ballesteros in 1979. Victory at The Masters came in 1961, with a one-stroke victory over favorite Arnold Palmer, followed by the 1962 PGA Championship. Three years later in 1965, Player became the first foreign golfer to win the U.S. Open.

4. **Jack Nicklaus**: In 1962, 22-year-old Nicklaus turned professional and promptly won the U.S. Open, besting Arnold Palmer. The following year he won both The Masters and the PGA Championship and then cinched the Grand Slam with his 1966 British Open victory.

5. **Tiger Woods**: Woods began with his now-legendary 1997 victory at The Masters, scoring an 18-under par 270, the lowest score in the tournament's history. The youngest player ever to win The Masters (he was 21) and the first African American to take home the coveted prize, Woods followed this with the 1999 PGA Champi-

onship and the 2000 U.S. Open, where he added more records to his resume: he was the first player to finish the 72 holes at double digits under par (12 under); his score of 272 was the lowest ever at the Open; and to top it off, his 15-stroke lead went down as the largest margin of victory in a major championship. His incredible streak continued at the 2000 British Open, with a 19-under par 269 win—a new tournament record. At 24, Woods also became the youngest pro golfer ever to win the Grand Slam.

Sources: golfonline.com; garyplayer.com; encarta.msn.com; abcnews.go.com

# LPGA CHAMPIONSHIP

## All-Time Highest Winning Scores

With today's LPGA pros regularly scoring between 280 and 270, these past LPGA Championship scores pale in comparison; for instance, Sandra Post's 1968 score of 294 would rank only as high as 66th in 2001. Of course, the nature of the game has changed considerably since these players won the LPGA Championship, due to advances in equipment and training methods.

| | | Tournament | | |
|---|---|---|---|---|
| **Player** | | **Year** | **Score** | **Par** |
| 1. | Sandra Post | 1968 | 294 | +2 |
| | Mickey Wright | 1963 | 294 | +10 |
| 3. | Kathy Ahern | 1972 | 293 | +1 |
| | Betsy Rawls | 1969 | 293 | +1 |
| 5. | Mickey Wright | 1960 | 292 | NA |
| 6. | Marlene Hagge | 1956 | 291 | NA |
| 7. | Sandra Haynie | 1974 | 288 | −4 |
| | Mary Mills | 1973 | 288 | −4 |
| | Betsy Rawls | 1959 | 288 | NA |
| | Kathy Whitworth | 1971 | 288 | −4* |
| | Mickey Wright | 1958 | 288 | NA |

*Whitworth also scored 288 to win the 1975 LPGA Championship.
Source: lpgatour.com

# LPGA CHAMPIONSHIP

## All-Time Lowest Winning Scores

A year after turning professional in 1977, Nancy Lopez won her first LPGA Championship title with a final score of 275. An extremely popular LPGA player who's long been a media favorite, Lopez has 48 victories to her credit, including three of the all-time lowest winning scores in LPGA Championship history—more than any other player on the list.

Number 1 on the list is Hall of Famer Betsy King, who was the first player in LPGA Tour history to hit four rounds in the sixties, scoring 68-66-67-66 to take the 1992 title with a final score of 267. Twenty-five years after turning pro in 1977, King remains a top competitor, with a recent victory in the Shoprite LPGA Classic in 2001.

| | | Tournament | | |
|---|---|---|---|---|
| **Player** | | **Year** | **Score** | **Par** |
| 1. | Betsy King | 1992 | 267 | −17 |
| 2. | Juli Inkster | 1999 | 268 | −16 |
| 3. | Karrie Webb | 2001 | 270 | −14 |
| 4. | Patty Sheehan | 1984 | 272 | −16 |
| 5. | Nancy Lopez | 1985 | 273 | −15 |
| | Se Ri Pak | 1998 | 273 | −11 |
| 7. | Nancy Lopez | 1989 | 274 | −14 |
| | Meg Mallon | 1991 | 274 | −10 |
| 9. | Jane Geddes | 1987 | 275 | −13 |
| | Nancy Lopez | 1978 | 275 | −13 |

Source: www.lpgatour.com

# LPGA CHAMPIONSHIP

## First and Last Place Finishes, 1991–2001

For the years 1991 to 2001, Dina Ammaccapane has the dubious distinction of finishing last in the LPGA Championship *twice*. Not to cast aspersions on Ms. Ammaccapane's golf game (she at least made the cut), but a strong finish in the LPGA Championship continues to elude her grasp, as it does so many other pro golfers.

Below are the first and last place finishers, 1991–2001.

| Year | Place | Player | Par | Rating |
|---|---|---|---|---|
| 1991 | First | Meg Mallon | 274 | −10 |
|  | Last | Diana Daugherty | 303 | +19 |
| 1992 | First | Betsy King | 267 | −17 |
|  | Last | (tie) Laura Baugh, Gail Graham and Kris Tschetter | 299 | +15 |
| 1993 | First | Patty Sheehan | 275 | −9 |
|  | Last | Dina Ammaccapane | 302 | +18 |
| 1994 | First | Laura Davies | 279 | −5 |
|  | Last | (tie) Sue Bianco and Laura Rinker Graham | 305 | +21 |
| 1995 | First | Kelly Robbins | 274 | −10 |
|  | Last | Lori Tatum | 300 | +16 |
| 1996 | First | Laura Davies | 213 | Even |
|  | Last | Michelle Estill | 232 | +19 |
| 1997 | First | Chris Johnson | 281 | −3 |
|  | Last | Vickie Odegard | 302 | +18 |
| 1998 | First | Se Ri Pak | 273 | −11 |
|  | Last | Heather Daly Donofrio | 298 | +14 |
| 1999 | First | Juli Inkster | 268 | −16 |
|  | Last | Karen Lunn | 299 | +15 |
| 2000 | First | Juli Inkster | 281 | −3 |
|  | Last | Dina Ammaccapane | 305 | +21 |
| 2001 | First | Karrie Webb | 270 | −14 |
|  | Last | Cathy Gerring | 301 | +17 |

Source: lpga.com

# LPGA CHAMPIONSHIP

## Players with Most Wins

Now sponsored by McDonald's, the LPGA Championship was first played in 1955, making it the second oldest of the LPGA "Majors." In the tournament's 46-year history, Mickey Wright reigns as the top winner with four victories under her belt. Named one of the top players of the 20th century by the Associated Press, Wright won 82 tournaments before retiring at age 34.

Here are the players who've won the LPGA Championship multiple times.

1. **Mickey Wright**
   4 victories: 1958, 1960, 1961, 1963
2. **Nancy Lopez**
   3 victories: 1978, 1985, 1989
   **Patty Sheehan**
   3 victories: 1983, 1984, 1993
   **Kathy Whitworth**
   3 victories: 1967, 1971, 1975
5. **Donna Caponi**
   2 victories: 1979, 1981
   **Laura Davies**
   2 victories: 1994, 1996
   **Sandra Haynie**
   2 victories: 1965, 1974
   **Julie Inkster**
   2 victories: 1999, 2000
   **Betsy Rawls**
   2 victories: 1959, 1969

Source: lpga.com

*Hall of Famer Nancy Lopez has won the LPGA Championship three times.*

# LPGA Grand Slam

## Career Winners

The tournaments that qualify as LPGA majors have changed since the tour's founding in 1950. The U.S. Women's Open has been the one constant, while others, such as the Titleholders Championship and the Western Open, haven't been considered majors since 1972 and 1967, respectively. Another, the du Maurier Classic, has since been replaced by the Weetabix Women's British Open. In addition to the Weetabix Women's British Open, three tournaments are currently designated LPGA majors: the U.S. Women's Open, the McDonald's LPGA Championship, and the Nabisco Dinah Shore Tournament. A prior victory at the du Maurier Classic, however, still counts towards the Career Grand Slam.

According to the LPGA, a player achieves the Career Grand Slam by winning each of the tournaments, that were classified as majors during their careers. For example, during Mickey Wright's LPGA heyday in the late fifties to early sixties, she needed to win the U.S. Women's Open, the LPGA Championship, the Titleholders, and the Western Open for the Career Grand Slam. Surprisingly, Hall of Famers Patty Berg, Kathy Whitworth, and Babe Zaharias never achieved a Career Grand Slam, though Zaharias came close with victories in the U.S. Women's Open, Titleholders, and the Western Open in 1950.

| Player | Date and Name of Major Victories |
|---|---|
| 1. **Pat Bradley** | 1980 du Maurier Classic, 1986 McDonald's LPGA Championship, 1986 Nabisco Dinah Shore, and the 1981 U.S. Women's Open. |
| 2. **Juli Inkster** | 1984 du Maurier Classic, 1999 McDonald's LPGA Championship, 1984 Nabisco Dinah Shore, and the 1999 U.S. Women's Open. |
| 3. **Louise Suggs** | 1957 LPGA Championship, 1954 Titleholders Championship, 1952 U.S. Women's Open, and the 1953 Western Open.* |
| 4. **Karrie Webb** | 1999 du Maurier Classic, 2001 McDonald's LPGA Championship, 2000 Nabisco Dinah Shore, and the 2000 U.S. Women's Open. |
| 5. **Mickey Wright** | 1958 LPGA Championship, 1961 Titleholders Championship, 1958 U.S. Women's Open, and the 1962 Western Open. |

*Suggs also won the U.S. Open, Titleholders, and Western Open prior to the LPGA's founding in 1950.
Source: lpga.com

# LPGA Grand Slam

## Players on the Verge

The LPGA counterpart to Tiger Woods, Aussie Karrie Webb has chalked up some records of her own since joining the tour in 1996. She became the first LPGA rookie to earn over $1 million in one year and later achieved a Career Grand Slam in less than two years—faster than any player in the tour's history.

Although Webb and archrival Annika Sorenstam generate the most media buzz on the tour, several other LPGA players are fast closing in on Career Grand Slams. They only need to win one more of the majors to join that select group, which so far includes four Hall of Famers: Pat Bradley, Juli Inkster, Louise Suggs, and Mickey Wright.

1. **Amy Alcott**: Alcott needs to win the McDonald's LPGA Championship, having already won the 1979 incarnation of the

du Maurier Classic (then called the Peter Jackson Classic,) the 1983 Nabisco Dinah Shore, and the 1980 U.S. Women's Open.

2. **Laura Davies**: Britisher Davies lacks a victory at the Nabisco Dinah Shore. Past victories include the 1996 du Maurier Classic, the 1994 McDonald's LPGA Championship, and the 1987 U.S. Women's Open, which she won before joining the LPGA.

3. **Betsy King**: The two-time winner of the Vare Trophy, King has yet to win the Weetabix Women's British Open. She previously won the 1992 Mazda LPGA Championship, the 1987 Nabisco Dinah Shore and the 1989 U.S. Women's Open.

4. **Meg Mallon**: Massachusetts-native Mallon has her sights on the Nabisco Dinah Shore. She has won the 2000 du Maurier, the 1991 Mazda LPGA Championship, and U.S. Women's Open.

5. **Se Ri Pak**: Victory at the Nabisco Dinah Shore has so far eluded Pak, who won both the McDonald's LPGA Championship and the U.S. Women's Open in 1998, her rookie year. Pak recently won the 2001 Weetabix Women's British Open.

6. **Patty Sheehan**: Elected to the Hall of Fame in 1993, Sheehan won the 1992 Weetabix Women's British Open before it was classified a major tournament. She won the 1983 LPGA Championship, the 1992 U. S. Women's Open, and the 1996 Nabisco Dinah Shore.

7. **Jan Stephenson**: On the LPGA Tour since 1976, Stephenson has never won the Nabisco Dinah Shore. Past victories include the 1981 Peter Jackson Classic (precursor to the du Maurier), the 1982 LPGA Championship, and the 1983 U.S. Women's Open.

Source: lpga.com

# LPGA GRAND SLAM

## *Purses and Prizes, Then and Now*

It's not just the PGA players taking home the big bucks—the purses and prize money of the LPGA majors have increased significantly since Patty Berg won the first U.S. Women's Open in 1946. Here's a rundown of the four LPGA Grand Slam tournaments.

### U.S. Women's Open

1946: Patty Berg received $5,600 from a total cash purse of $19,700.
2001: Karrie Webb earned $520,000 from a total cash purse of $2.9 million, the richest of the LPGA majors.

### LPGA Championship

1955: Beverly Hanson won $1,200 from a total cash purse of $6,000.
2001: Karrie Webb received $225,000 from a total cash purse of $1.5 million.

### Nabisco Championship

1972: Jane Blalock received $20,050 from a total cash purse of $110,000.
2001: Annika Sorenstam earned $225,000 from a total cash purse of $1.5 million.

### Weetabix Women's British Open

1994: Liselotte Neumann took home $80,325 from a total cash purse of $500,000.
2001: Se Ri Pak earned $221,650 from a total cash purse of $1.5 million.

Source: lpga.com

# MAJOR TOURNAMENTS

## *Come-From-Behind Wins*

In opera, they say it's never over until "the fat lady sings." And who hasn't watched at least one ballgame where a last minute Hail Mary pass or grand-slam home run in the bottom of the ninth changed the outcome of the game?

Since pro golfers play a game of relatively small numbers, they aren't able to make up four strokes in one hole like a bases-loaded home run can do for baseball. In fact, it's not uncommon for the final round leader to hold on and win it all. On the other hand, a few birdies have been known to boost a play's ranking, especially if his competitor runs into a streak of bogeys.

The 1960 U.S. Open saw one of the most dramatic comebacks when Arnold Palmer surged from 15th place and seven strokes back to win in the final round. Thirty years later at another U.S. Open, Hale Irwin improved his position from a lowly 20th place to 1st. Ironically, he only cut four strokes in his exciting win.

Here's a look at some of the biggest comebacks in The Masters, U.S. Open, British Open, and PGA Championship tournaments.

| Player | Strokes Behind | Players Passed |
|---|---|---|
| **THE MASTERS** | | |
| Art Wall, 1959 | 6 | 12 |
| Gary Player, 1978 | 7 | 9 |
| Jack Burke Jr., 1956 | 8 | 3 |
| Nick Faldo, 1989 | 5 | 8 |
| Jack Nicklaus, 1986 | 4 | 8 |
| Fuzzy Zoeller, 1979 | 6 | 3 |
| **U.S. OPEN** | | |
| Arnold Palmer, 1960 | 7 | 14 |
| Hale Irwin, 1990 | 4 | 19 |
| Johnny Miller, 1973 | 6 | 12 |
| Byron Nelson, 1939 | 5 | 11 |
| Johnny Farrell, 1928 | 5 | 5 |

| | | |
|---|---|---|
| **British Open** | | |
| Gary Player, 1959 | 4 | 12 |
| Tommy Armour, 1931 | 5 | 5 |
| Jock Hutchinson, 1921 | 4 | 7 |
| Denny Shute, 1933 | 3 | 9 |
| Willie Park Jr., 1887 | 5 | 3 |
| **PGA Championship** | | |
| Payne Stewart, 1989 | 6 | 10 |
| Bob Rosberg, 1959 | 6 | 5 |
| Steve Elkington, 1995 | 6 | 4 |
| Larry Wadkins, 1977 | 6 | 3 |

Source: *Golf Magazine*

# MAJOR TOURNAMENTS

## *Oldest and Youngest Winners*

With his 1997 victory at The Masters at the tender age of 21, Tiger Woods became that tournament's youngest winner, displacing previous record-holder Seve Ballesteros. Rightly hailed as a prodigy, Woods still isn't the youngest player ever to win one of the majors. That honor belongs to Tom Morris Jr., or Young Tom Morris as he was affectionately called, who won the British Open in 1868 while a mere 17. A legend in golf circles, Morris went on to win the British Open three more times before dying prematurely at age 24 in 1875.

Although he didn't join the pro circuit until he was nearly 30, Julius Boros went on to win both the U.S. Open and the PGA Championship, the latter when he was 48 years old. With that victory in 1968, Boros became the oldest player to win a major tournament.

| | | | |
|---|---|---|---|
| | **BRITISH OPEN** | | |
| **Oldest Winner:** Tom Morris Sr. | | 46 years old | 1867 |
| **Youngest Winner:** Tom Morris Jr. | | 17 years old | 1868 |
| | **THE MASTERS** | | |
| **Oldest Winner:** Jack Nicklaus | | 46 years old | 1986 |
| **Youngest Winner:** Tiger Woods | | 21 years old | 1997 |
| | **PGA CHAMPIONSHIP** | | |
| **Oldest Winner:** Julius Boros | | 48 years old | 1968 |
| **Youngest Winner:** Gene Sarazen | | 20 years old | 1922 |
| | **U.S. OPEN** | | |
| **Oldest Winner:** Hale Irwin | | 45 years old | 1990 |
| **Youngest Winner:** John McDermott | | 19 years old | 1911 |

Source: http://sportsillustrated.com

# Masters

## *All-Time Highest Winning Scores*

Sam Snead's 1954 win at The Masters is one of the most discussed in the tournament's history. He faced stiff competition from defending champion Ben Hogan and remarkable amateur Billy Joe Patton, who was the tournament's early leader, much to the surprise and chagrin of his fellow competitors. Patton's quest to become the first amateur to win The Masters ended on the back nine. As his fortunes faded, Snead's prevailed. He defeated Hogan in a playoff the next day to win a third Masters and set a tournament record for the all-time highest winning score which was matched by Jack Burke Jr. in 1956.

| Player | Year | Score |
|---|---|---|
| 1.　Jack Burke Jr. | 1956 | 289 |
| 　　Sam Snead | 1954 | 289 |
| 3.　Jack Nicklaus | 1966 | 288 |
| 4.　Jack Nicklaus | 1963 | 286 |
| 　　Jack Nicklaus | 1972 | 286 |
| 　　Sam Snead | 1952 | 286 |
| 7.　Larry Mize | 1987 | 285 |
| 　　Henry Picard | 1938 | 285 |
| 　　Horton Smith | 1936 | 285 |
| 10.　Arnold Palmer | 1958 | 284 |
| 　　Horton Smith | 1934 | 284 |
| 　　Craig Stadler | 1982 | 284 |
| 　　Art Wall | 1959 | 284 |

Source: sportsillustrated.cnn.com/augusta/ history/ news/2001/03/31/playoffs_1950 (reprint of article that originally appeared in *The Augusta Chronicle*: "Masters Playoffs—1950s Amateur's error opens door for vets" by John Boyette

# Masters

## *All-Time Lowest Winning Scores*

Tiger Woods' winning score of 270 at the 1997 Masters broke a record that had stood since 1965. That year, Jack Nicklaus defeated defending champion, Arnold Palmer and Gary Player to win his second Masters with a final score of 271 and 18 under par. Palmer and Player tied for second with 280, a decent finish that was nonetheless completely overshadowed by the Golden Bear's record-setting victory. Thirty-two years would pass before the game's reigning golden boy shot 70-66-65-69 to set a new all-time lowest winning score at The Masters.

| Player | Year | Score |
|---|---|---|
| 1.　Tiger Woods | 1997 | 270 |
| 2.　Raymond Floyd | 1976 | 271 |
| 　　Jack Nicklaus | 1965 | 271 |
| 4.　Tiger Woods | 2001 | 272 |
| 5.　Ben Crenshaw | 1995 | 274 |
| 　　Ben Hogan | 1953 | 274 |
| 7.　Seve Ballesteros | 1980 | 275 |
| 　　Fred Couples | 1992 | 275 |
| 9.　Nick Faldo | 1996 | 276 |
| 　　Jack Nicklaus | 1975 | 276 |
| 　　Arnold Palmer | 1964 | 276 |
| 　　Tom Watson | 1977 | 276 |

Source: masters.org; sportsillustrated.com

# Masters

## *First and Last Place Finishes, 1991–2001*

Every April since 1934, eligible golfers from all over the world have descended upon the Augusta National Golf Club to vie in The Masters. The competition for slots is fierce; at the 2001 Masters, only 46 of the starting field of 93 golfers survived the cut to compete for the celebrated green jacket. Such PGA stars past and present as Sergio Garcia, Davis Love III, and Jack Nicklaus were among the unlucky 47 who could only watch the rest of The Masters from the sidelines.

　　The margin between first and last place at The Masters is often substantial, if not downright embarrassing for the also-rans. Check out the following scores/par ratings for the first and last place finishers from 1991 to 2001, which is shown on the table on the opposite page.

### The Masters, First and Last Place, 1991–2001

| Year | Place | Golfer | Score | Par Rating |
|------|-------|--------|-------|------------|
| 1991 | 1st Place | Ian Woosnam | 277 | −11 |
|      | Last Place | Manny Zerman | 299 | 11+ |
| 1992 | 1st Place | Fred Couples | 275 | −13 |
|      | Last Place | Rodger Davis | 301 | 13+ |
| 1993 | 1st Place | Bernhard Langer | 277 | −11 |
|      | Last Place | Billy Andrade | 303 | 15+ |
| 1994 | 1st Place | Jose Maria Olazabal | 279 | −9 |
|      | Last Place | (tie) John Harris and Jeff Maggert | 305 | 17+ |
| 1995 | 1st Place | Ben Crenshaw | 274 | −14 |
|      | Last Place | Rick Fehr | 297 | 9+ |
| 1996 | 1st Place | Nick Faldo | 276 | −12 |
|      | Last Place | Alex Cejka | 302 | 14+ |
| 1997 | 1st Place | Tiger Woods | 270 | −18 |
|      | Last Place | Frank Nobilo | 303 | 15+ |
| 1998 | 1st Place | Mark O'Meara | 279 | −9 |
|      | Last Place | Gary Player | 302 | 14+ |
| 1999 | 1st Place | Jose Maria Olazabal | 280 | −8 |
|      | Last Place | Trevor Immelman | 305 | 7+ |
| 2000 | 1st Place | Vijay Singh | 278 | −10 |
|      | Last Place | Tommy Aaron | 313 | 25+ |
| 2001 | 1st Place | Tiger Woods | 272 | −16 |
|      | Last Place | Robert Allenby | 295 | 7+ |

Source: masters.org; sportsillustrated.com

# MASTERS

## Most Wins

One of the Grand Slam tournaments, The Masters is the creation of golfing legend Bobby Jones and businessman Clifford Roberts. Cofounders of the Augusta National Golf Club, the men approached the United States Golf Association in 1933 about hosting the U.S. Open. When the USGA declined their offer, Jones and Roberts promptly created the Augusta National Invitation Tournament, which was first played on March 22, 1934. Five years later, Roberts convinced Jones to rename the tournament "The Masters." Except for a three-year period during World War II (1943–1945), The Masters has been held the first week of April every year since 1940. The following players have donned the green winner's jacket the most times at The Masters.

1. Jack Nicklaus, 6 wins: 1963, 1965, 1966, 1972, 1975, 1986

2. Arnold Palmer, 4 wins: 1958, 1960, 1962, 1964

3. Four players tied for 3rd with 3 wins apiece:
   Jimmy Demaret: 1940, 1947, 1950
   Sam Snead: 1949, 1952, 1954
   Gary Player: 1961, 1974, 1978
   Nick Faldo: 1989, 1990, 1996

*In 1972, Jack Nicklaus won the fourth of his record six victories at The Masters.*

4. Eight players tied for 4<sup>th</sup> with 2 wins apiece:

Horton Smith: 1934, 1936
Byron Nelson: 1937, 1942
Ben Hogan: 1951, 1953
Tom Watson: 1977, 1981
Seve Ballesteros, 1980, 1983
Bernhard Langer: 1985, 1993
Ben Crenshaw: 1984, 1995
Jose Maria Olazabal: 1994, 1999

Source: www.masters.org

# MASTERS

## Oldest Winners

Jack Nicklaus's victory at the 1986 Masters is widely regarded as one of the Golden Bear's finest moments. Competing against many of the tour's hottest young players, the veteran edged out Greg Norman and Tom Kite with a final score of 279 to their second place tie of 280. With this win, 46-year-old Nicklaus heads the list of the oldest winners of the prestigious Masters.

| Player | Age | Year | Score |
|---|---|---|---|
| 1. Jack Nicklaus | 46 | 1986 | 279 |
| 2. Ben Crenshaw | 43 | 1995 | 274 |
| 3. Gary Player | 42 | 1978 | 277 |
| 4. Sam Snead | 41 | 1954 | 289 |
| Mark O'Meara | 41 | 1998 | 279 |
| 6. Ben Hogan | 40 | 1953 | 274 |
| 7. Jimmy Demaret | 39 | 1950 | 283 |
| Sam Snead | 39 | 1952 | 286 |
| Craig Wood | 39 | 1941 | 280 |
| Bob Goalby | 39 | 1968 | 277 |

Source: masters.org

# MASTERS

## Youngest Winners

By now, Tiger Woods' record-setting victory at the 1997 Masters has become legendary in the world of professional golf. At the tender age of 21, Woods donned the winner's green jacket with an all-time low score of 270; runner-up Tom Kite trailed far behind with a score of 282.

Just old enough to drink champagne legally for his first Masters win, Woods tops yet another list, this time of the youngest winners of The Masters.

| Player | | Age | Year | Score |
|---|---|---|---|---|
| 1. | Tiger Woods | 21 | 1997 | 270 |
| 2. | Seve Ballesteros | 23 | 1980 | 275 |
| | Jack Nicklaus | 23 | 1963 | 286 |
| 3. | Byron Nelson | 25 | 1937 | 283 |
| | Jack Nicklaus | 25 | 1965 | 271 |
| | Gary Player | 25 | 1961 | 280 |
| | Horton Smith | 25 | 1934 | 284 |
| | Tiger Woods | 25 | 2001 | 272 |
| 9. | Seve Ballesteros | 26 | 1983 | 280 |
| | Jack Nicklaus | 26 | 1966 | 286 |

Source: masters.org

# NABISCO CHAMPIONSHIP

## *All-Time Highest Winning Scores*

One of the most gifted women golfers of all time, Mickey Wright effectively curtailed her career after a 1969 win at the Bluegrass Invitational. She was only 34, but the stress of competing had taken its toll and she began making only sporadic appearances on the tour. Her last LPGA Tour victory came at the 1973 Colgate Dinah Shore (as it was then known,) which she won with a final score of 284; it was her 84th LPGA Tour victory.

Wright's winning score, recorded the year the tournament switched from three to four rounds of play, is one of the all-time highest winning scores in the tournament's 30 year history. Here are some other players with high winning scores.

*Tiger Woods, the youngest player ever to win The Masters.*

| Player | Year | Par | Final Score |
|---|---|---|---|
| 1. Jo Ann Prentice | 1974 | +1 | 289 |
| Kathy Whitworth | 1977 | +1 | 289 |
| 3. Nanci Bowen | 1995 | −3 | 285 |
| Judy Rankin | 1976 | −3 | 285 |
| 5. Helen Alfredsson | 1993 | −4 | 284 |
| Mickey Wright | 1973 | −4 | 284 |
| 7. Betsy King | 1987 | −5 | 283 |
| Betsy King | 1990 | −5 | 283 |
| Sandra Palmer | 1975 | −5 | 283 |
| Sandra Post | 1978 | −5 | 283 |

Source: lpgatour.com; wgv.com

# NABISCO CHAMPIONSHIP

## *All-Time Lowest Winning Scores*

A 1994 inductee in the World Golf Hall of Fame, Dinah Shore has long been considered one of the LPGA's biggest champions. In 1972 she lent her name to this tournament, which was then known as the Colgate Dinah Shore. Nabisco took over as the corporate sponsor in 1982; a year later, it officially became one of the tour's major competitions. Although it has been known as the Nabisco Championship since 2000, Shore's contributions have not been forgotten by the tournament's current organizers. The 18th hole at the Mission Hills Country Club has been designated the "Dinah Shore Walk of Champions."

*Dinah Shore's generous support of the LPGA earned her a spot in the World Golf Hall of Fame.*

In addition to drumming up national awareness of the LPGA, Shore also launched a tradition at this championship: the winner takes a victory swim in the lake off the 18th hole. Amy Alcott joined Shore for the first dip and others have happily followed.

| Player | Year | Par | Final Score |
|---|---|---|---|
| 1. Dottie Pepper | 1999 | –19 | 269 |
| 2. Amy Alcott | 1991 | –15 | 273 |
| 3. Amy Alcott | 1988 | –14 | 274 |
| Karrie Webb | 2000 | –14 | 274 |
| 5. Donna Caponi | 1980 | –13 | 275 |
| Alice Miller | 1985 | –13 | 275 |
| 7. Donna Andrews | 1994 | –12 | 276 |
| Betsy King | 1997 | –12 | 276 |
| Sandra Post | 1979 | –12 | 276 |
| 10. Nancy Lopez | 1981 | –11 | 277 |

Source: lpgatour.com

# NABISCO CHAMPIONSHIP

## *First and Last Place Finishes, 1991–2001*

Every player has his or her "off" day on the course—too bad it sometimes happens during a major tournament. For instance, in 1997, Betsy King won the Nabisco Championship with a final score of 276, one of the 10 lowest in the tournament's history. Five years later, she finished 74th, dead last. Although she has certainly rebounded from that defeat, King would probably like to forget her final score of 309, a whopping 21 over par.

### Nabisco Champions and Last Place Finishers, 1991–2001

| Year Rating | Place | Player | Score | Par |
|---|---|---|---|---|
| 1991 | 1st Place | Amy Alcott | 273 | −15 |
| | Last Place | Bonnie Lauer | 307 | +19 |
| 1992 | 1st Place | Dottie Pepper | 279 | −9 |
| | Last Place | Kate Rogerson | 308 | +20 |
| 1993 | 1st Place | Helen Alfredsson | 284 | −4 |
| | Last Place | (tie) Shirley Furlong and Vicki Goetze | 308 | +20 |
| 1994 | 1st Place | Donna Andrews | 276 | −12 |
| | Last Place | Ann Marie Palli | 307 | +19 |
| 1995 | 1st Place | Nanci Bowen | 285 | −3 |
| | Last Place | Jody Anschultz | 311 | +23 |
| 1996 | 1st Place | Patty Sheehan | 281 | −7 |
| | Last Place | (tie) JoAnne Carner and Cindy Mackey | 305 | +17 |
| 1997 | 1st Place | Betsy King | 276 | −12 |
| | Last Place | (tie) Amy Benz and Tracy Kerdyk | 305 | +17 |
| 1998 | 1st Place | Pat Hurst | 281 | −7 |
| | Last Place | Kris Monaghan | 311 | +23 |
| 1999 | 1st Place | Dottie Pepper | 269 | −19 |
| | Last Place | (tie) Sophie Gustafson and Val Skinner | 302 | +14 |
| 2000 | 1st Place | Karrie Webb | 274 | −14 |
| | Last Place | Dale Eggeling | 309 | +21 |
| 2001 | 1st Place | Annika Sorenstam | 281 | −7 |
| | Last Place | Betsy King | 309 | +21 |

Source: lpga.com

# PGA CHAMPIONSHIP

## *All-Time Top Moneymakers*

*Vijay Singh has made $768,034 from nine appearances in the PGA Championship.*

Even the last-place finisher at the PGA Championship would turn up his nose at what the tournament's first winner received in 1916: $500 and a diamond clip. At the 2001 PGA Championship, Colin Montgomerie was disqualified, but still took home $2,000, only slightly less than 1916's total cash purse.

Like the other majors, the PGA Championship can be lucrative for winners and also-rans alike. Just ask Greg Norman, Nick Faldo, and Justin Leonard, who've all racked up six-figure earnings without a single victory among them. Leonard just edges out five-time winner Jack Nicklaus, who's pocketed $434,788 in 36 PGA Championship appearances.

| Player | PGA Appearances | Earnings | PGA, Year(s) Won |
|---|---|---|---|
| 1. Tiger Woods | 4 | $1,612,625 | 1999, 2000 |
| 2. Nick Price | 17 | $1,009,011 | 1994 |
| 3. Steve Elkington | 11 | $828,978 | 1995 |
| 4. Vijay Singh | 9 | $768,034 | 1998 |
| 5. Davis Love III | 14 | $726,938 | 1997 |
| 6. Paul Azinger | 15 | $552,481 | 1993 |
| 7. Mark Brooks | 13 | $535,031 | 1996 |
| 8. Greg Norman | 19 | $522,329 | None to date |
| 9. Nick Faldo | 19 | $452,527 | None to date |
| 10. Justin Leonard | 6 | $436,917 | None to date |

Source: sportsillustrated.com

# PGA CHAMPIONSHIP

## *First and Last Place Finishes, 1991–2001*

When he coined the term "survival of the fittest" to describe evolution, Charles Darwin couldn't have known how applicable his theory would be to professional golf tournaments, particularly the majors. Unlike the animal kingdom, however, the food chain in golf exists in flux—how else to account for the poor showings made by defending champions over the years in the PGA Championship? If you want hard evidence, look to John Daly's 82nd place finish in 1992, the year after he won the title. His fall from grace is only of many examples of the fickle nature of the game.

| Year | Place | Golfer | Score | Par Rating |
|---|---|---|---|---|
| 1991 | 1st Place | John Daly | 276 | −12 |
| | Last Place | Kenny Perry | 300 | +12 |
| 1992 | 1st Place | Nick Price | 278 | −6 |
| | Last Place | Neal Lancaster | 300 | +23 |
| 1993 | 1st Place | Paul Azinger | 272 | −12 |
| | Last Place | John Adams | 296 | +12 |
| 1994 | 1st Place | Nick Price | 269 | −11 |
| | Last Place | (tie) Brian Henninger and Hajime Meshiai | 298 | +18 |
| 1995 | 1st Place | Steve Elkington | 267 | −17 |
| | Last Place | (tie) Wayne Defrancesco and Curt Byrum | 291 | +7 |
| 1996 | 1st Place | Mark Brooks | 277 | −11 |
| | Last Place | (tie) Howard Clark and John Reeves | 298 | +10 |
| 1997 | 1st Place | Davis Love III | 269 | −11 |
| | Last Place | (tie) Pete Jordan and Kevin Sutherland | 297 | +17 |
| 1998 | 1st Place | Vijay Singh | 271 | −9 |
| | Last Place | Tim Herron | 298 | +18 |
| 1999 | 1st Place | Tiger Woods | 277 | −11 |
| | Last Place | Fred Funk | 300 | +12 |
| 2000 | 1st Place | Tiger Woods | 270 | −18 |
| | Last Place | Frank Dobbs | 313 | +25 |
| 2001 | 1st Place | David Toms | 265 | −15 |
| | Last Place | Steve Pate | 294 | +14 |

Source: sportsillustrated.com

# PGA CHAMPIONSHIP

## Highest Winning Scores

What a difference a year makes. In 1987 Larry Nelson took the PGA Championship with a whopping final score of 287 at the PGA National in Palm Beach. Defending his title the following year at Oak Tree Golf Club, Nelson again scored 287 and finished in a tie for 38th place and considerably less prize money than the $150,000 he took home in 1987.

A two-time winner of the PGA Championship, Nelson tops the list of the tournament's highest winning scores since the PGA switched to the stroke play format in 1958. Coming in fourth is Julius Boros, whose 1968 victory at age 48 makes him the tournament's oldest winner.

| Player | Year | Par | Final Score |
|---|---|---|---|
| 1. Larry Nelson | 1987 | 287 | −1 |
| 2. Wayne Grady | 1990 | 282 | −6 |
| Lanny Wadkins | 1977 | 282 | −6 |
| 4. Julius Boros | 1968 | 281 | +1 |
| Jay Hebert | 1960 | 281 | +1 |
| Don January | 1967 | 281 | −7 |
| Jack Nicklaus | 1971 | 281 | −7 |
| Gary Player | 1972 | 281 | +1 |
| Dave Stockton | 1976 | 281 | +1 |
| 10. Al Geiberger | 1966 | 280 | Even |
| Dave Marr | 1965 | 280 | −4 |

Source: espn.go.com

# PGA CHAMPIONSHIP

## Lowest Winning Scores

And now for something completely different: a top-10 list *not* headed by Tiger Woods. Strange but true, Woods' winning score of 270 at the 2000 PGA Championship is the fifth lowest in the tournament's history since stroke play was implemented in 1958. Of course, Woods still makes history as one of only two players to win the PGA Championship twice in a row. His predecessor was Denny Shute, who won back-to-back victories in 1936 and 1937, the era of match play.

Among the players, Bobby Nichols stands out as a bona-fide giant killer. At the 1964 PGA Championship, Nichols defeated both Jack Nicklaus and Arnold Palmer for the title. This must have particularly stung 1963 winner Nicklaus, since the 1964 PGA Championship was played in his hometown of Columbus, Ohio. Nicklaus subsequently won the PGA Championship in 1971, 1973, 1975, and 1980.

| Player | Year | Par | Final Score |
|---|---|---|---|
| 1. David Toms | 2001 | 265 | −15 |
| 2. Steve Elkington | 1995 | 267 | −17 |
| 3. Davis Love III | 1997 | 269 | −11 |
| Nick Price | 1994 | 269 | −11 |
| 5. Tiger Woods | 2000 | 270 | −18 |
| 6. Bobby Nichols | 1964 | 271 | −9 |
| Vijay Singh | 1998 | 271 | −9 |
| 7. Paul Azinger | 1993 | 272 | −12 |
| Raymond Floyd | 1982 | 272 | −8 |
| David Graham | 1979 | 272 | −8 |
| Jeff Sluman | 1988 | 272 | −12 |

Source: espn.go.com, *The Golfer's Sourcebook* by Cliff Schrock

# PGA CHAMPIONSHIP

## *Most Wins*

Except for the years 1917, 1918, and 1943, when the event was canceled due to World Wars I and II, the PGA Championship has been held annually since 1916. The PGA itself was then just coming together, but the fledgling association was determined to sponsor a national tournament equal in prestige to the British Open. Now considered one of golf's "Grand Slam" tournaments, the PGA Championship has come a long way since department store tycoon Rodman Wanamaker gave a check for $2,580 and a trophy bearing his name to the tournament's first winner, Englishman Jim Barnes. Players today compete for a cash prize worth millions of dollars.

The following players have won the Wanamaker Trophy the most times in PGA Championship history.

1.  **Walter Hagen**, 5 times: 1921, 1924, 1925, 1926, 1927

*When he wasn't busy living it up, legendary bon vivant Walter Hagen chalked up a record five victories in the PGA Championship.*

**Jack Nicklaus**, 5 times: 1963, 1971, 1973, 1975, 1980

2.  **Gene Sarazen**, 3 times: 1922, 1923, 1933
    **Sam Snead**, 3 times: 1942, 1949, 1951

3.  **Jim Barnes**, 2 times: 1916, 1919
    **Leo Diegel**, 2 times: 1928, 1929
    **Paul Runyan**, 2 times: 1934, 1938
    **Denny Shute**, 2 times: 1936, 1937
    **Byron Nelson**, 2 times: 1940, 1945
    **Ben Hogan**, 2 times: 1946, 1948
    **Gary Player**, 2 times: 1962, 1972
    **Dave Stockton**, 2 times: 1970, 1976
    **Raymond Floyd**, 2 times: 1969, 1982
    **Lee Trevino**, 2 times: 1971, 1984
    **Larry Nelson**, 2 times: 1981, 1987
    **Nick Price**, 2 times: 1992, 1994
    **Tiger Woods**, 2 times: 1999, 2000

Source: usatoday.com

# PGA GRAND SLAM OF GOLF

## *Most Appearances*

With his fifth consecutive appearance (and fourth victory, another record) at the 2001 PGA Grand Slam of Golf, Tiger Woods tied Greg Norman for the most appearances at this popular match play event. Whether or not he makes it six for six in 2002, Woods will undoubtedly continue to be a major player at the PGA Grand Slam of Golf in years to come.

Of the players who've made multiple appearances at the PGA Grand Slam, 1979's cowinner, Andy North, had to wait the longest for his second appearance. Eleven years after sharing first place with Gary Player, North qualified for 1990's competition, which he also won—making him the only player to win both times he participated in the PGA Grand Slam of Golf.

| Player | Number of Appearances | Years |
|---|---|---|
| Greg Norman | 5 | 1986, 1988–1989, 1993–1994 |
| Tiger Woods | 5 | 1997–2001 |
| Jack Nicklaus | 3 | 1979, 1981, 1986 |
| Ian Baker-Finch | 2 | 1989, 1991 |

| | | |
|---|---|---|
| John Daly | 2 | 1991, 1995 |
| Ernie Els | 2 | 1994, 1997 |
| Nick Faldo | 2 | 1992, 1996 |
| Davis Love III | 2 | 1997, 1999 |
| Larry Nelson | 2 | 1982, 1988 |
| Andy North | 2 | 1979, 1990 |
| Nick Price | 2 | 1992, 1994 |
| Vijay Singh | 2 | 1998, 2000 |
| Craig Stadler | 2 | 1989–1990 |
| Payne Stewart | 2 | 1990–1991 |

Source: pga.com

# PGA GRAND SLAM OF GOLF

## *Winners*

In 1979 the winners of the four majors gathered at the Oak Hill Country Club in Rochester, New York, to compete in the first PGA Grand Slam of Golf. Despite the presence of such greats as Jack Nicklaus, Andy North, Gary Player, and John Mahaffey, the tournament generated little excitement; even the players themselves had a hard time summoning much enthusiasm during 18 holes of play, which ended in a tie between Player and North. With so little prize money at stake, they skipped the play-off and left it a draw.

Despite the inauspicious beginning, the PGA Grand Slam of Golf has gradually become a "must-see" event, due in part to the tournament's $1 million purse. Players who once routinely skipped the PGA Grand Slam of Golf now compete for the $400,000 first place prize money, and no one walks away empty-handed. The last-place finisher pockets $150,000 for two days work (the tournament has doubled from 18 to 36 holes in 1991). Tiger Woods (no surprise) has dominated the PGA Grand Slam in recent years, winning four consecutive victories from 1998 to 2001. Here are the winners and runners-up in order of finish for the PGA Grand Slam, which has been played annually since 1979, except for the years 1983–1985 and 1987.

**1979**: Winner: a tie between Gary Player and Andy North. Runners-up: Jack Nicklaus and John Mahaffey tied for second.

**1980**: Winner: Lanny Wadkins. Runners-up: Hale Irwin; David Graham and Fuzzy Zoeller tied for third.

**1981**: Winner: Lee Trevino. Runners-up: Tom Watson, Jack Nicklaus, and Seve Ballesteros.

**1982**: Winner: Bill Rogers. Runners-up: David Graham, Larry Nelson, and Tom Watson.

**1986**: Winner: Greg Norman. Runners-up: Fuzzy Zoeller; Jack Nicklaus, and Bob Tway tied for third.

**1988**: Winner: Larry Nelson. Runners-up: Larry Mize and Scott Simpson tied for second; Greg Norman.

**1989**: Winner: Curtis Strange. Runners-up: Craig Stadler, Ian Baker-Finch. and Greg Norman.

**1990**: Winner: Andy North. Runners-up: Craig Stadler and Payne Stewart. Curtis Strange withdrew from the tournament.

**1991**: Winner: Ian Woosnam. Runners-up: Ian Baker-Finch, Payne Stewart, and John Daly.

**1992**: Winner: Nick Price. Runners-up: Tom Kite, Fred Couples, and Nick Faldo.

**1993**: Winner: Greg Norman. Runners-up: Paul Azinger, Lee Janzen, and Bernhard Langer.

**1994**: Winner: Greg Norman. Runners-up: Nick Price, Ernie Els, and Jose Maria Olazabal.

**1995**: Winner: Ben Crenshaw. Runners-up: Steve Elkington and Cory Pavin tied for second; John Daly.

**1996**: Winner: Tom Lehman. Runners-up: Steve Jones, Nick Faldo, and Mark Brooks.

**1997**: Winner: Ernie Els. Runners-up: Tiger Woods, Davis Love III. and Justin Leonard.

**1998**: Winner: Tiger Woods. Runners-up: Vijay Singh, Lee Janzen. and Mark O'Meara.

**1999**: Winner: Tiger Woods. Runners-up: Davis Love III, Jose Maria Olazabal. and Paul Lawrie.

**2000**: Winner: Tiger Woods. Runners-up: Vijay Singh, Paul Azinger, and Tom Lehman.

**2001**: Winner: Tiger Woods. Runners-up: David Toms, Retief Goosen, and David Duval.

Sources: pga.com, *Golfwatching: A Viewer's Guide to the World of Golf* by George Peper

# PGA TOUR QUALIFYING TOURNAMENT

## *Notable Tournament Graduates*

Often referred to as "Q School," the PGA Tour Qualifying Tournament is universally acknowledged as a grueling, intense experience for both the entrants and observers. Since the first tournament was held in 1965, thousands of wannabe professional golfers have competed annually for their PGA eligibility card. On average, approximately 170 entrants survive the preliminary qualifying tournaments to compete in the final tournament, which sounds like the golfing equivalent of running a marathon barefoot on hot asphalt: six rounds, 108 holes. Is it any wonder that many exhausted golfers have been reduced to angry, frustrated tears by "Q School?"

At the end of the PGA Tour Qualifying Tournament, eligibility is given to the players who finish in the top 35 positions, including ties. The rest will qualify to play on the Buy.com Tour. Those players who earlier fell by the wayside sometimes return year after year, determined to make the grade. But even if they make it to the proverbial bitter end and earn PGA eligibility, success is not guaranteed. Some lose their eligibility and are forced to compete again. And for every Fuzzy Zoeller or Ben Crenshaw who went on to win the majors, scores of "Q School" graduates disappear from the PGA roster. Here are 20 of the more celebrated golfers who survived this PGA version of hazing.

| Golfer | Qualifying Year |
|---|---|
| 1.  Lee Elder | 1967 |
| 2.  Hale Irwin | 1968 |
| 3.  Johnny Miller | 1969 |
| 4.  Lanny Wadkins | 1971 |
| 5.  Tom Watson | 1971 |
| 6.  Tom Kite | 1972 |
| 7.  Ben Crenshaw | 1973 |
| 8.  Fuzzy Zoeller | 1974 |
| 9.  Calvin Peete | 1975 |
| 10.  Peter Jacobsen | 1976 |
| 11.  Curtis Strange | 1976 |
| 12.  Craig Stadler | 1976 |
| 13.  Mark O'Meara | 1980 |
| 14.  Fred Couples | 1980 |
| 15.  Payne Stewart | 1981 |
| 16.  Paul Azinger | 1981 |
| 17.  Nick Price | 1982 |
| 18.  Davis Love III | 1985 |
| 19.  Lee Janzen | 1989 |
| 20.  Jesper Parvenik | 1993 |

Source: *Q School Confidential* by David Gould

# PRESIDENTS CUP

Seen by some as the "poor man's Ryder Cup," the Presidents Cup has nonetheless overcome initial resistance to emerge as an often exciting international team match-play competition. The top 12 players from the United States square off against a team comprised of 12 players from outside Europe; no European players eligible for the Ryder Cup can participate in this series of 32 matches, which consists of ten foursomes, ten four-ball matches, and 12 singles matches. If the teams are even in points at the end of the singles matches, players from each team compete in a sudden-death playoff to determine the winner.

First played in 1994 at the Robert Trent Jones Golf Club in Gainesville, Virginia, the Presidents Cup offers no prize money to the winners. All revenues generated by the competition are instead donated to various charities. Former Presidents Gerald Ford, George Bush, and Bill Clinton have all served as honorary chairman of the biennial competition, which is never played the same year as the Ryder Cup.

Here are the results of the Presidents Cup tournaments since 1994:

**1994**: The United States team, led by captain Hale Irwin, defeated the international team with a final score of 20–12. Aussie David Graham captained the international team.

**1996**: Arnold Palmer led the United States team to a second victory over the international team headed by Aussie Peter Thomson, 16–15.

**1998**: Peter Thomson returned to lead the victorious international team, which defeated Jack Nicklaus and his teammates with a final score of 20–11.

**2000**: The United States regained the title under the leadership of Ken Venturi, whose team finished the competition with a score of 21 to the international team's 10. Peter Thomson again captained the international team.

Source: presidentscup.com

# RYDER CUP

After 75 years, the Ryder Cup may finally be on the verge of shedding its effete image and blossoming into a truly classic sporting event that will generate excitement instead of yawns.

Founded in 1927, and named after British seed merchant Samuel Ryder, for its first four decades the event pitted 12-member teams from the United States and Britain against each other in match play. The U.S. dominated, winning 16 of the first 19 cups. Irish players were added to strengthen the British team in 1973, but it didn't help. The Yanks kept winning.

Finally, in 1979 an all-European team was assembled to oppose the U.S. That change made all the difference. Suddenly, the cup became competitive. Going into the 1999 Ryder Cup at Brookline, Massachusetts, the teams were tied at five victories each, and public interest was mounting, undoubtedly spurred by Tiger Woods playing for the U.S. team.

Entering the final day of 1999 Cup play, the Americans were trailing badly. But U.S.

Captain Ben Crenshaw vowed that his team would fight on and pull victory from the abyss. And lightning struck! Stroke by stroke, match by match, U.S. golfers squeezed out victories. As the final foursome reached the 17th green, few in the gallery thought that Justin Leonard had a prayer of sinking a difficult 45-foot birdie putt. But Leonard struck the putt firmly, and the ball traced a twisting path to the cup and fell in. That moment sealed one of the most dramatic comebacks in sports history, and the world watched on television as normally reserved professional golfers celebrated jubilantly, like a team of college kids who had won the NCAA basketball championship. That day the Ryder Cup came of age, giving golf fans a memory for the ages and an event to anticipate in years to come.

# The Ryder Cup Matches

| | |
|---|---|
| 2001 | Postponed by terrorist attacks; rescheduled for September 2002 |
| 1999 | USA 14$\frac{1}{2}$–13$\frac{1}{2}$ |
| 1997 | Europe 14$\frac{1}{2}$–13$\frac{1}{2}$ |
| 1995 | Europe 14$\frac{1}{2}$–13$\frac{1}{2}$ |
| 1993 | USA 15–13 |
| 1991 | USA 14$\frac{1}{2}$–13$\frac{1}{2}$ |
| 1989 | Draw 14–14 |
| 1987 | Europe 15–13 |
| 1985 | Europe 16$\frac{1}{2}$–11$\frac{1}{2}$ |
| 1983 | USA 14$\frac{1}{2}$–13$\frac{1}{2}$ |
| 1981 | USA 18$\frac{1}{2}$–9$\frac{1}{2}$ |
| 1979 | USA 17–11 |

Source: *ESPN Sports Almanac*; rydercup.com

# RYDER CUP

## *Best Two-Man Teams, 1979–1999*

The first two days of the Ryder Cup competition pit two-man teams from the United States and Europe in a series of morning foursomes and afternoon four-play matches. This opening section of the biennial event has featured some memorable pairings over the years. At the 1993 Ryder Cup, for example, Americans Paul Azinger and Fred Couples played Nick Faldo and Colin Montgomerie in a marathon match that lasted well past sunset, forcing the players to quit for the day and reconvene the next morning to finish!

In the last 20 years of the Ryder Cup, five two-man teams deserve special mention for their excellent records. Each of these records reflects a team's list of victories, losses and halved matches for that year's Ryder Cup.

| Players | Team | Year | Wins | Losses | Halved Matches |
|---|---|---|---|---|---|
| 1. Lanny Wadkins/ Larry Nelson | United States | 1979 | 4 | 0 | 0 |
| 2. Nick Faldo/ Ian Woosnam | Europe | 1987 | 3 | 0 | 1 |
| 3. Seve Ballesteros/ Jose Maria Olazabal | Europe | 1989 | 3 | 0 | 1 |
| 4. Seve Ballesteros/ Jose Maria Olazabal | Europe | 1991 | 3 | 0 | 1 |
| 5. Sergio Garcia/ Jesper Parnevik | Europe | 1999 | 3 | 0 | 1 |

Source: *Golf Magazine*, October 2001 issue

**Viva España! Sergio Garcia in the 1999 Ryder Cup competition.**

# RYDER CUP

## Botched Shots

"So close, and yet so far" sums up that awful moment when a golfer's lead seemingly vanishes in the wake of one botched shot. In the history of the Ryder Cup competition, many players have bogeyed or missed a crucial putt in the clinch. Here are some of those moments that the players involved would like to forget, in chronological order.

1. **1933: Denny Shute** 3-putted for a double bogey on the 18th hole to lose to Syd Easterbrook.

2. **1953: Sam Snead** lost five holes, bogeying on four of them, and dropped the match against Harry Weetman.

3. **1953: Peter Alliss** duffed a chip on the 18th hole and then missed a 3-footer for a bogey 6.

4. **1983: Bernard Gallacher** double-bogeyed on the 17th hole and lost to Tom Watson.

5. **1989: Payne Stewart** sent his tee shot into the water's edge on the 18th hole and had to take two swings to get it free.

6. **1991: Mark Calcavecchia** bogeyed and triple-bogeyed on the last four holes to lose his advantage.

7. **1991: Bernhard Langer** missed his six-foot putt on the final green and effectively ended Europe's chances of winning the Ryder Cup.

8. **1995: Curtis Strange** bogeyed the last three holes, giving the European team the necessary break to win the competition.

Source: *Golf* Magazine, 10/01 issue

# RYDER CUP

## *European Team Captains*

The European team for the first Ryder Cup competition in 1927 got off to a shaky start. Original team captain Abe Mitchell was stricken with appendicitis and replaced by Ted Ray. The team was undermanned, forcing the organizers to recruit Channel Islands golf pro Herbert Jolly at the very last moment. Arriving in New York City four days after the rest of the team, Jolly raced to join them in Worcester, Massachusetts, where they lost to the Americans.

The Europeans later regrouped from that loss to win the 1929 Ryder Cup under the leadership of George Duncan. Some of Europe's finest players have since captained the team, which has won the Ryder Cup seven times. Here are all the captains of the European Ryder Cup teams in chronological order.

**Ted Ray** 1927

**George Duncan** 1929

**Charles Whitcombe** 1931, 1935, 1937, 1949

**J. H. Taylor** 1933

**Henry Cotton** 1947, 1953

**Arthur Lacey** 1951

**Dai Rees** 1955, 1957, 1959, 1961, 1967

**John Fallow** 1963

**Henry Weetman** 1965

**Eric Brown** 1969, 1971

**Bernard Hunt** 1973, 1975

**Brian Huggett** 1977

**John Jacobs** 1979, 1981

**Tony Jacklin** 1983, 1985, 1987, 1989

**Bernard Gallacher** 1991, 1993, 1995

**Seve Ballesteros** 1997

**Mark James** 1999

**Sam Torrance** 2001*

*Due to the events of 09/11/01, The 2001 Ryder Cup was postponed until 2002. Source: rydercup.com

# RYDER CUP

## *U.S. Team Captains*

At the 1927 Ryder Cup competition, United States team captain Walter Hagen led his teammates to victory, winning nine matches to the British team's two. The charismatic Hagen served as captain of the U.S. Ryder Cup team five more times before the outbreak of World War II interrupted his tenure. Once the Ryder Cup resumed play in 1947, such notables as Ben Hogan, Sam Snead, and Tom Watson all captained the United States team. Here are all the captains of the United States Ryder Cup teams, in chronological order.

**Walter Hagen** 1927, 1929, 1931, 1933, 1935, 1937

**Ben Hogan** 1947, 1949, 1967

**Sam Snead** 1951, 1959, 1969

**Lloyd Mangrum** 1953

**Chick Harbert** 1955

**Jack Burke Jr.** 1957, 1973

**Jerry Barber** 1961

**Arnold Palmer** 1963, 1975

**Byron Nelson** 1965

**Jay Hebert** 1971

**Dow Finsterwald** 1977

Billy Casper  1979

Dave Marr  1981

Jack Nicklaus  1983, 1987

Lee Trevino  1985

Ray Floyd  1989

Dave Stockton  1991

Tom Watson  1993

Lanny Wadkins  1995

Tom Kite  1997

Ben Crenshaw  1999

Curtis Strange  2001*

*Due to the events of 09/11/01, the 2001 Ryder Cup was postponed until 2002.
Source: rydercup.com

**England's Nick Faldo made the first of his 11 Ryder Cup appearances in 1977.**

# RYDER CUP

## Players with Most Appearances

Except for the years 1939–1945, teams from the United States and Europe have competed in the Ryder Cup every other year since the first competition was held in Worcester, Massachusetts, in 1927. The United States has dominated the Ryder Cup, winning 24 of the 33 competitions and battling Europe to a tie in 1969 and 1989.

In the Ryder Cup's history, many of golf's greatest players have competed for their respective countries. Here are the players who've chalked up the most Ryder Cup appearancees for both the United States and Europe.

### United States

| Golfer | Appearances |
| --- | --- |
| 1. Billy Casper | 9 |
| 2. Ray Floyd | 8 |
| 3. Lanny Wadkins | 8 |
| 4. Tom Kite | 7 |
| 5. Gene Littler | 7 |
| 6. Sam Snead | 7 |

### Europe

| Golfer | Appearances |
| --- | --- |
| 1. Nick Faldo | 11 |
| 2. Christy O' Connor Sr. | 10 |
| 3. Bernhard Langer | 9 |
| 4. Dai Rees | 9 |

Source: "Ryder Cup By Facts and Oddities," compiled by Sal Johnson and David Barrett, *Golf Magazine*

# SENIOR SKINS GAME

## Winners, 1988–2002

Five years after the PGA launched the Skins Game, the SPGA followed suit in 1988. Longtime crowd favorite Chi Chi Rodriguez won the first two Senior Skins competitions. From 1994 through 1998, Raymond Floyd dominated the field, winning this unofficial SPGA event five consecutive times. His streak ended in 1999, when Hale Irwin took the first of his three Senior Skins victories to date. On the opposite page is a list of SPGA Skins games winners.

### Senior Skins Game Winners, 1988–2002

| Player | Earnings | Year |
|---|---|---|
| 1.  Chi Chi Rodriguez | $40,000 | 1988 |
| 2.  Chi Chi Rodriguez | $90,000 | 1989 |
| 3.  Arnold Palmer | $140,000 | 1990 |
| 4.  Jack Nicklaus | $125,000 | 1991 |
| 5.  Arnold Palmer | $120,000 | 1992 |
| 6.  Arnold Palmer | $145,000 | 1993 |
| 7.  Raymond Floyd | $115,000 | 1994 |
| 8.  Raymond Floyd | $120,000 | 1995 |
| 9.  Raymond Floyd | $180,000 | 1996 |
| 10.  Raymond Floyd | $170,000 | 1997 |
| 11.  Raymond Floyd | $210,000 | 1998 |
| 12.  Hale Irwin | $160,000 | 1999 |
| 13.  Gary Player | $210,000 | 2000 |
| 14.  Hale Irwin | $260,000 | 2001 |
| 15.  Hale Irwin | $450,000 | 2002 |

Source: pgatour.com

# SKINS GAME

## Winners, 1983–2001

One of the more popular, if unofficial PGA, tournaments is the annual Skins Game, which has been drawing big television audiences since its debut in 1983. Created by Don Ohlmeyer and Barry Frank, the Skins Game pits four of the best players in a hole-by-hole competition for big bucks. Whoever wins a hole gets that hole's cash value. In the event of a tie, no one wins and the stakes increase at the next hole. With each hole worth thousands of dollars, the competition has gotten pretty cut-throat since Jack Nicklaus, Arnold Palmer, Gary Player, and Tom Watson met for the first Skins Game.

In 2001 the tournament's organizers decided to shake things up a bit. Even if a player won a hole, he wouldn't get to keep the money unless he won or halved the next hole. Under this new rule, a player could therefore only keep the money free and clear if he won the 18th hole. Playing against Tiger Woods, Jesper Parvenik, and defending champion Colin Montgomerie, Greg Norman ultimately won the Skins and $1 million, the largest purse in the tournament's history.

| Year | Player | Winnings |
|---|---|---|
| 1983 | Gary Player | $170,000 |
| 1984 | Jack Nicklaus | $240,000 |
| 1985 | Fuzzy Zoeller | $255,000 |
| 1986 | Fuzzy Zoeller | $370,000 |
| 1987 | Lee Trevino | $310,000 |
| 1988 | Raymond Floyd | $290,000 |
| 1989 | Curtis Strange | $265,000 |
| 1990 | Curtis Strange | $225,000 |
| 1991 | Payne Stewart | $260,000 |
| 1992 | Payne Stewart | $220,000 |
| 1993 | Payne Stewart | $280,000 |
| 1994 | Tom Watson | $210,000 |
| 1995 | Fred Couples | $270,000 |
| 1996 | Fred Couples | $280,000 |
| 1997 | Tom Lehman | $300,000 |
| 1998 | Mark O'Meara | $430,000 |
| 1999 | Fred Couples | $635,000 |
| 2000 | Colin Montgomerie | $415,000 |
| 2001 | Greg Norman | $1,000,000 |

Source: pgatour.com; sportsillustrated.com

# SOLHEIM CUP

## Results from 1990–2000

Named after the competition's late sponsor Karsten Solheim, the inventor of Ping golf clubs, the Solheim Cup is a biennial match-

**Kathy Whitworth, captain of the U.S. team for the inaugural Solheim Cup.**

**1998**: Making it three in a row, captain Judy Rankin and the United States team defeated Europe 16–12, in Muirfield Village, Ohio.

**2000**: Europe came back under captain Dale Reid to triumph over the United States 14–11, in Loch Lomond, Scotland.

Source: golftoday.co.uk

# SPECIALTY TOURNAMENTS

## *Unusual Play*

If you thought putt-putt golf was American sports kitsch at its best—or worst, depending on your sensibility—then get a load of these tournaments. With cheerful disregard for the venerable rules of The Royal and Ancient Golf Club, these tournaments' organizers have come up with some "novel" approaches to the game. In an inexplicable oversight, the PGA hasn't added any of these to the current tour; the Senior Citizen's Shoot-Your-Age event is certainly a natural for the SPGA.

1. **Senior Citizen's Shoot-Your-Age** event (Los Angeles): This par-3 event challenges seniors to shoot their age or less.

2. **April Foolish Open** (Mims, Florida): Temporary hazards such as ceramic frogs and clotheslines of laundry tied to a tree pose challenges to the golfers.

3. **Hawaiian Holiday Masters** (Honokaa, Hawaii): Golfers use Macadamia nuts coated with latex for balls, hitting them with rubber-padded clubs.

4. **Stop Watch Golf** (Walla Walla, Washington): Teams play a round of golf relay-style as fast as possible. The first event in 1949 was played in seven minutes, 24 seconds by 20 golfers, with a score of 41 for nine holes. Former President Bush, known to be a speedy golfer, would make a fine honorary chairman for this tournament.

play competition between teams of women professional golfers from the United States and Europe. Every other September since 1990, teams of 12 players have competed in the three-day event, which consists of eight foursome matches on the first day, six four-ball matches on the second, and twelve single matches on the last. Here are the results for the Solheim Cup through the 2000 competition:

**1990**: The United States team, led by Kathy Whitworth, defeated the European team 11–4, in Lake Nona, Florida.

**1992**: European captain Mickey Walker led her team to victory over the United States, 11–4, in Edinburgh.

**1994**: The United States team bounced back under captain JoAnne Carner, beating Europe 13–7, in Greenbrier, West Virginia.

**1996**: Victorious again, the United States team led by Judy Rankin defeated Europe 17–11, in Wales.

5. **Nitelite Golf Tournaments** (various locations): Players play in the dark using glow-in-the-dark balls, tees, putters, necklaces, and bracelets.

Source: *Offbeat Golf* by Loeffelbein

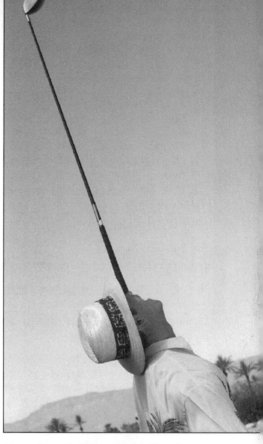

No matter what your talent, there's probably a golf tournament for you.

# SPECIALTY TOURNAMENTS PART II

Truth is truly stranger than fiction when it comes to these actual golf tournaments, which run the gamut from downright silly to serious. Catering to some extremely narrow golf demographics, these tournaments nonetheless demonstrate how the game's appeal transcends all barriers. Even if you're doing time behind bars, you can still play golf; just don't expect any lucrative endorsements coming your way if you win the Pros and Cons Invitational.

So if you don't make it through the demanding PGA Qualifying School, relax. As long as you meet their specific entry requirements, you can always compete in tournaments for . . .

1. **Bald-headed men** in Clarkston, Washington.

2. **Public links players** in Hershey, Pennsylvania.

3. **Vietnam POW-MIA bracelet wearers** in Corpus Christi, Texas.

4. **Hoboes** in Shawnee, Oklahoma.

5. **Obese men** in Baton Rouge, Louisiana.

6. **Maitre d's** in Las Vegas, Nevada.

7. **Blind players** in Fenton, Michigan.

8. **Penitentiary inmates** and touring pros in the Pros and Cons Invitational.

9. **Bionic Invitational**—those who have had a joint surgically replaced—in Aiken, South Carolina.

Source: *Offbeat Golf* by Loeffelbein

# SPGA CHAMPIONSHIP

## *Highest Winning Scores Since 1958*

If the late Gene Sarazen had been around to shoot 288 (his 1958 winning score) in the 2001 Senior PGA Championship, he would've only tied for 15th place, 14 points higher than winner Tom Watson, whose 274 brought him the coveted Bourne Trophy *and* $360,000 in prize money.

In the years since the Senior PGA Championship added a fourth round, the winners' scores have fluctuated wildly. Although Sam Snead's score of 290 in the 1970 tournament still ranks as the highest winning score, he's certainly in good company, as the following list demonstrates.

| Player | Year | Score |
|--------|------|-------|
| 1. Sam Snead | 1970 | 290 |
| 2. Jack Fleck | 1979 | 289 |
| Arnold Palmer | 1980 | 289 |
| 4. Don January | 1982 | 288 |
| Gene Sarazen | 1958 | 288 |
| 6. Freddie Haas | 1966 | 286 |
| Joe Jimenez | 1978 | 286 |
| Sam Snead | 1972 | 286 |
| Peter Thomson | 1984 | 286 |
| 10. Julius Boros | 1971 | 285 |

Source: golfweek.com

# SPGA CHAMPIONSHIP

## *Lowest Winning Scores Since 1958*

Since 1958 the Senior PGA Championship has been a four-round tournament played on some of the most challenging courses in Florida (and dangerous to boot—watch out for those alligators!).

That year, "the Squire" Gene Sarazen won his second Senior PGA Championship with a final score of 288, beating Charles Sheppard by three strokes to take home $1,200 from a total purse of $10,000. His score now ranks as one of the highest in the tournament's history, right up there with Sam Snead's all-time high of 290 in 1970 (foul weather apparently hindered Snead's game). Slammin' Sam redeemed himself three years later, however, shooting a record 268 in a 15-stroke victory over Julius Boros. Almost 30 years later, Snead's 1973 final score still heads the list of the tournament's lowest winning scores since 1958.

| Player | Year | Score |
|--------|------|-------|
| 1. Sam Snead | 1973 | 268 |
| 2. Don January | 1979 | 270 |
| 3. Jack Nicklaus | 1991 | 271 |
| 4. Herman Barron | 1963 | 272 |
| 5. Roberto De Vicenzo | 1974 | 273 |
| 6. Allen Doyle | 1999 | 274 |
| Hale Irwin | 1997 | 274 |
| Tom Watson | 2001 | 274 |
| 9. Hale Irwin | 1998 | 275 |
| Tom Wargo | 1993 | 275 |

Source: golfweek.com

# SPGA CHAMPIONSHIP

## *Players With Most Victories*

Forty-three years before the Senior PGA Tour officially launched in 1980, golf legend Bobby Jones held a tournament for golfers over 50 at the Augusta National Golf Club in 1937. Thanks to Jones and golf patron Alfred S. Bourne, who contributed $1,500 towards the tournament's purse of $2,000, veteran golfers could compete against their peers instead of the upstarts on the PGA circuit.

Jock Hutchinson won the first Senior PGA Championship, which was played over 54 holes. Aside from 1939, 1943, and 1944, the tournament has been played yearly, usually at the PGA National Golf Club in Palm Beach Gardens, Florida. In 1979 and 1984, the tournament was played twice. While some of the tournament's early winners are little more than footnotes in golf history today (Otto Hackbarth?), the following luminaries have won the Senior PGA Championship the most times in the tournament's 60-plus year history.

1. **Sam Snead**: 6 victories: 1964, 1965, 1967, 1970, 1972, 1973

2. **Hale Irwin**: 3 victories: 1996, 1997, 1998

*Elder statesman Sam Snead won the SPGA Championship six times.*

**Gary Player**: 3 victories: 1986, 1988, 1990
**Al Watrous**: 3 victories: 1950, 1951, 1957
**Eddie Williams**: 3 victories: 1942, 1945, 1946

6. **Julius Boros**: 2 victories: 1971, 1977
**Jock Hutchinson**: 2 victories: 1937, 1947
**Don January**: 2 victories: 1979, 1982
**Arnold Palmer**: 2 victories: 1980, 1984
**Paul Runyan**: 2 victories: 1961, 1962
**Gene Sarazen**: 2 victories: 1954, 1958
**Lee Trevino**: 2 victories: 1992, 1994

Source: golfweek.com

*The legendary amateur Bobby Jones with one of his many trophies.*

# U.S. Amateur Championship

## *Multiple Winners*

The oldest golf tournament in the United States, beating the U.S. Open by one day, the U.S. Amateur Championship was first played in 1895. Charles Blair MacDonald, acknowledged today as the father of golf course architecture, won the tournament's Havemeyer Cup (named after the first USGA president, Theodore Havemeyer) at the Newport Country Club.

From 1895 to 1965, the U.S. Amateur Championship was a match-play tournament. The tournament organizers then switched to stroke play format for the next nine years, when such future pros as Lanny Wadkins and Bruce Fleisher won the competition. The match-play format was reinstated in 1973.

Many of the game's all-time greats launched their careers with victories at the U.S. Amateur Championship: Arnold Palmer, Jack Nicklaus, and Tiger Woods, to name a few. The most famous U.S. Amateur Champion is none other than Bobby Jones, who took the Havemeyer Cup a record five times between 1924 and 1930. Jones heads the list of players with multiple U.S. Amateur victories.

| | Player | Number Of Victories | Years |
|---|---|---|---|
| 1. | Bobby Jones | 5 | 1924–1925, 1927, 1928, 1930 |
| 2. | Jerry Travers | 4 | 1907–1908, 1912–1913 |
| 3. | Walter Travis | 3 | 1900–1901, 1903 |
| | Tiger Woods | 3 | 1994–1996 |
| 4. | Deane Berman | 2 | 1960, 1963 |
| | Charles Coe | 2 | 1949, 1958 |
| | Gary Cowan | 2 | 1966, 1971 |
| | H. Chandler Egan | 2 | 1904–1905 |
| | Chick Evans | 2 | 1916, 1920 |
| | Lawson Little | 2 | 1934–1935 |
| | Jack Nicklaus | 2 | 1959, 1961 |
| | Francis Ouimet | 2 | 1914, 1931 |
| | Jay Sigel | 2 | 1982–1983 |
| | William Turnesa | 2 | 1938, 1948 |
| | Bud Ward | 2 | 1939, 1941 |
| | Harvie Ward | 2 | 1955–1956 |
| | H. J. Whigham | 2 | 1896–1897 |

Source: hickoksports.com

# U.S. OPEN

## All-Time Moneymakers

Now that the purses at the majors all hover around $5 million, even the fifth and sixth-place finishers walk away with six figures for their less-than-stellar efforts. Gone are the days when everyone but the winner went away empty-handed. At the 2001 U.S. Open, last-place finisher Stephen Gangluff received $8,110 for scoring 301 and shooting 21 over par, a nice chunk of change for basically surviving the cut.

As the following stats reveal, the top moneymakers aren't necessarily the players who've won the U.S. Open the most. In fact, three of the tournament's all-time top 10 moneymakers, Tom Lehman, Colin Montgomerie, and Phil Mickelson, have *never* won. What these three players have done is finish in the top 10 or higher several times, which has done wonders for their bank accounts, if not their trophy cases.

| | Player | Number of Appearances | Earnings | Years Won |
|---|---|---|---|---|
| 1. | Payne Stewart | 16 | $1,455,880 | 1999 |
| 2. | Ernie Els | 8 | $1,307,306 | 1994, 1997 |
| 3. | Tiger Woods | 6 | $1,070,540 | 2000 |
| 4. | Lee Janzen | 11 | $952,780 | 1998 |
| 5. | Tom Lehman | 12 | $750,883 | None to date |
| 6. | Colin Montgomerie | 9 | $694,565 | None to date |
| 7. | Curtis Strange | 22 | $608,185 | 1988, 1989 |
| 8. | Phil Mickelson | 10 | $588,169 | None to date |
| 9. | Hale Irwin | 31 | $501,264 | 1974, 1979, 1990 |
| 10. | Steve Jones | 8 | $496,058 | 1996 |

Source: sportsillustrated.com

# U.S. OPEN

## Amateur Champions

In the annals of golf, there have been many underdogs—players who seemingly come out of nowhere and defy both the odds and more experienced players to emerge victorious. At the 1913 U.S. Open, spectators watched in awe as 20-year-old, self-taught amateur Francis Ouimet defeated favorites Harry Vardon and Ted Ray in a play-off at The Country Club in Brookline, Massachusetts. Ouimet's surprise victory thrust the young amateur from modest circumstances into the spotlight. He would later play on eight Walker Cup teams and become the first American captain of The Royal and Ancient Golf Club in 1951. Here are some other amateurs who came out on top against the pros.

- **Jerome Travers**: Two years after Ouimet's victory, Jerome Travers became the second amateur to win the U.S. Open at Baltrusol Golf Club in Springfield, New Jersey. The four-time U.S. Amateur champion, Travers quit playing competitive golf after his 1915 U.S. Open Victory.

- **Charles Evans Jr.**: The following year, Charles "Chick" Evans Jr. became the third amateur U.S. Open champion with a score of 286, a course record for 20 years. That same year, Evans made history by becoming the first player to win both the U.S. Open and the U.S. Amateur championship.

- **Bobby Jones**: Certainly the most celebrated of all the U.S. Open amateur champions is Bobby Jones, who won his first of four titles in 1923 at the Inwood Country Club in Inwood, New York. He was also the tournament runner-up four times before retiring from competitive golf in 1930.

- **John Goodman**: The last amateur to win the U.S. Open was John Goodman in 1933 at the North Shore Golf Club in Glenview, Illinois. A poor Nebraska orphan who had previously defeated Bobby Jones in the first round of the 1929 National Amateur competition, Goodman slew another giant, Walter Hagen, at the 1933 U.S. Open.

Source: sportsillustrated.com

# U.S. OPEN

## First and Last Place Finishes, 1991–2001

Since 1991, three players have twice won the U.S. Open: Ernie Els, Lee Janzen and the late Payne Stewart, who tragically died in a plane crash just months after taking the 1999 title at the historic Pinehurst Country Club. In his 16 starts at the tournament, Stewart made the cut 12 times and twice finished as the runner-up—an impressive legacy for a golfer sadly cut down in his prime. Like "Champagne" Tony Lema, who died in a plane crash in the sixties, Stewart had the makings of an all-time great. His two U.S. Open victories in 1991 and 1999 guarantee him a spot in the history books.

### U.S. Open, First and Last Place Finishes, 1991–2001

| Year | Place | Golfer | Score | Par Rating |
|------|-------|--------|-------|------------|
| 1991 | 1st Place | Payne Stewart | 282 | −3 |
|      | Last Place | (tie) Wayne Grady, Lanny Wadkins and Terry Snodgrass | 305 | +17 |
| 1992 | 1st Place | Tom Kite | 285 | −3 |
|      | Last Place | Kirk Triplett | 305 | +17 |
| 1993 | 1st Place | Lee Janzen | 727 | −8 |
|      | Last Place | Robert Gamez | 298 | +18 |
| 1994 | 1st Place | Ernie Els | 279 | −4 |
|      | Last Place | (tie) Emlyn Aubrey, Mike Smith and Ed Humenik | 302 | +18 |
| 1995 | 1st Place | Corey Pavin | 280 | Even |
|      | Last Place | Joey Gullion | 301 | +21 |
| 1996 | 1st Place | Steve Jones | 278 | −2 |
|      | Last Place | Shawn Kelly | 309 | +29 |
| 1997 | 1st Place | Ernie Els | 276 | −4 |
|      | Last Place | Slade Adams | 306 | +26 |
| 1998 | 1st Place | Lee Janzen | 280 | Even |
|      | Last Place | Tom Sipula | 305 | +25 |
| 1999 | 1st Place | Payne Stewart | 279 | −1 |
|      | Last Place | John Daly | 309 | +29 |
| 2000 | 1st Place | Tiger Woods | 272 | −12 |
|      | Last Place | Robert Damron | 313 | +29 |
| 2001 | 1st Place | Retief Goosen | 276 | −4 |
|      | Last Place | Stephen Gangluff | 301 | +21 |

Source: golfonline.com

# U.S. OPEN

## Foreign-Born Winners of U.S. Open

The first winner of the 1895 U.S. Open was Englishman Horace Rawlins. Sixteen years would pass before an American golfer, John J. McDermott, ended British rule of the tournament with his 1911 victory. The Americans came on strong in the subsequent years, most spectacularly with Bobby Jones' four wins between 1923 and 1930. But foreign-born golfers have played a big part in the tournament's history. Here are all the foreign-born winners of the U.S. Open in chronological order.

| Year | Golfer | Country |
|------|--------|---------|
| 1895 | Horace Rawlins | England |
| 1896 | James Foulis | Scotland |
| 1897 | Joe Lloyd | England |
| 1898 | Fred Herd | Scotland |
| 1899 | Willie Smith | Scotland |
| 1900 | Harry Vardon | England |
| 1901 | Willie Anderson | Scotland |
| 1902 | Laurence Auchterlonie | Scotland |
| 1903 | Willie Anderson | Scotland |
| 1904 | Willie Anderson | Scotland |
| 1905 | Willie Anderson | Scotland |
| 1906 | Alex Smith | Scotland |
| 1907 | Alex Ross | Scotland |
| 1908 | Fred McLeod | Scotland |
| 1909 | George Sargent | England |
| 1910 | Alex Smith | Scotland |
| 1920 | Edward Ray | England |
| 1921 | James Barnes | England |
| 1924 | Cyril Walker | England |
| 1925 | William Marfarlane | Scotland |
| 1927 | Tommy Armour | Scotland |
| 1965 | Gary Player | South Africa |
| 1970 | Tony Jacklin | England |
| 1981 | David Graham | Australia |
| 1994 | Ernie Els | South Africa |
| 1997 | Ernie Els | South Africa |
| 2001 | Retief Goosen | South Africa |

Source: usopen.com

*Gary Player, seen here with longtime rivals Jack Nicklaus and Arnold Palmer, was the first South African golfer to win the U.S. Open.*

# U.S. OPEN

## Highest Winning Scores

Three years after the first U.S. Open was held in 1895, the number of tournament rounds was doubled from two to four. At the 1898 U.S. Open in South Hamilton, Massachusetts, Fred Herd shot a 328 for the victory. Playing the same course three years later, Willie Anderson won the 1901 U.S. Open with a final score of 331. Maybe their high scores can be attributed in part to the venue: the Myopia Hunt Club!

Anderson and Herd are the U.S. Open winners with the two highest scores in tournament history. The first American winner of the U.S. Open, Francis Ouimet comes in 10th on the following list with a score of 304.

| Golfer | Year | Score |
|--------|------|-------|
| 1. Willie Anderson | 1901 | 331 |
| 2. Fred Herd | 1891 | 328 |
| 3. Fred McLeod | 1908 | 322 |
| 4. Willie Smith | 1899 | 315 |
| 5. Willie Anderson | 1904 | 314 |
| 6. Harry Vardon | 1900 | 313 |
| 7. Willie Anderson | 1903 | 307 |
| Laurie Auchterlonie | 1902 | 307 |
| John McDermott | 1911 | 307 |
| 10. Francis Ouimet | 1913 | 304 |

Source: golfstats.usopen.com

# U.S. Open

## Lowest Winning Scores

For one of the few times in his meteoric career, Tiger Woods has tied rather than broken a previous tournament record. Matching the score shot by Jack Nicklaus and Lee Janzen in the 1980 and 1993 U.S. Opens respectively, Woods scored 272 to win the Open in 2000. The trio heads the list of the tournament's all-time-lowest winning scores, which includes South African Retief Goosen, who won the 2001 tournament despite missing a three-foot putt on the 18th hole.

*Seen here in his trademark knickers, Payne Stewart won his second U.S. Open title in 1999, just months before he died in a tragic plane crash.*

| Player | | Year | Score |
|---|---|---|---|
| 1. | Lee Janzen | 1993 | 272 |
| | Jack Nicklaus | 1980 | 272 |
| | Tiger Woods | 2000 | 272 |
| 4. | David Graham | 1981 | 273 |
| 5. | Jack Nicklaus | 1967 | 275 |
| | Lee Trevino | 1968 | 275 |
| 7. | Ernie Els | 1997 | 276 |
| | Retief Goosen | 2001 | 276 |
| | Ben Hogan | 1948 | 276 |
| | Fuzzy Zoeller | 1984 | 276 |

Source: golfstats.usopen.com

# U.S. Open

## Most Wins

Since the first U.S. Open in 1895, many pros have hoisted the trophy in victory on two or more occasions. Here are the golf pros that have won the U.S. Open the most times in the tournament's history.

| Player | | Victories | Years |
|---|---|---|---|
| 1. | Willie Anderson | 4 | 1901, 1903, 1904, 1905 |
| | Bobby Jones | 4 | 1923, 1926, 1929, 1930 |
| | Ben Hogan | 4 | 1948, 1950, 1951, 1953 |
| | Jack Nicklaus | 4 | 1962, 1967, 1972, 1980 |
| 5. | Hale Irwin | 3 | 1974, 1979, 1990 |
| 6. | Alex Smith | 2 | 1906, 1910 |
| | John J. McDermott | 2 | 1911, 1912 |
| | Walter Hagen | 2 | 1914, 1919 |
| | Gene Sarazen | 2 | 1922, 1932 |
| | Ralph Guldahl | 2 | 1937, 1938 |
| | Cary Middlecof | 2 | 1949, 1956 |
| | Julius Boros | 2 | 1952, 1963 |
| | Billy Casper | 2 | 1959, 1966 |
| | Lee Trevino | 2 | 1969, 1971 |
| | Andy North | 2 | 1978, 1985 |
| | Curtis Strange | 2 | 1988, 1989 |
| | Ernie Els | 2 | 1994, 1997 |
| | Lee Janzen | 2 | 1993, 1998 |
| | Payne Stewart | 2 | 1991, 1999 |

Source: golfstats.usopen.com

# U.S. SENIOR OPEN

## Winners, 1980–2001

The U.S. Senior Open opened with a whimper, not a bang, in 1980. Just over 500 spectators showed up at the Winged Foot Golf Club in Mamaroneck, New York, to watch Roberto De Vincenzo pocket $20,000 and the title. Despite the presence of such pros as Julius Boros and Tommy Bolt among the qualifiers, neither the media nor the public exhibited much interest in the fledgling SPGA Tour. This collective indifference gave way to enthusiasm the following year, when the USGA lowered the cut-off age to 50, which paved the way for Arnold Palmer to qualify. Suddenly the U.S. Senior Open got a much-needed dose of pizzazz. Today it is widely regarded as the most prestigious event on the SPGA Tour.

| | Player | Tournament Year | Par | Final Score |
|---|---|---|---|---|
| 1. | Roberto De Vincenzo | 1980 | +1 | 285 |
| 2. | Arnold Palmer | 1981 | +9 | 289 |
| 3. | Miller Barber | 1982 | −2 | 282 |
| 4. | Billy Casper | 1983 | +4 | 288 |
| 5. | Miller Barber | 1984 | +6 | 286 |
| 6. | Miller Barber | 1985 | −3 | 285 |
| 7. | Dale Douglass | 1986 | −5 | 279 |
| 8. | Gary Player | 1987 | −14 | 270 |
| 9. | Gary Player | 1988 | Even | 288 |
| 10. | Orville Moody | 1989 | −9 | 279 |
| 11. | Lee Trevino | 1990 | −13 | 275 |
| 12. | Jack Nicklaus | 1991 | +2 | 282 |
| 13. | Larry Laoretti | 1992 | −9 | 275 |
| 14. | Jack Nicklaus | 1993 | −6 | 278 |
| 15. | Simon Hobday | 1994 | −14 | 274 |
| 16. | Tom Weiskopf | 1995 | −13 | 275 |
| 17. | Dave Stockton | 1996 | −11 | 277 |
| 18. | Graham Marsh | 1997 | Even | 280 |
| 19. | Hale Irwin | 1998 | +1 | 285 |
| 20. | Dave Eichelberger | 1999 | −7 | 281 |
| 21. | Hale Irwin | 2000 | −17 | 267 |
| 22. | Bruce Fleisher | 2001 | Even | 280 |

Source: *Golfwatching: A Viewer's Guide to the World of Golf* by George Peper; USGA

# U.S. WOMEN'S OPEN

## All-Time-Highest Winning Scores

Murle Breer, Kathy Cornelius, Fay Crocker: their names may draw a blank among today's golf fans—unless they're golf historians, of course—but each achieved their 15 minutes of fame with victories at the U.S. Open in the fifties and sixties. Along with such better known players as Betsy Rawls and Sandra Haynie, these golfers make the list of the 10 highest winning scores in the tournament's history.

## U.S. Women's Open, All-Time-Highest Winning Scores

| Player | | Tournament Year | Score | Par Rating |
|---|---|---|---|---|
| 1. | Kathy Cornelius | 1956 | 302 | Not available |
| | Betsy Rawls | 1953 | 302 | Not available |
| 3. | Murle Breer | 1962 | 301 | Not available |
| 4. | Babe Zaharias | 1948 | 300 | Not available |
| 5. | Susie Berning | 1972 | 299 | +11 |
| | Fay Crocker | 1955 | 299 | Not available |
| | Betsy Rawls | 1957 | 299 | Not available |
| 8. | Sandra Spuzich | 1966 | 297 | +9 |
| 9. | Sandra Haynie | 1974 | 295 | +7 |
| | Sandra Palmer | 1975 | 295 | +7 |

Source: lpga.com

# U.S. WOMEN'S OPEN

## All-Time-Lowest Winning Scores

As the U.S. Women's Open purses get bigger, the winners' scores fall lower. Back in the forties and fifties, the winning scores regularly topped 290 or more. In 1948, the year the tournament switched from match play to stroke play, winner Babe Zaharias scored 300. Only in the 20 years have players scored consistently between 270 and 280. Pat Bradley was the first winner to score below 280, shooting 279 and 9-under-par to take the 1981 title. A breakthrough at the time, Bradley's score currently ranks ninth in the top-10 list of all-time-lowest winning scores.

## U.S. Women's Open, All-Time-Lowest Winning Scores

| Player | | Tournament Year | Score | Par Rating |
|---|---|---|---|---|
| 1. | Juli Inkster | 1999 | 272 | −16 |
| | Annika Sorenstam | 1996 | 272 | −8 |
| 3. | Karrie Webb | 2001 | 273 | −7 |
| 4. | Alison Nicholas | 1997 | 274 | −10 |
| 5. | Liselotte Neumann | 1988 | 277 | −7 |
| | Patty Sheehan | 1994 | 277 | −7 |
| 7. | Betsy King | 1989 | 278 | −4 |
| | Annika Sorenstam | 1995 | 278 | −2 |
| 9. | Pat Bradley | 1981 | 279 | −9 |
| 10. | Amy Alcott | 1980 | 280 | −4 |
| | Kathy Baker | 1985 | 280 | −8 |
| | Patty Sheehan | 1992 | 280 | −4 |
| | Lauri Merten | 1993 | 280 | −8 |

Source: lpga.com

# U.S. WOMEN'S OPEN

## First and Last Place Finishes, 1991–2001

For the last 56 years the U.S. Women's Open has been challenging the LPGA's best and qualified amateurs to survive four rounds of often grueling play. Many of the game's most-celebrated players have failed to make the cut, while comparative unknowns finish in the top 10. With the tournament purse worth nearly $3 million, the competition has gotten even fiercer in recent years. Just making the cut in the 2001 U.S. Women's Open earned the four last-place finishers over $8,000 apiece.

### U.S. Women's Open, First and Last Place, 1991–2001

| Year | Place | Golfer | Score | Par Rating |
|------|-------|--------|-------|-----------|
| 1991 | 1st Place | Meg Mallon | 283 | −1 |
|      | Last Place | Susan Sanders | 309 | +25 |
| 1992 | 1st Place | Patty Sheehan | 280 | −4 |
|      | Last Place | Missie Berteoitti | 313 | +29 |
| 1993 | 1st Place | Lauri Merten | 280 | −8 |
|      | Last Place | Jennifer Myers | 305 | +17 |
| 1994 | 1st Place | Patty Sheehan | 277 | −7 |
|      | Last Place | Sarah McGuire | 304 | +20 |
| 1995 | 1st Place | Annika Sorenstam | 278 | −2 |
|      | LastPlace | Alison Munt | 306 | +26 |
| 1996 | 1st Place | Annika Sorenstam | 272 | −8 |
|      | Last Place | (tie) Eva Dahllof and Nina Foust | 300 | +20 |
| 1997 | 1st Place | Alison Nicholas | 274 | −10 |
|      | Last Place | Page Dunlop | 303 | +19 |
| 1998 | 1st Place | Se Ri Pak | 290 | +6 |
|      | Last Place | Kim Bauer | 316 | +32 |
| 1999 | 1st Place | Juli Inkster | 272 | −16 |
|      | Last Place | Tammie Green | 299 | +11 |
| 2000 | 1st Place | Karrie Webb | 282 | −6 |
|      | Last Place | Michelle McGann | 311 | +23 |
| 2001 | 1st Place | Karrie Webb | 273 | −7 |
|      | Last Place | (tie) Yu-Ping Lin, Jamie Hullett, Lynnette Brooky and Lisa Strom | 299 | +19 |

Source: lpga.com

# U.S. WOMEN'S OPEN

## Most Victories

First played in 1946, the U.S. Women's Open is the longest-running tournament for professional women golfers; it even predates the founding of the LPGA by four years.

Arguably the most difficult of the LPGA "Majors," the U.S. Women's has been overseen by the United States Golf Association since 1953. Among the tournament's many illustrious winners, two Hall of Famers are conspicuously missing: neither Kathy Whitworth nor Nancy Lopez has ever won the U.S. Women's Open. Whitworth finished second to JoAnne Carner in 1971, while Lopez has been the runner-up four times since 1975, when she played as an amateur and lost to Sandra Palmer.

Here are the LPGA players who've won the U.S. Women's Open the most times in the tournament's 56-year history.

## U.S. Women's Open, Most Victories

| Player | Victories | Years |
|--------|-----------|-------|
| 1. Betsy Rawls | 4 | 1951, 1953, 1957, 1960 |
| Mickey Wright | 4 | 1958, 1959, 1961, 1964 |
| 3. Susie Berning | 3 | 1968, 1972, 1973 |
| Hollis Stacy | 3 | 1977, 1978, 1984 |
| Babe Didrikson Zaharias | 3 | 1948, 1950, 1954 |
| 6. Donna Caponi | 2 | 1969, 1970 |
| JoAnne Carner | 2 | 1971, 1976 |
| Betsy King | 2 | 1989, 1990 |
| Patty Sheehan | 2 | 1992, 1994 |
| Annika Sorenstam | 2 | 1995, 1996 |
| Louise Suggs | 2 | 1949, 1952 |
| Karrie Webb | 2 | 2000, 2001 |

Source: lpga.com

# WALKER CUP

When George Herbert Walker first broached the idea of an international team competition to the USGA Executive Committee in the early twenties, golfers were already criss-crossing the Atlantic to play on American and British courses. What had been unheard of prior to World War I was now commonplace—that is, if you were a wealthy man of leisure who could afford the pricey transatlantic fare.

Viewing golf as a means of fostering better international relations, Walker even donated the trophy for the tournament, which was first played in 1922 at the National Golf Links in Southampton, Long Island. America's finest amateurs, including Francis Ouimet, squared off against the British contingent sent by the Royal and Ancient Golf Club. At the end of the second day of tournament play the Americans emerged victorious, with a score of 8 to Great Britain's 4.

Since 1924 the Walker Cup has been played every two years on courses in the United States, Great Britain, and Ireland. The teams are composed of 10 amateurs, who are selected by the USGA and the Royal and Ancient, respectively. Jack Nicklaus, David Duval, Davis Love III, and Phil Mickelson are among the many golfers who competed in the Walker Cup before turning professional.

Here are the results of the last 10 Walker Cup tournaments, which the American team has won six times.

| Year | Score |
|------|-------|
| 1983 | America 13, Great Britain and Ireland 10½ |
| 1985 | America 13, Great Britain and Ireland 11 |
| 1987 | America 16, Great Britain and Ireland 7½ |
| 1989 | Great Britain and Ireland 12, America 11½ |
| 1991 | America 14, Great Britain and Ireland 10 |
| 1993 | America 19, Great Britain and Ireland 5 |
| 1995 | Great Britain and Ireland 14, America 10 |
| 1997 | America 18, Great Britain and Ireland 6 |
| 1999 | Great Britain and Ireland 15, America 9 |
| 2001 | Great Britain and Ireland 15, America 9 |

Source: walkercup.org; hickoksports.com

## LES KRANTZ

Les is a former staff member of *Golf Magazine* and the author of dozens of books including *What the Odds Are, The Art of the Market, Their First Time in the Movies,* and *The Best and Worst of Everything*. He is also the author of several books from the *Wall Street Journal*, including the *Jobs Rated Almanac*.

## TIM KNIGHT

Tim is a freelance editor and writer and has worked on several projects with Krantz including *Their First Time in the Movies* and several *Wall Street Journal* books.